U0917742

本书出版受以下项目资助：

1. 国家社科基金项目《中国社会科学研究伦理审查制度缺失问题及对策研究》（15BSH032）；

2. 湖南省社科基金项目《伦理审查在中国社科领域中的本土适应性研究》（12YBA031）；

3. 国防科技大学本科教育教学研究课题《小班教学改革试点课程发展性评价体系构建纵向质性研究》（U2015105）。

中国学生跨国学习经历研究

——以中英合作办学项目为例

侯俊霞 著

中国社会科学出版社

图书在版编目(CIP)数据

中国学生跨国学习经历研究：以中英合作办学项目为例／侯俊霞著．—北京：中国社会科学出版社，2016．12

ISBN 978－7－5161－8281－9

Ⅰ．①中…　Ⅱ．①侯…　Ⅲ．①高等教育—国际合作—联合办学—研究—中国　Ⅳ．①G649．2

中国版本图书馆CIP数据核字(2016)第116720号

出 版 人　赵剑英
选题策划　刘　艳
责任编辑　刘　艳
责任校对　陈　晨
责任印制　戴　宽

出　　版　中国社会科学出版社
社　　址　北京鼓楼西大街甲158号
邮　　编　100720
网　　址　http://www.csspw.cn
发 行 部　010－84083685
门 市 部　010－84029450
经　　销　新华书店及其他书店

印　　刷　北京君升印刷有限公司
装　　订　廊坊市广阳区广增装订厂
版　　次　2016年12月第1版
印　　次　2016年12月第1次印刷

开　　本　710×1000　1/16
印　　张　19.75
插　　页　2
字　　数　321千字
定　　价　72.00元

凡购买中国社会科学出版社图书,如有质量问题请与本社营销中心联系调换
电话:010－84083683

Contents

Figures

Tables

Chapter 1 Introduction

1.1 Research Background

Recent changes in China owing to economic reforms have been dramatic (Guthrie, 2009). Since the 'open-door policy' started in 1978, the Chinese economy has achieved a growth rate of around 9.5 per cent per year (Chow, 2007) and in 2008 China was the second largest economy in the world in terms of Gross Domestic Product at Purchasing Power Parity (World Bank, 2009). The accession to the World Trade Organisation (WTO) in 2001 marked an acceleration in China's integration with the globalised economy. This has not only enabled the access to international markets and capital, but also to technology, requiring China to put more emphasis on improvements in productivity and technology (Stiglitz, 2006). As a result, the Chinese government is engaging in a process of reform to its entire education system to prepare its 1.3 billion people for the knowledge economy which has become crucial in China's sustainable development.

In response to globalisation, higher education is experiencing internationalisation. Cooperation between Chinese educational institutions and those from other countries delivering foreign awards to Chinese citizens started in the 1990s and has developed considerably over the past two decades. These education joint ventures have become a major part of China's higher education system (Zhou, 2006). In order to encourage and also to standardise this kind of transnational cooperation, the State Council of the Chinese Government enacted the *Regulations of the People's Republic of China on Chinese-Foreign*

Cooperation in Running Schools in 2003, and in 2004 the Ministry of Education(MoE) issued the *Implementation Measures for Regulations of the People's Republic of China on Chinese-Foreign Cooperation in Running Schools*. The enactment of the Regulations aims to make China's education system globally competitive by converting the government's WTO commitments into solid domestic legislation following the three basic principles of WTO: non-discrimination, transparency and fair competition(Zhou, 2006:271).

These regulations state that high-quality cooperation in the field of higher education and vocational education is an undertaking beneficial to public interest. Britain, as one of the countries which enjoys a good reputation for the quality of its higher education, has become a preferred partner for Chinese institutions. Articulation programmes at undergraduate level are one of the most common forms of collaboration between China and the UK, both for recruitment and educational reasons. These are programmes whereby Chinese students recruited through the National Higher Education Entrance Examination study in a Chinese partner institution for one to three years, then progress to the UK to complete their studies.

Institutions in the UK increasingly recognise the value of building partnerships with Chinese institutions (Oxford, 2008). In 2005 – 2006, there were approximately 11,000 Chinese students studying in China for a UK higher education award, 3,000 of whom were on articulation programmes that would involve their transferring from a Chinese institution in order to complete their studies with a UK partner (Quality Assurance Agency for Higher Education, 2006). The overall numbers of students taking part in articulation programmes are still low, but growing. This can be evidenced by the increasing number of China-UK cooperative institutions and programmes, which has increased from 40 in 2002 (MoE, 2004a) to 114 in 2010 (MoE, 2010a and 2010b). China, with its huge potential market, has become a favourite source country for international students. Numbers of Chinese students have continued to rise; they have become the largest group represented amongst international students in the UK (UKCISA, 2013). China currently operates

1,979 transnational education programmes, which amount to a total of 450,000 students enrolled in Transnational Higher Education (TNHE) and 1.5 million graduates from TNHE (MoE, 2013a). The Chinese Government is reluctant to accept the current role of the country being a sender in TNHE, although the recent announcement that China will open its first branch campus in Malaysia in 2015 demonstrates a gradual sea change in this respect.

The Chinese Government emphasises that the essence of the cooperation should be for the Chinese institutions to introduce and absorb high-quality educational resources through which their own education system can be improved (MoE, 2007 and 2013a). It should not be simply about sending Chinese citizens abroad. However, the quality audit system was not set up until 2012 when the Chinese Ministry of Education conducted an experimental audit on TNHE programmes and institutions in three provinces (Liaoning, Jiangsu and Henan) and one municipality directly under the Central Government (Tianjin). Those who failed in the audit were ordered to terminate the cooperation. Lacking statistical figures from the Government, the general results of the audit are not clear. But it is certain that in the audit, not only students' satisfaction was given importance, but the actual introduction of high quality of education resources was considered as one of the crucial standards to be met (MoE, 2013a). The Chinese Government intended to order Chinese universities to import one third of core modules for each TNHE programme, invite foreign staff to deliver one third of the core modules and bear one third of the teaching hours (MoE, 2006). However, to save the cost, some Chinese universities and their partners did not provide these resources to the students and damaged the reputation of TNHE in China. Therefore, another round of audit is being carried on 314 TNHE programmes and institutions in 23 provinces and municipalities since the early of 2013 (MoE, 2013a). Students and their parents can check their registration information on the official website (www.crs.jsj.edu.cn) to increase the public participation in the audit. Therefore, only partner institutions who pay attention to the quality can get the licence from the Chinese Government.

As a Chinese educator who was involved in three China-UK articulation programmes, I was eager to know how to prepare the Articulation Programme Students for their study abroad. How will they cope with their study? Can the preparations facilitate their transition? In which ways? What more could be done before their leaving for the UK? What will the English counterparts think of these students' performance? How are their teaching practices different from ours? How do the differences affect students' learning approaches? Are there better ways to bridge the two stages of teaching and learning? In 2006, I had a chance to pursue my Masters degree in Education Studies in the UK. During that year, I met many other overseas Chinese students, including students coming through articulation programmes. In the summer of 2007, I became a visiting lecturer in the School of Health, Community and Education Studies, teaching Articulation Programme Students from China. My dual role as an international student and a part-time lecturer offered me a valuable chance to understand students' learning experience on the programmes. Whilst there is a great deal of research on international students overall, research focusing on their experiences on undergraduate articulation programmes is rare, perhaps due to the complexity involved in scrutinising educational activities in two countries. This is an under-researched area, therefore, a relevant topic area for my PhD research project.

1.2 Research Overview

The main research question of this study is:

How do Chinese Articulation Programme Students experience their transitional stage from China to the UK?

This study aims to explore Transnational Articulation Programme Students' transition experience between the educational context in China and the UK, with the objectives to investigate the factors that have influenced students' transition and the impact of students' transition on the educational context in both higher education institutions.

The '2 +2' articulation programme researched in this study was set up by a university in the southeast of China and a university in the north of England in 2004 for two courses: *BEng (Hons) Electrical and Electronic Engineering (EEE)* and *BEng (Hons) Communication and Electronic Engineering (CEE)*. To protect the confidentiality of the field setting, the two universities are referred to here as Southeast China University and North Britain University. The participants in this study (n = 50) registered in 2006 on the Articulation Programme in Southeast China University, where they spent two years studying the core modules imported from North Britain University, as well as the compulsory modules required by the Chinese Ministry of Education. These students came to North Britain University in 2008 for their final two years' study. After successfully finishing the four years' study, they were awarded two undergraduate degrees, one from each university. Students who preferred to undertake a work placement before the final year need one extra year to obtain their degrees.

A longitudinal ethnographic study was designed to explore the intercultural transition experiences of this group of students, based on on-site and online fieldwork carried out over 15 months in China and the UK. I went to Southeast China University in early 2008 when students were in their last semester in China. I stayed in student accommodation and participated in students' academic and social activities, then followed them through a whole academic year in the UK, carrying out observations on the students' in-class and out-of-class activities. Sixteen students were interviewed on three occasions. The first round of interviews were conducted in China before students' leaving the country. The second and third interviews were carried out, respectively, two months after their arrival in Britain and the month after their first academic year. In addition to this, ten Chinese staff members, eight British staff members, five English students, two international students, and two Chinese parents were interviewed. I also conducted cyber observations on students' online chat and used their blogs and coursework to obtain a comprehensive picture of students' experience in their transitional stage.

1.3 The Organisation of the Book

This book is presented in seven chapters:

Chapter One: introduces the whole project with a brief description of the research background followed by the rationale, the derivation of the research question, and a review of the research study.

Chapter Two: analyses the current situation of Transnational Higher Education (TNHE) in China by conducting a comprehensive documentary analysis. It first situates the phenomenon in global transnational mobility in higher education and then explores the diverse motivations of importing and exporting countries taking China and the UK as linked examples. The documentary analysis carried out for this part suggests that China has stated aims to promote Transnational Higher Education as a public good, whereas UK motivations for Transnational Education are ostensibly more driven by financial reasons. The chapter also identifies three features of the current situation in China: first showing that the distribution of the Transnational Higher Education in China is imbalanced; second, partner institutions are based in 21 economic developed countries or regions; third, the prominent cooperative arrangements are strongly focused in particular disciplines. The chapter argues that these features have led to unfair competition in some areas. Therefore, it appears that there are some inconsistencies and tensions between the stated aims of Chinese TNHE policy and the way in which TNHE is spreading and developing in practice.

Chapter Three: provides a critical review of the literature in relation to intercultural transition. This literature review was drafted after I finished an independent data analysis and generated a substantive theory in order to avoid importing preconceived ideas and imposing them on my work (Charmaz, 2006). It first reviews existing models and theories, including cultural shock theory, U-shaped curve theory, stress-adaptation-growth model, and developmental models, leading to the conclusion that international students' transition experience is a complex journey and cannot be oversimplified by any of the existing models. This chapter then discusses national cultural theory and culture of learning theory, which argues that understanding individuals' intercultural transition experience from the perspectives of these theories has the potential to fall into the traps of stereotyping. This chapter tries to understand the transition from both a microscopic perspective, focusing on individual factors, as well as a contextual perspective focusing on situational factors. The final part of this chapter examines the social interactions between members of the host community and sojourners, and interprets the intergroup relations by social identity theories. Possible ways to reduce intergroup bias are explored at the end.

Chapter Four: first presents my philosophical assumptions, which consist of ontological orientation, my epistemological consideration, and my intention to be an inside learner with a balance to be an outside expert in understanding my participants' social world. It then moves on to a discussion of the rationale of my choice of a qualitative research strategy: ethnography. My data collection methods, including participant observation, in-depth interviews and document analysis, are described and followed by an explanation of the data analysis process. My ethical concerns and critical reflexivity on the research process are also discussed.

Chapter Five: focuses on the individual transition experience across two universities. Although the students on the programme came from the same country and had the similar educational experience, there were a lot of factors which made individuals' transition experiences and their response to those experiences very different. We should not overgeneralise their experiences based on their nationality and 'culture of learning'. However, there were some significant patterns. Three broad response categories were identified which represented the key types of experience found within the group. They encompassed different motivations for studying abroad and strategies and attitudes towards the pre-departure preparation which particularly influenced their interaction with the new learning environment and their outcomes of academic performance. Three patterns of interaction with the new learning environment were identified and presented in terms of Direct Interaction, Indirect Interaction and Avoiding Interaction. These patterns show, how in the new learning environment, some factors can be 'double-edged' in that they may have negative or positive impacts depending upon the student's transition response. Examples are: 'internet', 'privacy' and 'peer support'.

Chapter Six: Because of the unique feature of the Articulation Programme, the participants studied abroad as a group of 50 and came across another group of students, primarily home students in the course at North Britain University. The interaction experience between these two groups in the class unavoidably influenced the participants' intercultural transition experience. Therefore, this chapter focuses on the Articulation Programme Students' interaction with the existing cohort of students and the impact of their participation on the learning environment at both universities. Participants' interaction experiences with their flatmates are also explored. This chapter blends the perspectives of home students, other international students and the staff to provide a holistic view of the Articulation Programme Students' transition experiences. The chapter first analyses how the home-based students and Chinese students in the same class were divided into two social and psychological groups, Us & Them. Then, it moves on to investigate how their own shared group membership influenced their social relations and behaviour in the class. Finally, the current structured interventions to improve students' integration were explored at the university, school, and staff level.

Chapter Seven: provides a critical discussion on the findings presented in the previous two chapters by relating them with the existing literatures. It first explores the connections of personal factors (motivations for studying abroad, attitudes towards pre-departure preparation, language competence, and autonomy) with the transition process. The functions of social factors in transition are then emphasised. It moves on to a discussion on the impact of the unique feature of the Articulation Programme, studying abroad as a group, on the students' interaction with the home students. The final part of this chapter answers the research question by providing a conclusion from the evidence collected in the study. The contribution to knowledge is specified, followed by the implications for practice and recommendations for further research.

Chapter 2 Chinese-Foreign Cooperation in Running Schools—Setting the Scene

2.1 Introduction

This chapter analyses the current situation of Transnational Higher Education (TNHE) in China by conducting a comprehensive documentary analysis. It first situates the phenomenon in global transnational mobility in higher education and then explores the diverse motivations of importing and exporting countries taking China and the UK as linked examples. The documentary analysis carried out for this part suggests that China has stated aims to promote Transnational Higher Education as a public good, whereas UK motivations for Transnational Education are ostensibly more driven by financial reasons. The chapter also identifies three features of the current situation in China: first showing that the distribution of the Transnational Higher Education in China is imbalanced; second, partner institutions are based in 21 economic developed countries or regions; third, the prominent cooperative arrangements are strongly focused in particular disciplines. The chapter argues that these features have led to unfair competition in some areas. Therefore, it appears that there are some inconsistencies and tensions between the stated aims of Chinese TNHE policy and the way in which TNHE is spreading and developing in practice.

2.2 Globalisation, Internationalisation & Transnational Higher Education

The process of globalisation is pushing 21st century higher education towards greater international involvement (Altbach and Knight, 2007) and this has turned higher education into 'a global business engaging in marketing strategies to sell their knowledge-based products, attract foreign students, and establish international branches' (Spring, 2009: 100). Worldwide there is a growing demand for access to higher education combined with increasing need for more diversified and flexible types of course delivery (van der Wende, 2003) with international cooperation in higher education becoming a key feature of development in today's global market (Chan, 2004). Universities in different countries are forging alliances to compete in the global and mass higher education market (*ibid.*) and therefore, as Leask (2008) has argued, Transnational Higher Education has become an agent of globalisation. In recent years, Transnational Higher Education has grown in scope and been engaged in recruitment campaigns for international students and faculty, as well as the race to create successful and competitive regional education hubs (Knight and Morshidi, 2011).

Transnational Higher Education (TNHE) is the kind of education that the learners are located in a country which is different from the one where the awarding institution is based (Huang, 2007; McBurnie and Ziguras, 2007; Wilkins and Huisman, 2012). Developed countries and larger European Union (EU) countries now provide most of the services as selling partners, while middle-income countries in Asia and Latin America have become the 'buying' partners (Altbach and Knight, 2007). In the English-speaking world, international operations have become the primary mode of development for some HE institutions (Marginson and van der Wende, 2009). Transnational Higher Education is becoming a popular format within international student mobility in the 21st century, especially now that TNHE practice need not always involve a change of location given new opportunities such as online learning.

The providers in exporting higher education products and services often experience barriers to trade in education, such as national legislation which may prevent foreign providers from obtaining a license to operate in the country (van der Wende, 2003). Unstable regulations in the host country may turn opportunities into threats (Wilkins and Huisman, 2012). Since the Uruguay Round of trade negotiations (1986 to 1993), educational services have been integrated into the General Agreement on Trade in Services (GATS) and Western countries have since tried to reduce barriers and gain better access to foreign educational markets through these negotiations (van der Wende, 2003). One of the landmark achievements of the Uruguay Round of trade negotiations (1986 – 1993) was the creation of the General Agreement on Trade in Services (GATS) which was implemented in January 1995 (WTO, 2006).

> The GATS is a multilateral agreement through which WTO members commit to voluntary liberalisation of trade in services, including education (Ziguras, 2003: 89).

GATS aims to 'establish a multilateral framework of principles and rules for trade in services with a view to the expansion of such trade under conditions of transparency and progressive liberalisation and as a means of promoting the economic growth of all trading partners and the development of developing countries' (WTO, 1995: 285). The GATS Agreement distinguishes between four modes of supplying services which are also applied to the international trade in education, as demonstrated in Table 2-1.

Table 2-1 Four Modes of Supply in GATS

Mode	Definition	International Trade in Education Examples
Mode 1 Cross-border Trade	Supply from the territory of one Member (of WTO) in the territory of any other Member	Distance education (e-learning), Franchise courses

(contd.)

Mode	Definition	International Trade in Education Examples
Mode 2 Consumption Abroad	Supply in the territory of one Member to the service consumer of any other Member	Student studying abroad
Mode 3 Commercial Presence	Supply by a service supplier of one Member, by means of commercial presence in the territory of any other Member	Branch campuses, Joint ventures with local institutions
Mode 4 Presence of Natural Persons	Supply by a service supplier of one Member, through the presence of natural persons of a Member in the territory of any receiving Member	Professors and researchers providing educational services in other countries (known as 'flying faculty')

(Source: adapted from Altbach and Knight, 2007; van der Wende, 2003; WTO, 2006)

Through GATS or other bilateral free trade agreements, trade liberalisation has been realized in higher education (van der Wende, 2003). As mentioned above, Transnational Higher Education has become a global phenomenon whose scale of activity has grown significantly in recent years (Naidoo, 2009). The main form of cross-border higher education, in terms of numbers engaged, however, is still international student mobility (Mode 2). International mobility of programmes (Mode 3) has, however, become the second most common form and 'may mark the beginning of an in-depth transformation of higher education in the long term' (Vincent-Lancrin, 2009: 68). The Chinese programmes focused upon later in this article in Figures 2-1, 2-2, and 2-3 below belong to Mode 3. This mode enables the exporting countries to recruit students and deliver their education programmes in students' home countries through setting up branch campuses, such as the University of Nottingham Ningbo China, or establishing joint ventures with local institutions, such as '3 + 1' or '4 + 0' programmes, in which students undertake some of their education in their home countries and some in the foreign providing country.

2.3 Chinese-British Cooperation in Transnational Higher Education

Chinese Transnational Higher Education has been greatly enhanced following China's accession to the World Trade Organisation in 2001 and the enactment of the *Regulations of the People's Republic of China on Chinese-Foreign Cooperation in Running Schools* in 2003. The United Kingdom, together with other major English-speaking destination countries such as America, Australia, Canada, and New Zealand, hosted 46 per cent of the foreign students in the world in 2004 (Gürüz, 2008: 238). These countries have become the most prominent exporters of programme mobility, with Mainland China operating alongside Singapore, Hong Kong, Malaysia, and India as the largest markets importing higher education programmes (Naidoo, 2009). Whilst this part is not a comparative study as such it was considered important to contextualise the Chinese documentary analysis against an exploration of a providing country's TNHE provision. As indicated above, since the UK is a major provider of TNHE this section will briefly explore the UK context of TNHE.

2.3.1 The UK Story

The UK currently operates 1,395 TNE programmes and has built 73 overseas campuses, which amounts to a total of 454,473 students enrolled and involved in TNHE and this excludes Distance Learning students (British Council, 2013). The UK's top partners for provision of TNHE are quoted by the British Council and HESA statistics as being Malaysia, Singapore, Pakistan, Mainland China and Hong Kong (*ibid.*). Current practices and activities in TNHE in different universities and countries are quite complex and it is not easy to give a commonly agreed glossary of the types of programmes available. Table 2-2 presents an overview of the four main practices of Chinese-British Transnational Higher Education, including the terms that are commonly used by the British universities. Naidoo(2009:315) explains the definitions applying to all countries, while the following table was adapted to be specific to the cooperation between China the UK and a third column to indicate how qualifications are awarded has been added.

Table 2-2 Current Practices and Activities in Transnational Higher Education Between China and the UK

Programmes	Modalities	Qualifications
Franchising	An institution in the UK(the franchiser) grants a Chinese university the right to deliver the franchiser's educational programmes in China or other countries. Students undertake the entire programme in China or a third country	Awarded by the franchiser in the UK
Twinning Degrees	An arrangement where an institution in the UK collaborates with another institution in China allowing students studying at the latter institution to transfer their course credits to the institution in the UK.	Awarded by the institution in the UK
Programme Articulations	Students undertake part of a British qualification in China and then transfer to the British institution with 'advanced standing' in terms of study credits and credit transfer to complete the qualification at the British institution in the UK	Awarded by the institution in the UK or joint/double degrees from both institutions.
Branch Campus	A subsidiary/satellite campus is established by a British education institution in China to deliver its own education programmes, via joint venture partnerships with local Chinese partners	Awarded by the institution in the UK. (graduation certificates are normally awarded by the joint venture)

(Source: adapted from Naidoo, 2009:315)

Although the practices and activities of collaboration among higher education institutions between China and the UK are prospering, the aims and purpose of carrying out the cooperation are very different. In the UK, over the last decade political debate has led to claims that overall levels of public funding for higher education have become increasingly inadequate and the government has repeatedly cut public funding on higher education. Higher education export has been identified as a promising economic activity and an important source of additional income(van der Wende,2003:195). Previously the British government has aimed to increase its share in the global market for international students to 25% (van der Wende, 2003), and the Prime Minister's Initiative(2006) urged British universities to increase the number of international students by 100,000 by 2011(Brown and Holloway,2007). Universities have been encouraged to generate international ventures and extend their market in developing and middle-income countries via branch campuses,franchised degree programs,and partnerships with local institutions (Altbach and Knight,2007). Economic benefit has thus become a key motive for transnational projects in most of the universities (Altbach and Knight, 2007) and this is being reflected in the motivations and philosophies driving the development of UK TNHE. Some evidence for this can be found in UK universities' internationalisation and transnational policy statements. The University of Manchester's policy statement is an example stating that:

> An underlying principle of our TNE activities is that they must not risk the University's potential to maximise international student fee income(University of Manchester,2014).

In addition to emphasising the motivation of TNHE as being economic, the University of Manchester's policy also underlines the overriding importance of the quality of the international student experience 'at home' in Manchester.

It is important to note that there may be a differentiation in the way that research-oriented universities and teaching-oriented universities (or 'Russell Group' and 'new universities' in the UK) approach transnational education. In the early 1990s in the UK, the university-polytechnic divide was ended, and this promoted the development of competitive education and training markets (Bennell and Pearce,2003). The new universities which emerged are more prepared to set up overseas validated courses than the older universities who are concerned that the collaboration with overseas institutions might tarnish their long-established reputation (*ibid.*). This distinction between the TNHE behaviour of research and teaching universities is also the case in China (Fang, 2012) and this is also highlighted in the next section. It should be acknowledged that there are also perceived political and cultural benefits of TNHE (Fernandes, 2006) and these include universities maintaining an influential position on the world stage and reaping the benefits of special links of international alumni.

> Maintaining a global network of people in power who have experience and understanding of the UK through its education system continues to be a way of facilitating continued global influence indirectly (Fernandes, 2006: 135).

These international alumni act as ambassadors for universities abroad and also benefit institutions by providing positive testimonies of career advancement (*ibid.*). A recent survey has shown that the alumni generally hold positive attitudes towards their study in the UK and not only would recommend others to undertake a similar experience, but also are loyal to UK brands which may benefit the UK's economy (Mellors-Bourne *et al.*, 2013). These alumni are potential professional networks and can 'offer the possibility of future business transactions and collaborations of economic value to the UK' (*ibid*: xi). Other benefits for institutions listed by Olcott (2008) include internationalising the curriculum, preparing students for a global society, collaborative research, and creating a multicultural campus. However, the above rhetoric cannot disguise the fact that economic benefit is the main motivation for British institutions to host international students (Olcott, 2008). Meanwhile, in comparison with recruiting international students onto courses individually, Transnational Higher Education initiatives such as articulation programmes, can bring in more sustainable numbers of students with better preparation for study abroad. Therefore, considerable numbers of institutions in the UK have focused on these transnational programmes to enhance their revenue generation.

2.3.2 The Chinese Story

The Chinese Government define Transnational Higher Education as 'Chinese-Foreign Cooperation in Running Schools', which means:

> The cooperation between foreign educational institutions and Chinese educational institutions in establishing educational institutions within the territory of China to provide education service mainly to Chinese citizens (State Council of the People's Republic of China, 2003: Article 2).

'Running schools' is the English translation of Chinese 'Ban Xue' in the government regulation. It refers to the phenomenon that Chinese universities and foreign universities cooperate to set up programmes or institutions to recruit Chinese students. These students either stay in China to finish the whole course or go abroad in their later stage of study. The cooperation of institutions in Taiwan, Hong Kong and Macao with the institutions in mainland China is also considered part of Chinese TNHE.

Chinese TNHE cooperation can appear in two formats: setting up institutions or setting up programmes. The Chinese Government sees TNHE as 'a component of China's educational cause' and a benefit to the public interest (State Council of the People's Republic of China, 2003: Article 3). The fundamental stated aim of TNHE is to introduce high quality education resources from other countries to enhance the international competiveness of Chinese institutions (Zhou, 2006). The Chinese Government strongly advocates that education should support the public interest (MoE, 2006 and 2013a). Some of the foreign partners may focus on the profits from the cooperation, and even reduce their standard of recruitment and degrees, which is not what the Chinese partners want (Ke, 2010). The Chinese Government may tend to reach an agreement with Skelly's (2009) argument that higher education is not a commodity, but a service for public interest. This aim stands in contrast to the UK motivation for TNHE as noted above.

In 2010, the Chinese Government published the *National Plan for Medium and Long-term Education Reform and Development (2010 – 2020)*, which shows that the Chinese Government will encourage its schools and institutions to conduct international communication and cooperation in various ways and successfully manage some examples of Transnational Higher Education in order to explore how to make use of the excellent education resources generated by TNHE (Central People's Government of People's Republic of China, 2010). This shows that TNHE has been considered as an 'experimental field' for an innovative mode of talent cultivation (Ke, 2010). In the more recently published documents, the Chinese Government encourages students to receive foreign education in China to save their own expenditure and push the internationalisation of Chinese universities (MoE, 2013a). This represents a financial motivation for TNHE which meshes more closely with the UK aim outlined above.

> Transnational Higher Education has offered a way for Chinese students to receive foreign education without going abroad, which has saved the expenditure on education. The average annual tuition fee of TNHE is around 25,000 RMB, while studying in the UK, USA, Canada and Australia will cost students around 90,000 RMB per year. 450,000 students enrolled in TNHE in 2012. If half of them choose to go abroad, we can save 15 billion RMB in tuition fee that year (MoE, 2013a: Part 2.2).

The motivations for the currently developing situation in Transnational Higher Education in China as represented in the documents analysed for this study can be characterised in three ways. First, the rapid development of the Chinese economy since 1978, especially through the accession to the World

Trade Organisation in 2001, requires China not only to convert the capital of its huge population into abundant human resources, but also to 'produce competent professionals at all levels, of all varieties, and ranging from the academically erudite to the practically skilled' (Zhou, 2006:281). Therefore, universities in China have become key agents in economic and social development (Willis, 2006). Collaboration with developed countries in higher education has been greatly encouraged to obtain world-leading experience and to improve Chinese research and innovation capacities. Through cooperative transnational higher education programmes, Chinese universities are expected to integrate urgently needed curricula and textbooks of world class levels and 'assimilate the strong points and successful governance expertise of foreign education institutions in light of China's actual conditions' (Zhou, 2006:273). Through this cooperation, Chinese universities can enhance their image, competitive position, and strengthen academic exchange to be part of a global academic community (Willis, 2006). Currently, there are 577 Chinese higher education institutions hosting TNHE, which accounts for 21% of the total number of Chinese higher education institutions. 79 are in the projects of 985 or 211 (the labels for prestigious research-intensive Chinese institutions), which only accounts for 16% of TNHE institutions (MoE, 2013a), demonstrating again that research-intensive institutions are less likely to engage in TNHE. These universities are defensive of their prestigious reputations and are looking for collaboration with universities within the top 100 around the world.

Second, the high value attached to education in Chinese culture is a driving social force. Chinese families are ready to make sacrifices to provide the best possible educational opportunities for their children (Welch, 2009). This desire has been heightened by the high number of single children in China, born under the 'One-Child Family Policy' (Zhou, 2006). At the same time, the development of the economy has led to the generation of a larger middle class in the last 30 years. The middle class is expanding with an estimated number of approximately 500 million by 2025 and this group has resources to pay tuition and other fees for admission to universities (Altbach,

2009). Their demand for access to higher education is diverse with respect to the places to go and subjects to take. Owing to the long-lasting influence of the high value of a western degree and the successful examples of professionals with overseas experiences, this group of people are trying to send their children to study abroad. This could be a way for the Chinese new middle class families to secure a generational reproduction of their class status and mobility(Tsang,2013).

> Acquisition of Western higher education becomes the imagined gateway to upward social and economic mobility in an increasingly unequal global system (Doherty and Singh, 2005: 57).

Transnational Higher Education gives these parents an alternative option to physically sending their children abroad. In view of the fact that Chinese students begin university at seventeen years of age(a parallel with the Scottish education system) they may be perceived as being too young to go abroad immediately after high school and some parents thus prefer the transnational programmes which will give their children a period of time to lay a foundation in a Chinese university before studying abroad. Both the parents and the students have taken the programmes as a kind of springboard for future education abroad and as a perceived key foundation for a pathway to a position with a large international company(Hou,Montgomery and McDowell,2011).

Third, the conflict between the strong domestic need for tertiary education and the limited supply of the Chinese universities has strengthened the development of Transnational Higher Education in China. In the late 1990s, China started to change its higher education from elite education to mass education. The gross enrolment rate for higher education has increased from 10.5% in 1999 to 23.3% in 2008 (MoE, 2009), and the Chinese Government is going to raise the rate to 40% in 2020 (Central People's Government of People's Republic of China, 2010). China runs the largest higher education system in the world with 2,263 higher education institutions and 20,210,000 university students in 2008 (National Bureau of Statistics of China, 2009). However, places at a desirable university are still very competitive. Students need to get a good result in the selective National Higher Education Entrance Examination in order to get into their preferred university. As a result of this and many other developing trends, an increasing number of potential students choose to study abroad through participation in the Transnational Higher Education programmes and institutions. The following section provides an analysis of the developing features of Chinese TNHE.

2.4 Features of Transnational Higher Education in China

This part is based on a comprehensive documentary analysis on the phenomenon of Transnational Higher Education aiming to identify significant features of the current situation in China. The sources of the documents are from the official website of the Chinese Ministry of Education (MoE) (http://www.moe.edu.cn). The documentary analysis used search strings and the results generated are shown in Table 2-3.

Table 2-3 Search History from the Official Website of MoE (http://www.moe.edu.cn)

Search Strings		Results
Keywords in Chinese	English Translation	
中外合作办学 Zhong Wai He Zuo Ban Xue	Chinese foreign cooperation in running schools (TNHE officially authorised by the Chinese Government)	1633
对外合作办学 Dui Wai He Zuo Ban Xue	foreign cooperation in running schools (Another term meaning TNHE officially authorized by the Chinese Government)	19
留学 Liu Xue	Study abroad	2351

(contd.)

Search Strings		Results
Keywords in Chinese	English Translation	
出国留学 Chu Guo Liu Xue	Chinese students study abroad	838
来华留学 Lai Hua Liu Xue	Foreign students study in China	373

Keywords related to Transnational Higher Education programmes or institutions officially authorised by MoE were used to find a total of 1,652 documents. The keywords of 'Liu Xue' (study abroad) were used to identify 2,351 documents, among which 'Chu Guo Liu Xue' (Chinese students study abroad) and 'Lai Hua Liu Xue' (foreign students study in China) were analysed respectively to research two of the trends both within the documents and drawing on the recent literature. These documents consisted of Government statistics, reports, notices, and regulations which were reviewed and analysed. The structured themes and issues drawn out of the analysis form the basis of the arguments in this chapter.

In addition to the themes generated from the documentary analysis above, an analysis was carried out on the data relating to 511 Transnational Higher Education programmes and institutions at undergraduate and postgraduate level identified and published on the Chinese Ministry of Education (MoE) Transnational Education website (http://www.crs.jsj.edu.cn) (see Figures 2-1, 2-2, and 2-3 for details). Some of the institutions and programmes were set up before the *Regulations of the People's Republic of China on Chinese-Foreign Cooperation in Running Schools* took effect in 2003, but they have been reviewed by the government. Because of to the lack of data on non-degree courses, the analysis is based solely on the degree courses of TNHE.

Scott's (1990) four criteria of analysis were kept in mind with attention paid to authenticity, credibility, representativeness and meaning in order to guarantee the quality of the documents. Data from different sources, such as the academic articles and the official documents, were cross-checked to see if there were any inconsistencies. As the documents were mainly in Chinese, the analysed results and tables were double checked by two professionals who are fluent in Chinese and English. In addition to this, the result of the negotiations between my two British supervisors and me regarding the culturally specific meanings of terms and the different national perspectives on the data is valuable and significant.

The Chinese Government encourages Chinese institutions to cooperate with foreign educational institutions which are well-recognised in terms of their academic level and education quality, and urges them to set up cooperation in emerging and urgently needed academic subjects required for the Chinese market (MoE, 2004b and 2013a). Cooperatively-run institutions or programmes can be made up of various types at various levels, but exclude the compulsory education service or special education services such as the military, police and political education services (State Council of the People's Republic of China, 2003: Article 6). Furthermore, 'foreign religious organizations, religious institutions, religious colleges and universities or religious workers' are not allowed to engage in the cooperative activities in China (State Council of the People's Republic of China, 2003: Article 7).

The following section is based on the analysis of the 511 programmes and institutions at undergraduate and postgraduate level published on the Chinese Ministry of Education (MoE) Transnational Education website (http://www.crs.jsj.edu.cn). The locations of the Chinese partner universities, the countries and regions of the foreign partner universities, and the cooperative courses are the main themes analysed in this part. Some of the features in the current practices of Transnational Higher Education are shown in the following examples.

2.4.1 The First Feature

The first feature relates to the imbalance in the distribution of the

Transnational Higher Education programmes and institutions shown in Figure 2-1. According to the statistics published in 2003, these institutions and programmes are mainly situated in the economically and culturally well-developed eastern coastal regions or large and medium-sized cities (MoE, 2003). In 2010, the general distribution has not changed greatly; however, there are two exceptions. Heilongjiang, which is not an economically well-developed province, has 152 undergraduate programmes and 4 postgraduate programmes, although 74 of them are in cooperation with institutions in Russia.

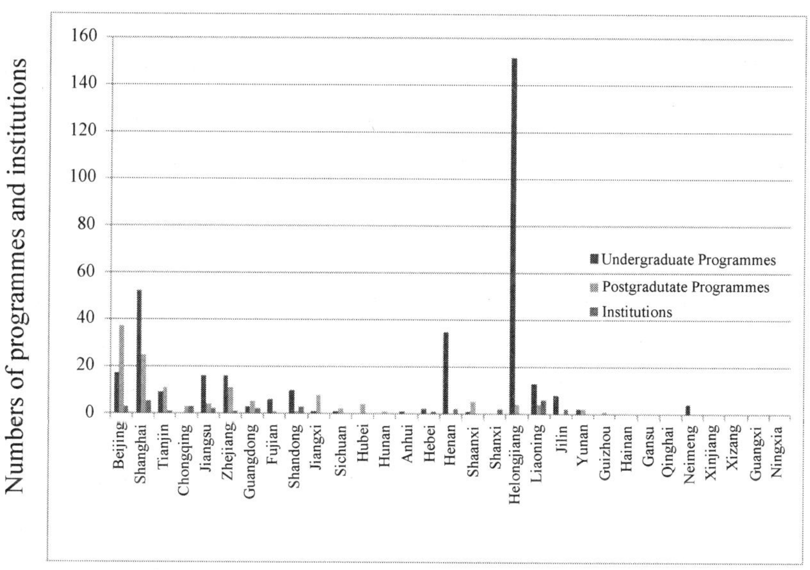

	Beijing	Shanghai	Tianjin	Chongqing	Jiangsu	Zhejiang	Guangdong	Fujian	Shandong	Jiangxi	Sichuan	Hubei	Hunan	Anhui	Hebei	Henan	Shaanxi	Shanxi	Helongjiang	Liaoning	Jilin	Yunan	Guizhou	Hainan	Gansu	Qinghai	Neimeng	Xinjang	Xizang	Guangxi	Ningxia
Undergraduate Programmes	17	52	9	0	16	16	3	6	10	1	1	0	0	1	2	35	1	0	152	13	8	2	0	0	0	0	4	0	0	0	0
Postgraduate Programmes	37	25	11	3	4	11	5	1	1	8	2	4	1	0	0	0	5	0	4	4	0	2	1	0	0	0	0	0	0	0	0
Institutions	3	5	1	3	2	1	2	0	3	0	0	0	0	0	1	2	0	2	0	6	2	0	0	0	0	0	0	0	0	0	0

Figure 2-1 TNHE Undergraduate and Postgraduate Degree Programmes and Institutions by 19th July, 2010

This is partly because of its location next to Russia, and partly due to its language foundation, as Russian is the second language in some of the middle schools. Henan, which is in the middle of China, is the other exception. It has 35 undergraduate programmes and 2 institutions. This has benefited from the proactive policies encouraging its universities to cooperate with the world's top 500 universities.

Shanghai has the second largest number of TNHE provisions with a diversity of partners. It has 5 TNHE institutions cooperating with universities in the USA, the UK, Germany, France and Belgium. Among its 52 undergraduate programmes, the partner universities are from 13 countries or regions: the USA(15), the UK(7), Germany(7), France(5), Australia(4), Canada(3), Netherland(2), Italy(2), Japan(2), New Zealand(1), South Korea(1) and Hong Kong(1). The capital city, Beijing, has the biggest number in postgraduate programmes. The USA(12), Australia(12) and Hong Kong(7) are the three most favoured cooperative countries or regions. However, among the five autonomous regions, only Neimeng(Inner Mongolia) has 4 undergraduate programmes with institutions in Australia and Canada. The other four regions, Tibet, Xinjiang, Guangxi and Ningxia do not have any TNHE degree courses. Although the government has encouraged more cooperation in the western and more remote areas of China since 2004, the situation has not changed. The lower level of economic development has made these areas less attractive to foreign universities. There is a tension here between China saying that TNHE is for the public good whilst not developing education where it is most needed, in the poorest areas of the country.

2.4.2 The Second Feature

The second feature is that partner institutions are based in 21 economic developed countries or regions. As shown in Figure 2-2, the UK ranks the first with 114 programmes and institutions. The USA and Australia are both runners-up with 84 each. The other top 10 countries or regions are Russia(75), Canada (39), Hong Kong(30), Germany(24), France(18), South Korea(8) and

Netherland(7). Ireland, New Zealand and Japan are the next in the league with 5 from each country. Other countries or regions, such as Belgium(3), Italy(2), Sweden(2), Singapore (2), Austria (1), Norway (1), South Africa (1) and Taiwan (1) have begun to expand their market in mainland China. As previously mentioned here, the UK is a leading provider of transnational education(McBurnie and Ziguras, 2009). However, its cooperative level needs to be extended in China. Most of the UK's cooperative programmes are at undergraduate levels. The UK has only 10 postgraduate programmes, while the USA has 33, the highest among the 21 countries and regions.

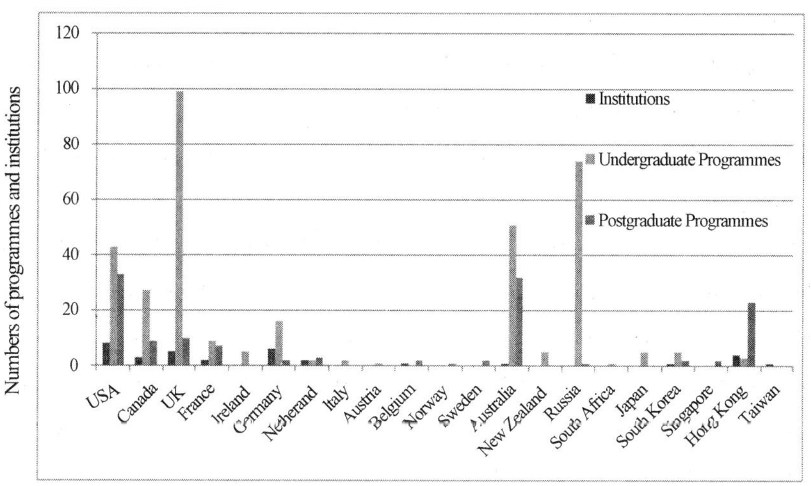

	USA	Canada	UK	France	Ireland	Germany	Netherland	Italy	Austria	Belgium	Norway	Sweden	Australia	New Zealand	Russia	South Africa	Japan	South Korea	Singrpore	Hong Kong	Taiwan
Undergraduate Programmes	43	27	99	9	5	16	2	2	1	0	0	0	51	5	74	1	5	5	0	3	0
Postgraduate Programmes	33	9	10	7	0	2	3	0	0	2	1	2	32	0	1	0	0	2	2	23	0
Institutions	8	3	5	2	0	6	2	0	0	1	0	0	1	0	0	0	0	1	0	4	1

Figure 2-2 Partner Countries and Regions in TNHE by 19th July, 2010

Hong Kong comes to the third with 23 postgraduate programmes. This evidence supports NG's (2011) argument that Hong Kong is ambitious to become the regional education hub through the internationalisation of its higher education campuses. Most of these countries and regions are English-speaking, due to the increasingly hegemonic role of English as a global language (Bennell and Pearce, 2003). In addition, in some of the non-English-speaking nations, English is spreading as a medium of instruction to attract foreign students (Marginson and van der Wende, 2009). As shown in Figure 2-2, other developed European countries, such as Russia, Germany, France, the Netherlands, Belgium, Italy, Sweden and Austria are actively seeking partner institutions in China. As mentioned before, Russia has located its priority market in the north-east of China, especially Heilongjiang Province. Apart from one undergraduate programme with Henan University, all of the other 74 programmes are in Heilongjiang. Germany has set up 6 TNHE institutions in Shanghai (1), Beijing (1), Shandong (2) and Shanxi (2). China-EU School of Law (CESL) in the China University of Political Science and Law, is built on cooperation with the University of Hamburg in Germany to 'offer high-level legal education to law students and legal professionals, to conduct Sino-European legal research and consultancy activities and to substantially contribute to the advancement of the rule of law in China' (China-EU School of Law, 2010).

2.4.3 The Third Feature

The third feature of Chinese TNHE that the analysis pinpointed is that the most prominent cooperative subjects are *Economy*, *Business Administration*, *Electrical Engineering and Computing Science*, and *Foreign Language Studies* (see Figure 2-3). Based on 'the Higher Education Institution Undergraduate Subject Catalogue' published by MoE (MoE, 1998), the 349 undergraduate programmes can be grouped into 33 categories and 87 subjects, among which, *Computing Science and Technology* ranks the first with 40 programmes. Seven countries have cooperation in this subject. The UK has set up 12 computing programmes, eight of which are in Helongjiang province. Meanwhile, all of the

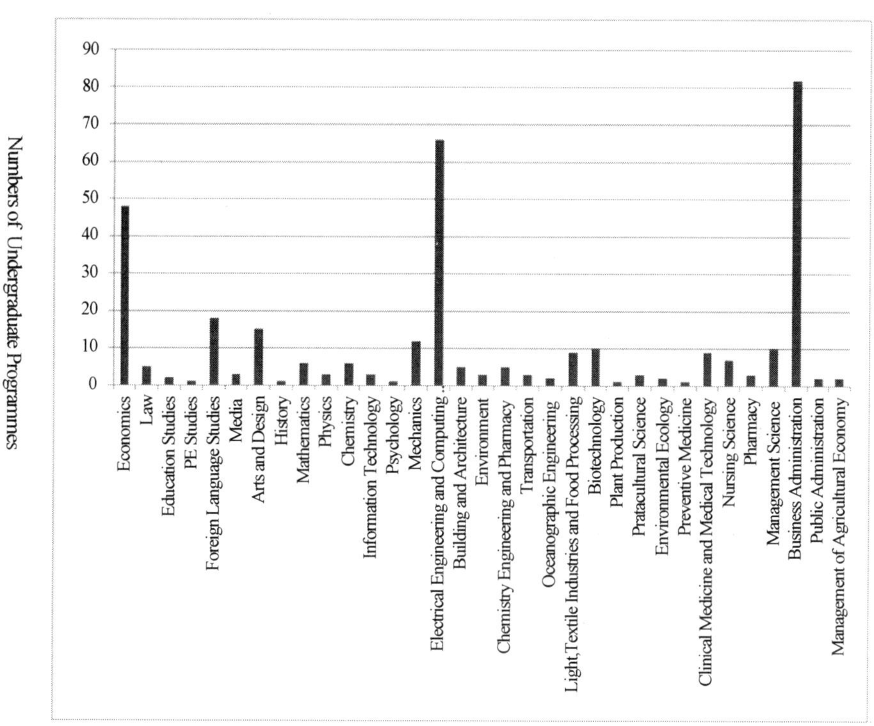

	Number of courses
Economics	48
Law	5
Education Studies	2
PE Studies	1
Foreign Language Studies	18
Media	3
Arts and Design	15
History	1
Mathematics	6
Physics	3
Chemistry	6
Information Technology	3
Psychology	1
Mechanics	12
Electrical Engineering and Computing Sciences	66
Building and Architecture	5
Environment	3
Chemistry Engineering and Pharmacy	5
Transportation	3
Oceanographic Engineering	2
Light,Textele Industries and Food Processing	9
Biotechnology	10
Plant Production	1
Prataculturial Science	3
Environmental Ecology	2
Preventive Medicine	1
Clinical Medicine and Medical Technology	9
Nursing Science	7
Pharmacy	3
Management Science	10
Business Administration	82
Public Administration	2
Management of Agricultural Economy	2

Figure 2-3 Subjects of TNHE Undergraduate Programmes by 19th July, 2010

eight Russian computing programmes are in the same province. The duplication of similar projects focusing on similar disciplines has caused severe competition within the same area. Some UK universities set up duplicated courses in different Chinese universities. When the Chinese students move on to their second part of study in the UK, they are most likely to be put in the same class. Thus, it is very common to see many UK classes with a high ratio of Chinese students compared to English home students. This not only destroys the Chinese students' expectation of making foreign friends, but may also have negative impacts on the home students' learning experience (Hou and McDowell, 2013).

2.5 Discussions

This study enables a consideration of the stated policies of the Chinese Government with respect to TNHE policies against the actual practices of TNHE. This reveals some inconsistencies between the stated aims and motivations of the policies and the way that TNHE is developing and spreading in practice.

One prominent contradiction is that there is a tension between stated Chinese Government Policy underlining that TNHE is for the public good but in reality TNHE is not developing education where it is most needed which is in the most socially and economically deprived areas of the country. Despite the Chinese Government's effort in shifting the balance of public resources to support education in western provinces (MoE, 2013b), the proposed development of TNHE activity in these areas is not prospering. The Chinese Government wants TNHE to support the wider public good in China, but provinces of China that are remote or not well developed economically are not generally benefiting from the TNHE currently available. TNHE programmes and institutions charge high tuition fees, which is part of the reason that foreign partners are more willing to cooperate with universities situated in wealthy areas with high level of household consumption expenditure. For example, a TNHE programme in southeast China charged RMB 19,200 for the annual tuition fee, which was about four times that of the non-programme students (Hou, Montgomery and McDowell, 2011). This may not be affordable for students from deprived families.

The second evident inconsistency is that the aim of the Government is to import the most urgently needed subjects to improve its education standards, but the duplication of similar projects focusing on similar disciplines has caused severe competition within the subjects favoured by providers and is thus an unnecessary waste of resources. This can be said to be undermining the public interest and therefore works against the development of TNHE for the public good. Some Chinese and foreign universities have lowered their recruitment standard to attract more students. Chinese high-school leavers are recruited into TNHE programmes or institutions through their results in the National Higher Education Entrance Examination. The enrolment standard for degree courses has three tiers and students need to get a high enough score to pass at the relevant standard. The intended recruitment number and score are required to be reported to the Ministry of Education before the Examination and cannot be changed casually. However, due to the severe competition in the same area, some universities illegally lower their recruitment standard to attract more students, which leads to the consequence that some of the foreign degrees cannot be authenticated by the Chinese Government.

Quality assurance has thus become a prominent issue because of the concerns about student enrolment standards and performance and as a result of this the Chinese Government has made the decision to slow the pace of development with respect to licenses for TNHE. A department to check the quality of Transnational Higher Education in China and to make sure that high standard programmes educating qualified students are in place has been created. To ensure the quality of the TNHE, the Chinese Ministry of Education asks institutions to adhere to the principle of public interest in TNHE and work against unreasonably high tuition fees (MoE, 2006). The Chinese Government is taking a stand against the commoditisation of education and restates that education services are not a commodity to trade. To prevent the reduction of enrolment standards, the government emphasises that the number of enrolments must be officially approved and listed in the national recruitment plan. If there are not enough potential students in the approved tier of the National Higher Education Entrance Examination, institutions are not allowed to recruit students for the programme in a lower tier. The teaching quality, standard of the curriculum and degrees awarded should be demonstrated as equivalent to those at the partner universities. For ' double campus ' programmes, foreign university staff should deliver at least one third of the core modules and teaching hours. However, this is very hard to implement for some of the programmes and has not yet been fully attained.

Therefore, in 2007, the Chinese Ministry of Education issued another notice to regulate the TNHE (MoE, 2007). This points out that some universities prefer to set up low cost programmes such as Commerce and Administration, Management, Computing and Information Technology. To be approved by the government, Chinese universities are encouraged to cooperate only with well-known universities or subjects. Eminent scholars in these institutions will also be considered as a criterion for approval. A specialised platform has been created to monitor TNHE (http://www.crs.jsj.edu.cn). Students and parents are able to check the legality and status of a programme or institution to help them make their decision about TNHE programmes. The analysis of the current features of TNHE in China presented here may guide the decisions of policy makers who intended to cooperate with Chinese institutes. The discussion here will enable institutions to understand the policy emphasis of the Chinese Government and this may help in different choices of TNHE destinations thus avoiding over emphasis in geographical areas and in specific subject disciplines.

2.6 Conclusions

This chapter contextualises the Transnational Articulation Programme studied in this research in the context of the globalisation and internationalisation of higher education. The rationale of current cooperation is explored through the discussion on the motivations of the host country (the UK) and the sender country (China). The chapter also provides an analysis of the current situation of Chinese-Foreign Cooperation in Running Schools (CFCRS) and examines the necessity of quality assurance in relation to this kind of transnational education cooperation, which further emphasises the importance of this research project.

TNHE is widely acknowledged as a growth area in higher education. However there is limited research investigating why and how TNHE is growing and the likely trends in its development. This chapter sets transnational higher education in the context of broader political and economic conditions. Research on TNHE has most frequently been undertaken at the institutional level, considering the practice and impact within universities and colleges, and at the individual, student experience level. However, an understanding of political and socio-economic conditions helps to explain the growth of TNHE and the directions of development.

The current state of development cannot be explained by the stereotypical view of English-speaking and Western countries regarding the various forms of international higher education as purely for income generation. The old geo-political configuration of TNHE and the view of some developed and, especially, English-speaking countries acting as suppliers of education and others receiving or purchasing their product is now more complex. It is likely that these distinctions in TNHE will become less clear cut, with perhaps many countries acting as both suppliers and receivers. New models of TNHE such as online and e-learning are also offering new opportunities with different ways to study and have an international experience.

The developments in China remind us that TNHE is not merely an economic operation. There are strong social and political drivers for TNHE operating in China which concern the upskilling of the workforce and the social and economic development of regions across the country. Although cost-effective forms of TNHE, some delivered using new models are important, the academic and social outcomes of higher education are of key concern. In order to achieve the basic goal to provide opportunities to study ' abroad ' importing countries have accepted the tendency for providers to trade upon reputation and the excellence of their standards has been largely assumed. We now see a strong interest in quality assurance with respect to TNHE. This is a development of key interest of both importing and exporting countries. Now, with so much more diversity, quality assurance systems offer a more evidence-based approach to the claims for quality provision and are becoming increasingly important.

As mentioned in the previous chapter, the Chinese Government emphasises that cooperation should benefit the quality enhancement of Chinese institutions and the whole education system (MoE, 2007). When the number of the programmes and institutions goes up, attention is paid to the teaching and learning aspect. Because Britain is the leading partner country and Engineering is one of the top three subjects, the Chinese-British Articulation Programme in Engineering, studied in this research project, will provide some valuable first-hand data on students' learning experience and give some insights into the teaching and learning practices. This will help policy-makers and practitioners uncover the complexity and have a better understanding of the core essence of TNHE in China and the United Kingdom.

Chapter 3 Intercultural Transition

3.1 Introduction

This chapter provides a critical review of the literature in relation to intercultural transition. This literature review was drafted after I finished an independent data analysis and generated a substantive theory in order to avoid importing preconceived ideas and imposing them on my work (Charmaz, 2006). It first reviews existing models and theories, including cultural shock theory, U-shaped curve theory, stress-adaptation-growth model, and developmental models, leading to the conclusion that international students' transition experience is a complex journey and cannot be oversimplified by any of the existing models. This chapter then discusses national cultural theory and culture of learning theory, which argues that understanding individuals' intercultural transition experience from the perspectives of these theories has the potential to fall into the traps of stereotyping. This chapter tries to understand the transition from both a microscopic perspective, focusing on individual factors, as well as a contextual perspective focusing on situational factors. The final part of this chapter examines the social interactions between members of the host community and sojourners, and interprets the intergroup relations by social identity theories. Possible ways to reduce intergroup bias are explored at the end.

3.2 Existing Models: Towards Happy-ending?

3.2.1 Cultural Shock

Sojourners are those who voluntarily go abroad for a set period of time associated with a specific assignment, contact or study, and are most likely to return home after the completion of their 'job' (Ward, Bochner and Furnham, 2001). As one of the main sojourner groups, international students stay overseas for the duration of their diplomas or degrees. The 'popular' idea of 'culture shock' is often used to describe the initial experience of their studying in a foreign country. It is said to be 'precipitated by the anxiety that results from losing all our familiar signs and symbols of social intercourse' (Oberg, 1960: 177). Oberg defines culture shock as an occupational disease. In the process of recovery, sojourners are expected to experience four stages of adjustment: the honeymoon stage followed by a crisis stage characterised by a hostile and aggressive attitude towards the host country, then move on to the recovery stage till the final stage of a complete adjustment (Oberg, 1960: 178-179). These four stages are similar to the U-shaped curve theory suggested by Lysgaard (1955: 51). His study on 200 Norwegian academic professions reviews that:

> adjustment is felt to be easy and successful to begin with; then follows a 'crisis' in which one feels less well adjusted, somewhat lonely and unhappy; finally one begins to feel better adjusted again, becoming more integrated into the foreign community (*ibid.*).

These early theories became popular and triggered the tendency to stage the intercultural transition experience. For example, Smalley (1963: 53-54) proposed a similar four-stage of culture shock. Gullahorn and Gullahorn (1963) expanded the U-shaped curve theory into W-shaped curve theory when they included the re-adjustment process back home.

These perfect U-shaped models have been challenged by some of the researchers. Ward *et al.* (1998:277) conducted a longitudinal study of the psychological and sociocultural adaptation of 35 Japanese students in New Zealand. Their results show that neither psychological nor sociocultural measurements of adaptation demonstrated the U-curve of adjustment. They argue that adjustment problems were greatest at entry point and decreased over time. This was supported by the studies of Brown and Holloway (2007), as well as Ying (2005). Brown and Holloway (2007) conducted an ethnographic study of 13 international students' adjustment journey in England and proposed that, at the early stage, international students were overwhelmed by negative symptoms largely related to culture shock. Ying (2005) argues that international students have various accesses to cross-cultural information before their arrival, and thus are less likely to demonstrate an initial euphoria. On the contrary, the evidence supported a gradual linear decline of acculturative stressors over time.

These clinically-oriented theories imply that these sojourners who experience difficulties require therapy and counselling in adjusting themselves to a new culture (Furnham and Bochner, 1982). Adjusting a person to a new culture is associated with cultural chauvinism which implies that the sojourners should abandon their original culture to embrace the values and customs of the host society (*ibid.*). These medical models not only focused on the negative features of the transition experience, and viewed 'culture shock' as a medical problem, but also regarded sojourners as passive victims in need of outside help (Ward, Bochner and Furnham, 2001:36-45). In intercultural transition studies, there are requirements for new theoretical approaches which view sojourners as active respondents who are dealing with their problems in constructive ways (*ibid.*).

3.2.2 Stress-Adaptation-Growth Model

The term *shock* in the above models is negative and implies that only difficulties will result from culture contact (Berry, 2006). *Stress* has 'a theoretical basis in studies of how people deal with negative experiences (*stressors*) by engaging in various *coping* strategies, leading eventually to some form of *adaptation*' (Lazarus and Folkman, 1984, cited in Berry, 2006: 43). Therefore, as Berry (2006) has argued, acculturation experiences can be advantageous as well from a stress perspective.

Berry's argument that stress can promote adaptation in a positive way is showed in Kim's (2001) acculturation model: stress-adaptation-growth. Kim (2005: 383) argues that *stress* is a kind of identity conflict essentially between the need for acculturation and the resistance to deculturation. It occurs when an individual's internal capabilities are not adequate to meet the demands of the environment (*ibid.*). Then, the creative forces of self-reflexivity of human mentation are triggered by each stressful experience and will help the individual to reorganise him/herself. Stress will be driven away when the individual works out new ways to handle problems and a 'leap forward' will be realised. Therefore the dynamic psychological movement consists of a three-pronged process: stress-adaptation-growth (Kim, 2005: 384). Stress is essential in the adaptation process and allows for self-(re)organisation and self-renewal (*ibid.*). Kim (2001) also points out that the stress-adaptation-growth dynamic plays out in dialectic, cyclic, and continual 'draw-back-to-leap' pattern, rather than a smooth, steady, and linear progression.

3.2.3 Developmental Models

Burnett and Gardner (2006: 68-70) advocate that developmental models of acculturation are more appropriate to explain the process their participants' experienced. The two models they reviewed are the stage-models of Bennett (1986) and Yoshikawa (1988). Bennett (1986: 181-186) suggests a six-stage continuum of personal growth: *denial* (the parochial denial of difference), *defense* (the evaluative defense against difference), *minimization* (the universalist position of minimization of difference), *acceptance* (the acceptance of difference), *adaptation* (the adaptation to difference) and *integration* (the integration of difference into one's world view). This developmental continuum moves from ethnocentrism to ethnorelativism. Burnett and Gardner(2006) point out that this model puts every stranger in a denial or defence position, presuming that they do not have any prior intercultural experience. This will lead to the danger of being judgemental in its view of those whom it assesses to be ethnocentric(*ibid.*).

Drawing on the philosophy of dialogue and Buddhistic perspectives on paradoxical relations, Yoshikawa(1987) constructs his double-swing model of intercultural communication, which is symbolised by the Möbius strip ' ∞ '. Yoshikawa's argument presents a non-western perception on the idea of intercultural communication. Yoshikawa (1987: 326-327) explains that his model is neither monistic nor dualistic, but an ' identity-in-unity '. It emphasises ' the act of meeting between two different beings without eliminating the otherness or uniqueness of each and without reducing the dynamic tension created as a result of meeting' (*ibid.*). One will neither be this side nor that side nor beyond both sides, but a dynamic, tension-laden ' between' in the balance of pull from the polarities of life. Later, Yoshikawa (1988) presents his five-stage model of cross-cultural adaptation: *contact*, *disintegration*, *reintegration*, *autonomy*, and *double-swing*. These stages are similar to Adler(1975)'s transition experience model. Yoshikawa substitutes Adler's fifth stage ' Independence ' with his pattern ' Double-Swing '. Adler's ' Independence ' stage shows that the individual's ' attitude, emotions and behaviours are independent but not independent of cultural influence' and is able to ' accept and draw nourishment from both cultural similarities and differences' (Adler, 1975: 144). His ' independent-interdependent ' stage embraces a new identity—the ' identity-in-unity ' or ' duality-in-unity ' (Yoshikawa, 1988: 142). However, this kind of in-betweenness(Double-swing or Integration) has not been confirmed by the research of Burnett and Gardner (2006: 88-89) on Chinese students' transition experience in UK universities. They argue that sojourners ' do internalise differences sufficiently so that they react as appropriate to the cultural context or situation in which they find themselves at any particular time'. They propose the end point of their acculturation model as 'Internalisation'.

3.3 National Cultures Perspective: a Suitable Way in Understanding Individuals?

3.3.1 National Cultural Theory and the Danger of Stereotyping Individuals

Collectivism versus individualism based on Hofstede's (1984) cultural theory is often considered as the main aspect in understanding Chinese students' transition experience in the UK. Hofstede (1984:21) defines culture as 'collective programming of the mind which distinguishes the members of one human group from another'. The main argument of his theory is that:

> People carry 'mental programs' which are developed in the family in early childhood and reinforced in schools and organization, and that these mental programs contain a component of national culture. They are most clearly expressed in the different values that predominate among people from different countries (Hofstede, 1984:11).

He called these 'mental programs' *software of the mind* (Hofstede, 1991: 4). The social environments one was brought up in are the sources of one's mental programs (*ibid.*). Hofstede surveyed staff in a large multinational business organization in 40 countries and identified four main dimensions along which dominant value systems in these countries can be ordered: *Power Distance* (from small to large), *Uncertainty Avoidance* (from weak to strong), *Collectivism versus Individualism*, and *Femininity versus Masculinity* (Hofstede, 1991: 14; Hofstede, 1984: 11). Bond and his Chinese colleagues in Hong Kong and Taiwan added a fifth dimension to Hofstede's 4-D framework: *long-term versus short-term orientation* (Hofstede and Hofstede, 2005: 31). These dimensions are believed to be able to affect human thinking, organisation, and institutions in predictable ways (Hofstede, 1984: 11).

Among these dimensions, *Collectivism versus Individualism* is always used as a main aspect in the comparison of the East and the West. Hofstede and Hofstede (2005: 33) think this is the least controversial of their dimensions. Mainland China was not on the Individualism index tables, but two regions, Hong Kong and Taiwan rank the 37th and 44th respectively in the league. The USA, Australia, the UK, Canada and Netherlands rank 1st to 5th. According to Hofstede (1991: 58-61), people from collectivist culture are more likely to avoid direct confrontation with another person to maintain harmony, respect group opinions rather than give personal opinion, be less independent and worry about losing face (being humiliated), while people from individualist cultures tend to speak one's mind to show honesty, develop their own opinion, be more independent and gain self-respect. Therefore, at school, collectivist culture students will hesitate to speak up in larger groups unless a teacher addresses their names, especially when there are outgroup members (Hofstede, 1991: 62). Because of to the large power distance in their culture, education tends to be teacher-centred with little interaction (*ibid.*).

Hofstede's work has a massive impact on intercultural studies, but is controversial as well. Holliday (2010: 260) criticises the presentation of national culture as the basic unit to describe and predict cultural behaviour in Hofstede's work. Montgomery (2010: 11) points out that suggesting a causal link between certain behaviours and particular nationalities is a kind of stereotype. Using the five dimensions of the framework to explain behaviour will create an essentialist picture, Which is inclined to cultural chauvinism because 'behavioural traits such as cheating are easily traced to the prioritising of group behaviour over personal choice, family structures, religion, political hierarchies and so on, so that not just cheating but a whole cultural system may be demonised' (Holliday, 2010: 260). This tendency is associated with Orientalism, which considers 'the long-standing Othering of the "exotic" East and the South as morally deficient' (*ibid.*).

Facing the increasing accusation of ' stereotyping ', Hofstede's first feedback to the criticism is that nations are 'usually the only kinds of units available for comparison, and they are better than nothing' (Hofstede, 2001: 73). In their latest version of 'Cultures and Organizations: Software of the Mind', Hofstede, Hofstede and Minkov (2010:40) notify that the association between personality and culture is not absolute, but statistical. Their support for the argument is via use of McCrae and Hofstede's self-scored personality test using the NEO Personality Inventory based on the Big Five (Neuroticism, Extraversion, Openness, Agreeableness, and Conscientiousness) to explore the relationship between personality dimension scores and national culture dimension scores (*ibid.*). The results show that a wide range of different personalities exist in every country, but the way the individuals describe themselves in personality tests is partly influenced by their national culture, which shows that culture and personality are not independent (*ibid.*). They also state that national culture scores are about national societies, rather than individuals. The re-explanation of their main arguments about mental programming is that national culture is not a combination of properties of the 'average citizen', or a 'modal personality; a set of likely reactions may not be shown by the same *individuals*, but only statistically more often in the same *society* (Hofstede, Hofstede and Minkov, 2010:191).

Therefore, both Hofstede and his critics have realised the danger of stereotyping individuals by their national cultures. In fact, as Montgomery (2010: 14-15) has pointed out, stereotypes act as a sort of selective filter through which people view others. 'Previously held beliefs relating to the culture and values of others are maintained by concentration on aspects of behaviour and interaction which support the stereotype, and evidence that contradicts the stereotype is ignored. Information that supports the stereotype is hoarded and information to the contrary is dismissed' (*ibid.*). Volet and Ang (1998) find that preconceived, negative, stereotyped views separate international students and home students. Both parties failed to benefit from learning from each other. The stereotypes in the learning context also influence the understanding of international students' intercultural transition which will be discussed in the following section.

3.3.2 Culture of Learning Theory and the Tendency to Stereotype Chinese Learners

Influenced by Hofstede's national culture theory on *Collectivism versus Individualism*, Cortazzi and Jin (1997) have proposed culture of learning theory to understand Chinese students' learning behaviours in the western educational context. Their work is well referenced, but might be the most contested in the literature on Chinese learning experience abroad. A culture of learning is the ' cultural beliefs and values about teaching and learning, expectations about classroom behaviour and what constitutes "good" teaching work' (Cortazzi and Jin, 1997:76). The main arguments of the theory are: students who are involved in a multi-cultural higher education environment will ' not only carry cultural behaviour and concepts into the classroom but that they also use the specific framework of their cultures to interpret and assess other people's words, actions and academic performance' (Cortazzi and Jin, 1997:77). The contrasted features of cultures of learning in the academic settings in China and the UK are listed in Table 3-1, which has been criticized as a way having strengthened the stereotypes of Chinese students.

Table 3-1 Different Emphases in Cultures of Learning: China & UK

CHINA	UK
Knowledge from teachers & textbooks	Skills in communicating & learning
Collective consciousness co-ordination, group support, social & moral learning	Individual orientation personal needs, attention, talent, uniqueness
Teaching & learning as performance Pace, variety, presentation, virtuosity	Teaching & Learning as organization Pairs, groups, activities, tasks
Learning through practice & memorization towards mastery preparation, repetition, confidence building	Learning through interaction & construction Experience, activities, tasks, initial creativity

(contd.)

CHINA	UK
Contextualized communication Listener/reader responsibility	Verbal explicitness Speaker/writer responsibility for communication
Hierarchical relations Agreement, harmony, face, respect	Horizontal relations Discussion, argument, informality
Teacher as model Expert, authority, parent, friend, teacher-centred	Teacher as organizer Mentor, guide, helper, learner-centred

(Source: Cortazzi and Jin, 1996a: 74)

They also argue that in the classroom, British university staff and Chinese students' expectations might have the following academic culture gaps shown in Table 3-2.

Table 3-2 Academic Culture Gaps Between the Expectations of British University Staff and Those of Some Overseas Students

British academic expectations	Academic expectations held by Chinese and other groups
Individual orientation	Collective consciousness
Horizontal relations	Hierarchical relations
Active involvement	Passive participation
Verbal explicitness	Contextualised communication
Speaker/writer responsibility	Listener/reader responsibility
Independence of mind	Dependence on authority
Creativity, originality	Mastery, transmission
Discussion, argument, challenge	Agreement, harmony, face
Seeking alternatives	Single solution
Critical evaluation	Assumed acceptance

(Source: Cortazzi and Jin, 1997: 78)

This culture of learning theory is in conflict with the findings of empirical studies and has been criticised by some researchers (Feng, 2009; Tian, 2008;

Gieve and Clark, 2005; Kumaravadivelu, 2003; Stephens, 1997). Stephens (1997) criticises Jin and Cortazzi's view as oversimplified and confirms 'the view of "culture" as an area of contested discourse rather than a reified construct' (p. 119). She points out the risk in overgeneralising about differences between the ways in which Chinese and British think.

> A broad brush view of the Chinese as collectively-oriented and the British as individualistic may say something about the historical development of ideology, but in relation to contemporary culture it may miss as much as it reveals (Stephens, 1997:120).

She argues that Chinese attitudes towards academic study are different and ideas about Chinese culture should be understood in a historical context.

Kumaravadivelu (2003) argues that classroom behaviours 'are the result of a complex interface between several social, cultural, economic, educational, institutional, and individual factors'. Therefore, '[i]t is almost impossible to control a multitude of variables in order to isolate culture as the sole variable that can be empirically studied to determine its impact on classroom behavior'. The author has doubts about Cortazzi and Jin's (1996b) research methodology, thinking that their research displays a 'lack of robust research design that can separate culture as a variable in order to investigate its causal connection to classroom behavior' and this kind of research 'predominantly through the cultural lens will result in nothing more than a one-dimensional caricature of these learners' (p. 714). He used the findings of Cheng's (2002) research to show a different story of a group of 167 Chinese students, who:

> are more concerned with the process of learning than with the product; they have realized that the ultimate goal of language learning is skills rather than knowledge; they prefer a student-centred approach to a teacher-centred approach; and they are willing to participate in interactive and cooperative language

learning activities (Cheng, 2002: 13, cited in Kumaravadivelu, 2003:715).

Cheng also finds that learner motivation and the importance they attached to their major subject shaped his subjects' expectations. This differs from Cortazzi and Jin's conclusion that the expectations and behaviour of Chinese learners are formed by a specific culture and social environment into which they have been socialised from an early age (Kumaravadivelu, 2003: 715). Kumaravadivelu (2003) points out that one of the reasons why teachers persist with cultural stereotypes is that:

> In our attempt to deal with the complexity of our task, we fall for simple, sometimes simplistic, solutions. We may be stereotyping our learners partly because it helps us reduce an unmanageable reality to a manageable label. ... So if our students fail to interact in class the way we expect them to, or if they fail to show that they engage their minds the way we want them to, we readily explain their behaviour in terms of culture and cultural stereotypes (Kumaravadivelu, 2003:716-717).

Gieve and Clark (2005) suggest that personal identity should be considered in the understanding of the different cultures of learning. Their research on Chinese students self-directed learning suggests that 'given appropriate conditions, what are apparently culturally determined dispositions towards a certain approach to learning can turn out to be quite flexible' (p. 261). Chinese participants respond well to forms of self-directed learning which are not only 'reactive and group-based', but also 'proactive and individual' (p. 265). They warn us of 'the danger of characterising groups of learners with reductionist categories' and suggest that attention must be paid to 'the heterogeneity in supposedly homogeneous cultures of learning' (p. 261).

Tian (2008) raises the issue that Jin and Cortazzi's work might not be freed from 'the accusation of homogenizing Chinese learners' and she supports

Stephens' s (1997) opinion that there is 'a tendency to dichotomize the West and the East' (p. 33). She points out the danger of over-generalisation and the tendency to use cultural stereotypes (p. 35). Tian, herself, adopts a qualitative multiple-case study method to explore the experiences of 13 Chinese postgraduate students in a UK university. Her findings challenge 'essentialist conceptualisation which sees individual students from China as undifferential collective members marked by a unique and fixed set of cultural scripts' (p. iii).

Another researcher who argues against the findings of Jin and Cortazzi is Feng(2009). He referenced the findings of Littlewood's(2001) survey, which was conducted among 2,656 students in 8 CHC(Confucian Heritage Culture) countries in Asia and 3 European countries, to 'suggest that difference in cultures of learning is perhaps an illusion as the students from different cultures seem to have the same perceptions and preferences as far as learning is concerned(Littlewood, 2001, cited in Feng, 2009: 78). This suggests that the 'Confucian culture of learning, like any form of culture, is context dependent' and 'essential features may be found evident in certain situations but not in others' (Feng, 2009: 78). In his view, 'contrastive studies do not seem to provide much valid insight into the dynamics of two cultures of learning in contact' and, in fact, questions 'whether the discussion on the notion makes any sense at all if little valid evidence of contrast or divergence is found between Confucian and Socratic cultures of learning, which have been traditionally believed to be vastly different' (p. 78).

Feng(2009) points out that the dominant 'standard' view of culture in the research of intercultural studies is 'an essentialist or reductionist approach to theorising culture', which 'is limited to locating essential features of a particular social group, that is the shared values, established norms and patterned behaviours' (Fay, 1996; Holliday, 1999, 2005 and Keesing, 1998, cited in Feng, 2009: 74). Instead, he proposes to adopt the third space theories in empirical studies to 'shed new light' on international students' learning experience abroad. Based on Bhabha's 'Third Space' theory, Feng

(2009) argues that:

> the third space perspective not only challenges traditional views of the elusive notion of culture but more importantly problematises our 'normal', polarised or binary perceptions of the relationships between, for examples, the West and the East, intercultural and intracultural communication, education and training, and deep learning and surface learning ... (Feng, 2009:75).

He analyses the experience of a group of CHC students at a UK university using the third space concepts. The findings show that both the CHC students and the lecturers in the UK perceived the differences between two cultures of learning discussed above. 'The perceived norms of learning and teaching associated with the Confucian culture of learning, their preliminary schemata, are useful as both students and lecturers seem to depend on them to make sense of the realities they face and use them as the basis for negotiating their identities and mediating learning and pedagogical strategies. During mediation, their preliminary schemata underwent a process of modification and transformation' (Feng, 2009:86). He finds that

> 'something new and something unrecognisable' did occur when the two cultures were in contact'. 'Some CHC students were exploring 'a new area of negotiation of meaning and representation' (Bhabha, 1990b:211) in a third space constituting the 'discursive conditions of enunciation' (Feng, 2009:87).

Therefore, Feng (2009) argues that 'the concepts of third space is particularly insightful when we study the experience of international mobile students' with 'its strong proposition to contest binary or polar opposites such as Confucian and Socratic cultures of learning' (p. 87). The notion of 'discursive conditions of enunciation' represented in third space allows researchers and theorists to investigate heterogeneity and ambivalence of culture and cultures in contact from different perspectives and from multidimentions' (p. 87).

The traditional cross-cultural approach ' is limited by its tendency to conceptualize culture as a static reality, rather than a dynamic and multi-faceted phenomenon' (Wang, 2008: 58). Contemporary China is demonstrating 'the fluidity and complexity of Chinese culture' due to the 'strange mix of socialist collectivism and market forces' evident under the trend of globalisation (Wang, 2008: 58-59). Moreover, the change of growing up in the family environment, education experience at school and living experience in society has added complexity to Chinese culture and certainly influenced the people inside it. Being the only child in the family, children receive more attention from parents and all four grandparents. Since 2001, the Ministry of Education launched a curriculum reform for basic education in China (Ho, 2006). The core of the curriculum reform was to cultivate ' new, advanced cultures and concepts to spread in schools and the society at large' (Xinhua News Agency, 2005, cited in Ho, 2006: 351). As discussed in the previous chapter, higher education institutions in China have gone through a fast changing period of internationalisation and cross border cooperation with partner universities all over the world. The province where the Southeast China University is situated is one of the leading and most rapidly developing areas in China. In 2007, the level of household consumption expenditure ranked third at the provincial level in mainland China (National Bureau of Statistics of China, 2008). Ninety per cent of the participants are from this province. They were born in the late 1980s, ten years after China implemented the policies of economic reform and opened up to the outside world; they have thus grown up during the process of China's globalisation. The occupations of their parents are managers, professors, doctors, civil servants, bankers or other professions with high income. These students either have a laptop or a computer and the internet is a part of their life. The environment these students grow up in might be largely different from those participants in Cortazzi and Jin's (1997) research. Via its overgeneralising and stereotyping the differences between frozen snapshots of cultures, the traditional comparative approach will not be useful in understanding teaching and learning practices in transnational programs (Wang, 2008).

3.4 A Microscopic Perspective: Focusing on Individual Factors

Discussions in the above sections demonstrate that the macro perspective, understanding international students' transition experience through their national cultures or cultures of learning, might lead to the tendency of stereotyping individuals. The dichotomy of East and West cultures pushes people into two sides, exaggerating the possible differences they might have and burying the similarities they are definitely experiencing in this globalised society. If I take this essentialist approach to understand the Articulation Programme Students' transition experiences, the only result I might get is a simplistic solution in terms of culture and cultural stereotypes for every unexplainable behaviour in the participants (Kumaravadivelu, 2003).

To avoid stereotypes imposed by essentialist and culturist perspectives, the contextualized approach should take a 'small cultures' approach, as suggested by Holliday (1999). Holliday (1999: 237-241) has distinguished the 'small cultures' from 'large cultures' by pointing out that the character of the former is 'non-essentialist', 'non-culturist', and related to 'cohesive behaviour in activities within any social grouping', whereas the latter is 'essentialist', 'culturist', and refers to 'prescribed ethnic, national and international entities'. Taking a 'small culture' perspective, the research orientation will be interpretive, focusing on process, rather than prescriptive, relying on the idea that specific ethnic, national or international groups have different cultures (Holliday, 1999: 241).

Intercultural transition is a complex issue. The experiences vary across different individuals. The overgeneralisations of students' transition experiences based on their nationalities and the cultural values behind them neglect the diversity of each student as an individual and their active agency in the transition process. Their personal factors, such as motivation, pre-departure knowledge, autonomy, and language competency, are crucial. Meanwhile, successful transition needs a supportive environment. The support they get from their peers and teaching practices cannot be neglected.

3.4.1 Motivation for Studying Abroad

Research has established a link between motivation and the outcome of the transition. For example, Chirkov *et al.* (2007: 215) applied constructs from Self-Determination Theory (SDT) to study international students' motivation for studying abroad. The results generally support their hypothesis that international students who are self-determined in their decision to study abroad adapt more successfully to a new cultural environment in comparison to those who are driven by non-self-determined reasons.

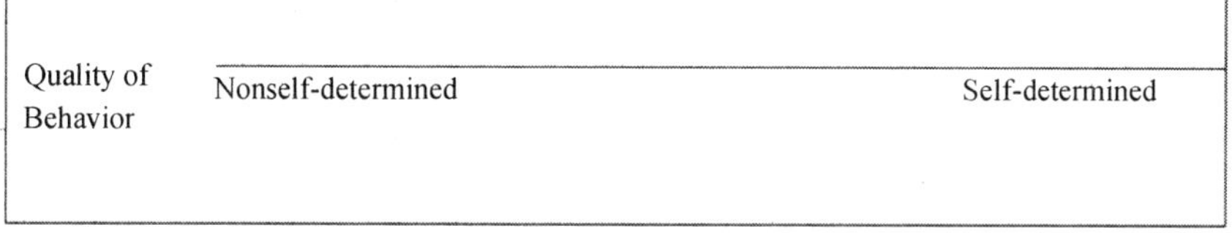

Type of Motivation	Amotivation	Extrinsic Motivation				Intrinsic Motivation
Type of Regulation	Non-Regulation	External Regulation	Introjected Regulation	Identified Regulation	Integrated Regulation	Intrinsic Regulation
Quality of Behavior	Nonself-determined					Self-determined

Figure 3-1 **The Self-Determination Continuum, with Types of Motivation and Types of Regulation (Source: Ryan and Deci**, 2002: 16)

Deci and Ryan's Self-Determination Theory highlights the social and environmental factors that facilitate versus undermine intrinsic motivation (Deci and Ryan, 2009; Ryan and Deci, 2000). *Intrinsic motivation* refers to doing an activity as it is inherently interesting or enjoyable, which results in high-quality learning and creativity. It is correlated with positive coping, as tested in Ryan and Connell's (1989) research, which is the prototype of autonomous or self-determined behaviour (Ryan and Deci, 2002). *Extrinsic motivation* means doing something because it leads to a separable outcome, which varies in different types, as shown in Figure 3-1.

External regulation is the classic type of extrinsic motivation, such as students who 'perform extrinsically motivated actions with resentment, resistance, and disinterest', and is considered as a pale and impoverished motivation compared with intrinsic motivation (Ryan and Deci, 2000:55). The behaviours are not representative of one's self, but are accompanied by the experience of pressure and control (Ryan and Deci, 2000: 65). This is the least autonomous form of extrinsic motivation (Ryan and Deci, 2002). Ryan and Connell (1989) find that it is related to poorer coping with failure and more anxiety. *Introjected regulation* is a type of extrinsic motivation which has only been partially internalised and has not been truly accepted as one's own (Ryan and Deci, 2002). Students' commitment toward an activity is based on feelings of guilt and compulsion (Koestner and Losier, 2002).

Identified regulation is a more self-determined form of extrinsic motivation in comparison with *introjected regulation* or *external regulation* (Ryan and Deci, 2002). Identification 'represents an important aspect of the process of transforming external regulation into true self-regulation' (Ryan and Deci, 2002: 17). This kind of extrinsic motivation involves 'a conscious valuing of a behavioural goal or regulation, an acceptance of the behaviour as personally important' (*ibid.*). Students' commitment toward an activity is based on its perceived meaning in relation to one's goals, values and identity (Koestner and Losier, 2002). Therefore, it is associated with a high degree of perceived autonomy (*ibid.*). However, some identification may not reflect the person's overarching values in a given situation (*ibid.*).

Integrated regulation is the most autonomous form of extrinsic motivation, which results in situations where 'identifications have been evaluated and brought into congruence with the personally endorsed values, goals, and needs that are already part of the self' (Ryan and Deci, 2002: 18). Students 'perform extrinsically motivated actions with an attitude of willingness that reflects an inner acceptance of the value or utility of a task', in which case 'the extrinsic goal is self-endorsed and thus adopted with a sense of volition' (Ryan and Deci, 2000: 55). The behaviours stem from one's sense of self which are accompanied by the experience of freedom and autonomy (Ryan and Deci, 2000: 65). It is related to more positive coping styles compared with other forms of extrinsic motivation. Although integrated extrinsic motivation shares many qualities with intrinsic motivation, the behaviours are still carried out to attain personally important outcomes rather than for inherent interest and enjoyment (Ryan and Deci, 2002: 18).

At the left end of the self-determination continuum shown in Figure 3-1 is *amotivation*, which is the state of lacking the intention to act (Ryan and Deci, 2002). Amotivated students either do not act at all or act passively (*ibid.*). The reasons for amotivated behaviours can be a lack of contingency or perceived competence or a lack of perceived value in the activity or outcomes (*ibid.*).

Therefore, apart from intrinsic motivation, internalisation can be another innate growth tendency to explain students' vitality, development, and psychological adaptation (Koestner and Losier, 2002: 101). Internalisation refers to 'the natural tendency to strive to integrate (or take into one's self) socially-valued regulations that are initially perceived as being external' (*ibid.*). *Identification* and *introjection* are two processes of the internalisation. The former describes 'the process wherein people accept the value of an activity as their own so that they can more easily assimilate it with their core sense of self (it becomes integrated with their values, beliefs, and personal goals)' (Koestner and Losier, 2002: 102). This results in a sense of personal endorsement of one's action (*ibid.*). The latter refers to 'a less successful internalisation in which a value or regulatory process is taken in but not accepted as one's own', which is theorised to be quite controlling and associated with the feelings of pressure or compulsion (*ibid.*). Koestner and

Losier(2002) conducted two separate longitudinal studies on transitions for high school students and college students. They argue that introjections placed students at risk when negotiating important developmental transition such as entering into or graduating from college. Their participants showed a pattern of heightened psychological distress when they were pursuing their education through internal pressures related to guilt avoidance and self-esteem maintenance(*ibid.*). Intrinsic and identified regulation can generate 'positive outcomes such as active information processing, the experience of positive emotions, and successful adaptation to school transitions' (Koestner and Losier, 2002: 113).

Ryan and Deci(2002) point out that to enhance successful internalization, the social environment should provide support for the three basic psychological needs of *relatedness*, *competence*, and *autonomy*. Their theory argues that through feelings related to the other person or the group, individuals will be more likely to engage in a behaviour endorsing an action, thus promoting the process of internalisation. For example, students, who feel securely connected to and cared for by their parents and teachers, tend to fully internalise the regulation of positive school-related behaviours (Ryan, Stiller and Lynch, 1994, cited in Ryan and Deci, 2002). If students feel incompetent to perform a target behaviour, they are unlikely to internalise the regulation of the behaviour and will be likely to find an excuse not to do the behaviour at all(Ryan and Deci, 2002). Self-determination theory advocates that support for autonomy is the critical factor promoting integrated regulation, which has been evidenced by empirical research studies(Deci, Connell and Ryan, 1989; Grolnick and Ryan, 1989; Deci, Nezlek and Sheinman, 1981).

> ... to integrate the regulation of a behaviour, people must grasp its meaning for themselves personally, and they must synthesize the meaning with other aspects of their psychic makeup. This type of engagement with the activity and with the process of internalization is most likely to occur when people experience a

> sense of choice, volition, and freedom from external demands. Accordingly, autonomy support is the basis for people's actively transforming a value and regulation into their own (Ryan and Deci, 2002:20).

According to self-determination theory, students who are overly controlled by parents or teachers are likely to lose initiative and learn less well, especially in a complex and creative learning process, than those who are autonomy supported. In comparison with those who grow up in a controlling environment, autonomy supported students are found to exhibit more autonomous self-regulation, less unknown control, higher perceived competence, and higher achievement (Grolnick, Ryan and Deci, 1991, cited in Grolnick and Apostoleris, 2002). These two forms of extrinsic motivation, *passive and controlling* versus *active and volitional* have different impacts on my participants' transition experience which will be illustrated in Chapter 5.

3.4.2 Pre-departure Preparation

Pre-departure knowledge of the new environment international students will live and study in is considered by Tsang (2001: 352-353) as a key background factor. His research supported Black's (1988) findings that this is important for sojourners' adjustment. Hall and Toll (1999:8) argue that pre-departure preparation should consider sojourners' prior experience and current knowledge, feelings and attitudes in order to influence what takes place during, and possibly after, the residence stage abroad (Hall and Toll, 1999: 8). Well-designed activities can help students to contextualise and learn from their prior and future experiences, which will raise their intercultural awareness by offering students insights into the transition processes and being 'intercultural people' ultimately (Hall and Toll, 1999:8). This will enhance sojourners' readiness and their ability to be open and flexible in new learning environments (Alred, 2003:18). Zhou, Topping and Jindal-Snape (2009) have found evidence in their study that an introduction to UK teaching and learning for Chinese students before their arrival may help them to be psychologically better prepared for and adapt to the UK educational system more quickly. Their participants identified that pre-departure preparations in their original countries are as important as post-arrival support from host countries in their transition experience. Their research supports Kennedy's(1999, cited in Zhou, Topping and Jindal-Snape, 2009) suggestion that pre-departure expectations would be closely related to sojourners' post-arrival adaption experiences.

During the transition, people will face a huge amount of uncertainty and newness, and when they 'exceed their absorption threshold they begin to display signs of dysfunction: fatigue, emotional burn out, inefficiency, sickness, drug abuse' (Conner, 1998: 12). Through increasing the predictability of the new situation and their anticipatory familiarity, such knowledge can reduce the uncertainty facing international students (Tsang, 2001: 352-353). Receiving universities are suggested to provide more detailed information about the institute and the country to facilitate anticipatory adjustment (Tsang, 2001: 365). Meanwhile, the sending universities should encourage and prepare would-be sojourners to engage in their transition(Alred, 2003: 18).

> Students are helped to appreciate the dimensions of their own cultural identity in order that they can understand how other belief systems and attitudes are encoded in other societies. The rationale is that the development of complex thinking about cultural difference through greater self-knowledge and awareness increases the self-confidences to be open to the challenges of living abroad(Alred, 2003: 19).

Educational transition is also a mutual adaptation which is experienced by all the stakeholders in the transition process. Petriwskyi *et al.* (2005, cited in Brooker, 2008) make this explicit in their definition of transition, which is considered as an ongoing process of mutual adaptations by students, families and educational institutions to facilitate students' moving from one setting to another. The transition period can be challenging for all the stakeholders, students and parents, as well as professionals (Jindal-Snape, 2010: 2). 'Professionals working with these children, young people, and families have to learn to implement new strategies according to their varying needs and ways of dealing with transition' (*ibid.*). When we argue that students should be ready for school, the school should be ready for students as well (Pianta and Cox, 1999, cited in Mayer, Amendum and Vernon-Feagans, 2010: 86). This readiness should be expanded to all the stakeholders involved in the transition.

Therefore, building a supportive environment needs cooperation from all stakeholders. For instance, the two educational institutions should exchange information at transfer, including more than just details of academic attainment (Jindal-Snape and Miller, 2010: 24). In the next stage institutions should receive information about individuals who might be more vulnerable at the transition stage (p. 24). Mayer, Amendum, and Vernon-Feagans (2010: 98) also argue that teacher cooperation between two institutions could build a more seamless transition for students. By which, they mean teachers in both settings should communicate to align classroom expectations, procedures, and processes and students could experience similar settings before moving on to the next stage. Once they get into the new school, the similarity across school cultures might facilitate an easier transition (*ibid.*). These two examples of earlier communication and preparation not only facilitate students' transition, but also the adaptation of staff as well. Thus, the transition process has become a shared experience for a variety of individuals, rather than an individual experience for the student him/herself (Dockett and Perry, 2001, cited in Mayer, Amendum and Vernon-Feagans, 2010: 97).

Considering transition process as mutual adaption will expand the benefit limitation from students to all the stakeholders in the process. In this kind of adaptation, all stakeholders could work together in building a supportive environment for all. As Jindal-Snape and Miller (2010: 27) illustrate:

> The internal attributes of the child or young person, a cohesive and supportive family, and an external support network in the form of nursery, school, or university, peers, and community all have a part to play in successful transition (*ibid.*).

The implication for this research is that holistic understanding of students' transition experience should include all the stakeholders in the process focusing on their mutual adaptations and the creation of the supportive environment facilitating successful transition.

3.4.3 Language Competency

International students' second language competency can influence their acculturation experience, which has been confirmed by some studies (Duru and Poyrazli, 2007; Lee, Koeske and Sales, 2004; Yeh and Inose, 2003; Poyrazli *et al.*, 2002; Mori, 2000). The language barrier might be the most significant problem for most international students (Mori, 2000: 137). Smalley (1963: 49) considers language problems as the core of much culture shock, and the very task of language learning carries perils. A lack of fluency in English can negatively affect academic and psychosocial adjustment (Duru and Poyrazli, 2007; Yeh and Inose, 2003). Yeh and Inose (2003: 23) report that lower levels of acculturative distress among international students is predicted by higher frequency of use, fluency level, and the degree to which the participants felt comfortable speaking English. This has been confirmed by the study of Duru and Poyrazli (2007: 108) which shows that English competency is a significant predictor of acculturative stress. Students with high levels of English competency are more likely to ask for help, meet new people and participate in class discussions, which in turn will reduce the level of their acculturative stress. Li, Chen and Duanmu (2010) find that English writing ability is a significant predictor for international students' academic performance.

Linguistic competence is also crucial for intergroup contact and interpersonal relationship development (Kim, 2001). A shared language can activate intergroup cues and influence interpersonal relationship development and maintenance(e. g. Kudo and Simkin, 2003, cited in Imamura, Zhang and Harwood, 2011 : 108). In the research of Japanese sojourners' attitudes toward Americans, Imamura, Zhang and Harwood(2011 : 114) found that participants' English competence, together with communication accommodation, positively predicted their relational solidarity with Americans. Mak and Tran(2001 : 197) found a significant effect of fluency in English on intercultural social self-efficacy.

A lack of linguistic competence will cause stress. Stress on the other hand will affect students' second language acquisition. MacIntyre(1995 : 92) argues that a demand to answer questions in a second language may cause a student to become anxious, which leads to worry and rumination. He uses the following figure to show the recursive relations among anxiety, cognition, and behaviour.

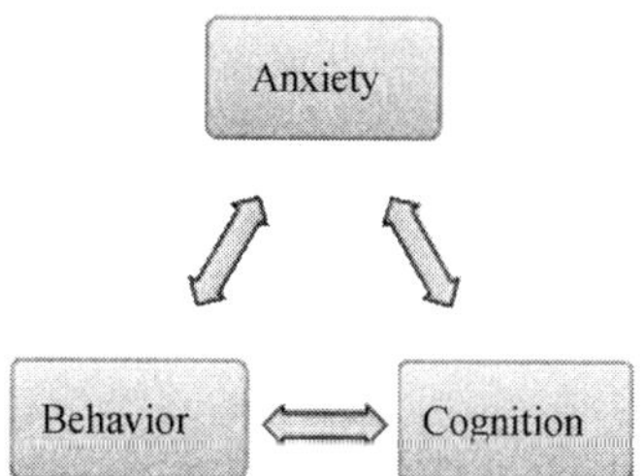

Figure 3-2 Recursive Relations Among Anxiety, Cognition, and Behaviour

(Source: MacIntyre, 1995 : 93)

Anxiety can create a divided attention scenario for anxious students who are focused on both the task at hand and their reactions to it (MacIntyre, 1995 : 96). The divided attention in answering questions in a second language can reduce cognitive performance, leading to negative self-evaluations and more self-deprecating cognition, which will further impair performance(*ibid.*). Thus, the recursive and cyclical pattern of the variables is: aptitude can influence anxiety, anxiety can influence performance, and performance can influence anxiety(*ibid.*). Anxious students do not learn as quickly as relaxed students(MacIntyre, 1995:96). This is verified by Allen and Herron's(2003) research on international students in France, which shows that international students who experience more anxiety have more difficulties in learning the language.

3.4.4 Personal Factors Related to Autonomy

For students at transition in education, the academic and social demand of the new environment can be a stressor. The ways how students appraise and cope with these stressors might be different and will greatly influence their transition to the new environment. This theoretical framework has influenced the literature on transition. Coping is defined by Lazarus and Folkman(1984: 141) as 'constantly changing cognitive and behavioural efforts to manage specific external and/or internal demands that are appraised as taxing or exceeding the resources of the person'. It is 'the process through which the individual manages the demands of the person-environment relationship that are appraised as stressful and the emotions they generate' (Lazarus and Folkman, 1984: 19). Reviewing the body of literature shows that many personal factors related to autonomy can influence the coping strategies related to transition. These include *locus of control* (Ward and Kennedy, 1992 and 1993), *self-efficacy* (Li and Gasser, 2005; Mak and Tran, 2001; Tsang, 2001; Fan and Mak, 1998; Harrison, Chadwick and Scales, 1996), *self-esteem* (Jindal-Snape and Miller, 2010; Brooker, 2008), *self-monitors* (Kosic, Mannetti and Sam, 2006; Harrison, Chadwick and Scales, 1996), *neuroticism* (Poyrazli, Thukral and Duru, 2010; Duru and Poyrazli, 2007; Ward, Leong and Low, 2004), and *resilience* (Wang, 2009).

The concept of *locus of control* was developed from Rotter's(1954) social learning theory. Rotter(1966) makes distinction between internal and external locus of control. Individuals with a high internal locus of control perceive that the positive and negative consequence of events are caused by their own behaviour and are under personal control; while those with high external locus of control believe that the consequences of these events are determined by factors under the control of powerful others such as luck, fate or chance (Rotter, 1990). Ward and Kennedy (1992) find *locus of control* to be a salient variable in acculturation research. Their analysis revealed that external locus of control was associated with greater mood disturbance. Ward and Kennedy (1993) find that internal locus of control is positively related to positive psychosocial adjustment.

Self-efficacy is defined by Bandura (1997) as the level of confidence that individuals have in their ability to accomplish tasks and produce desirable outcomes. Harrison, Chadwick and Scales (1996) find that high general self-efficacy is significantly related to greater degrees of general, interaction, and work adjustment in the process of cross-cultural adjustment. Tsang (2001: 364) also reports that self-efficacy is significant in the general adjustment of sojourners. Bandura's concept of self-efficacy has also been adapted to explore its significance in intercultural interaction (Li and Gasser, 2005; Mak and Tran, 2001; Fan and Mak, 1998). Intercultural social self-efficacy is strongly negatively associated with social avoidance among non-English speaking background migrant students (Fan and Mak, 1998). Mak and Tran (2001: 193) argue that intercultural social confidence or self-efficacy is important for Vietnamese Australian students to be successful in their university studies and future career. A significantly higher level of social self-efficacy in conational interactions was reported by these students. Li and Gasser (2005) argue that self-efficacy is especially important in the cross-cultural interaction. International students with high self-efficacy are confident that they can perform certain social functions successfully in another culture and achieve desirable outcomes (Li and Gasser, 2005: 566). Their research finds that contact with the hosts partially mediated the effect of cross-cultural self-efficacy on sociocultural adjustment. Mak and Tran (2001: 197) suggest that early intervention and intercultural training programs should address the development of intercultural social efficacy, the absence of which will hinder students' academic and occupational success.

Resilience is 'the ability to absorb high levels of change while displaying minimal dysfunctional behavior' (Conner, 1998: 219). Five basic characteristics of resilience are positive, focused, flexible, organised and proactive (Conner, 1998: 238). Wang (2009) considers transition as a change process and resilience characteristics are personal abilities to cope with change. Wang's (2009) study on the transition of international graduate students at U. S. universities find that *resilience* characteristics are highly negatively correlated with adjustment problems.

The successful transition is closely related to *self-esteem*, which is a personal characteristic of individuals (Jindal-Snape and Miller, 2010: 12). In the process of transitions, students will experience various challenges. For students who have high self-esteem, these challenges might stimulate them to think of new strategies to enhance their abilities to cope with difficulties. This could lead to the claim made by Brooker (2008) that 'transitions are a trigger for development and learning' (p. 7). However, for some students who are exposed to a new environment and required to make new responses and establish or lose significant relationships, the process of educational transition can significantly affect their self-esteem (Epstein, 1979, cited in Jindal-Snape and Miller, 2010: 15). In resilience literature, self-esteem is central to students' internal attributes, as pointed out by Jindal-Snape and Miller (2010: 27). They agree with Mruk's opinion that transition is a period of 'challenge of living', where an individual's sense of worth and competence are particularly vulnerable (p. 15). This self-worth and self-competence are two dimensions of Mruk's model of self-esteem theory, which indicates that

> an individual's self-esteem is dependent upon two types of judgement: the extent to which one feels worthy of respect from others, and competent to face the challenges which lie ahead (Jindal-Snape and Miller, 2010: 11).

Jindal-Snape and Miller argue that self-esteem is one of the internal protective factors in students' transition experience. When it is damaged, the external protective factors, such as positive relationships at home and school, are more crucial to walk students through the period of considerable uncertainty and potential stress (p. 23). Newman and Blackburn (2002, cited in Jindal-Snape and Miller, 2010: 23) also assert that a protective environment together with adequate coping skills is indispensable in a successful transition. By protective environment they mean an environment which protects students against excessive demands, but also provides students with opportunities to learn and adapt by exposing them to reasonable levels of risk (*ibid.*). It is hard to make a judgement on how protective the environment should be. As Lucey and Reay (2000, cited in Jindal-Snape and Miller, 2010: 23) have pointed out, the dilemma for students who are under educational transition is that they need to be able and willing to give up some protection in order to gain a level of autonomy.

Harrison, Chadwick and Scales (1996) find that high *self-monitors* expressed greater degrees of general and interaction adjustment than low self-monitors. Kosic, Mannetti and Sam (2006) report that self-monitoring was positively related to sociocultural and psychological adaptation. 'Individuals high on self-monitoring are characterized by high sensibility and sensitivity towards social occurrence' (Kosic, Mannetti and Sam, 2006: 143). They can learn new ways of reacting easily.

From the above review, consensus has emerged that in the process of transition, students who are 'convinced of their own efficacy at overcoming obstacles are more likely to appraise failures and stressors as challenges, to cope using problem-solving and strategizing, and to persevere and remain optimistic in the face of obstacles' (Skinner and Edge, 2002: 297-298). Meanwhile those 'who believe themselves to be incompetent tend to panic and show confusion when faced with setbacks, to become pessimistic and doubting, to ruminate and lose concentration, to escape the stressor if possible, and to expect the worst about future stressful encounters (*ibid.*).

3.5 A Contextual Perspective: Focusing on Situational Factors

Understanding the process of transition to higher education requires an examination from a multidisciplinary perspective (Goldrick-Rab, Carter and Wagner, 2007: 2470). Transition in higher education which involves academic and social integration into the university culture is a significant period for students' success all through their university life. Transition and retention are closely related (Yorke and Longden, 2007). Academic and social integration are vital to survival for new students (Billing, 1997: 132). Support has been highlighted relating to positive transitions in the first year university context (Ramsay, Jones and Barker, 2007: 248). Rather than identifying the difficulties and challenges students will come across, recent research in this area has focused on social and academic support to facilitate students' transition. As argued in the previous sections, transition is a complex issue. Experiences vary across different individuals and successful transition needs a supportive environment. From contextual perspective, situational factors such as social support and formative assessment have been linked closely to the development of supportive environments for students under transition.

3.5.1 Support from Conational, Host National and Other National Groups

Social support has been related to a lower level of acculturative stress (Duru and Poyrazli, 2007; Lee, Koeske and Sales, 2004; Yeh and Inose, 2003). Adelman (1988) argues that social support can help sojourners to cope with uncertainty and enhance perceived mastery and control. Berry *et al.* (1987), Searle and Ward (1990: 451) and Tsang (2001: 365) consider social support as a buffer against acculturative stress. This has been verified by Lee, Koeske and Sales (2004: 399) who report that students with high levels of social support were significantly less likely to report symptoms with increasing levels of acculturative stress. Ye (2006: 12) also found that international students who are more satisfied with their interpersonal support network are more likely to suffer less from acculturative stress.

Bochner(1982: 30) has found that the peer group is important in the academic sojourn, and exerts a major influence on the cultural orientation of the students. He and his colleges have conducted a series of studies to explore the social networks of international students' friendship patterns. They have identified three kinds of social networks that international students belong to. The primary conational network is *monoculture* and provides a place for international students to rehearse and express their ethnic and cultural values. The compatriot group was found to be the most important social network of sojourning overseas students. The secondary network of these students is *bicultural*, and consists of bonds with host nationals and will 'instrumentally facilitate the academic and professional aspirations of the sojourner' (Bochner, 1982:31). Academics, landlords, student advisers and government officials are also put into this category (Furnham and Bochner, 1982: 173). The third network is the *multicultural* circle of friends and acquaintances of international students, which provides 'companionship for recreational, non-culture and non-task oriented activities' (*ibid.*). It is predicted that appropriate host culture friends will help sojourners learn the skills of host culture more easily than those whose friends are all compatriots (Furnham and Bochner, 1982: 174). Ward and Kennedy(1994:333) examined Berry's four modes of acculturation in relation to the two adjustive outcomes of sojourners: psychological and sociocultural adaptations. The results revealed that sojourners with strong host national identification experienced less sociocultural adjustment difficulties, while those with strong co-national identification experienced less psychological adjustment problems. Separation was associated with the greatest level of social difficulty and integrated subjects experienced less depression than assimilated ones(*ibid.*). Kashima and Loh(2006:471) have verified that students with more international ties were better adjusted in general.

Support from the conational group, or the home network, has been identified by some researchers as the main effective source for international students to gain academic, emotional and other support abroad. It has helped Gill's (2007) participants to overcome loneliness and the sense of loss and disorientation at the initial stage. Her research suggests that the home network was considered as the first place where students looked for information on British culture and for orientation and support on arriving in the UK. It has also become a source of academic, emotional and moral support for understanding and reassurance (Gill, 2007: 174). Li, Chen and Duanmu (2010) find that social communication with compatriots is a significant predictor for international students' academic performance. However, Ward, Bochner and Furnham (2001: 87) argue that 'co-national relationships can be harmful or helpful, depending on the nature of individual supporters and their group's dynamics'. Poyrazli *et al.* (2004) prove that students who primarily socialised with non-Americans and that students from Asian countries experienced more acculturative stress compared with other subgroups. Kosic *et al.* (2004) argue that conational groups can limit the heritage worldviews of the individuals.

Furnham and Bochner (1986, cited in Searle and Ward, 1990: 451) point out that relationships with host nationals are more effective for some forms of sojourner adjustment. Li and Gasser (2005: 571) find that Asian students' contact with host nationals facilitated their sociocultural adjustment process because the contact with hosts enabled them to develop local networks, understand local cultures and acquire social skills. Kashima and Loh (2006: 471) illustrate that having personal ties with locals alleviated international students' psychological adjustment. For example, the support from academic staff has been emphasised greatly to help international students overcome initial challenges (Gill, 2007; Elsey, 1990).

Ramsay, Jones and Barker (2007) identify that international students, compared with local students, are facing greater risk of reduced opportunities for social companionship support, which highlights the importance of orientation programs that facilitate cross-cultural adjustment. Universities are suggested to help international students to build up the bonds with members of the host culture to enable benefit for both of the networks (Tsang, 2001; Bochner, 1982). However, some take-for-granted methods may not be effective. For example, some studies have found that internationally mixed accommodation can help students reduce prejudice in relation to other ethnic groups (eg. Pettigrew and Tropp, 2000). Murphy-Lejeune (2003: 108) also argues that shared accommodation and shared activities with native people generate closer contacts. However, Bochner, Hutnik and Furnham (1985: 690) argue that it might fail to be an ideal place for students to get to know each other and build long-standing cross-cultural friendships. They conducted research in England and found that only 17% of the friends of foreign students were English. The predominant friendship pattern of host students was for friendships with other English persons. Their results demonstrate that international houses are not overly successful in facilitating the creation of bonds between foreign students and host nationals.

From a pedagogic perspective, peer support networks are particularly important in the process of transition (Billing, 1997: 132). Well-adjusted students reported higher levels of social companionship support than less adjusted groups (Ramsay, Jones and Barker, 2007: 247). More opportunities for the development of supportive peer relationships should be considered. Failure in making compatible friendship networks may lead students to withdraw (Mackie, 2001). DeBerard, Spielmans and Julka (2004) find a significant relationship between perceived social support and academic achievement for first year students. Academic peer mentoring programmes have been identified as a positive way to support first-year students' academic transition. Studies conducted respectively by Loots (2009), Parkinson (2009), Longfellow *et al.* (2008) and Loke and Chow (2007) assigned senior students to a small group of mentees for different modules. Their results indicate that peer assisted learning support can greatly improve students' academic performance. Loke and Chow (2007) also prove that both tutors and tutees benefit from the peer-tutoring process. Peer support is pivotal to student success and retention. Peer assisted learning feedback is a kind of formative assessment practice. Reviewing literature in this area has led to a tentative conclusion that formative assessment is a way to nurture students' transition in higher education.

3.5.2 Formative Assessment and Transition in Higher Education

Commonly people make the distinction between formative assessment and summative assessment on the basis that marks are awarded in summative assessment, but not awarded in formative assessment. However, the distinction should be based on whether the assessment enhances students' learning during the learning process. Formative assessment in this thesis refers to any assessment and feedback that will enhance students' learning during their learning process. It is the process adopted by teachers in order to recognise and respond to student learning with the purpose of improving the learning in the process of learning (Cowie and Bell, 1999). Formative assessment can be part of individual research projects, self and peer assessment, oral presentations, group projects, poster presentations, simulated professional tasks, portfolios, profiles and other methods, aims to use learning-oriented assessment strategies to enhance student learning 'as opposed to validating or certifying learning through summative assessment' (Keppell *et al.*, 2006: 454).

McDowell (2001) asserts that innovative assessment methods will improve learning and change the culture of assessment because of the shift from the measurement approach to the educational approach. Several new features are essential to the process. The first is that the purpose of the assessment has changed from identifying and categorising intelligence, or ranking students and comparing them with their peers, to identifying and describing achievements against relevant criteria. The next is the change in assessment contents, where there has been a shift from the testing of 'discrete, de-contextualised elements of knowledge and skill' to the assessment of 'more holistic and complex activities' such as problem-based learning (p. 2). The most vital change is the shift from

> highly standardised and controlled testing methods which result in quantitative scores and where assessment is strongly separated from teaching and learning to a more diverse range of assessment methods, resulting in qualitative descriptions or judgements and where assessment is often integrated with teaching and learning and may involve students as active participants (p. 3).

The transfer from quantitative scores to qualitative descriptions shows that the feedback is more meaningful to students. Hattie (1999) affirms that the most powerful single moderator that enhances achievement is feedback. The provision of timely and diagnostic feedback is necessary for students making transition to higher education (McInnis, James and McNaught, 1995). In education, feedback is about 'the current level of performance in relation to the optimum level of performance, including advice on how to bridge the gap between the two', which simply means 'how to get to where you want to go' (Carless, 2003:14). In formative assessment practice, the use of feedback is encouraged to foster students' capabilities of 'evaluating, judging and improving their own performance' which are the core of 'autonomous learning and of the graduate qualities valued by employers and in professional practice' (McDowell *et al.*, 2006:3). It is widely and empirically argued that formative assessment has the greatest impact on learning and achievement (Elton and Johnston, 2002). Increasing the proportion of formative assessment is advocated as a guide to facilitate students to become autonomous learners during the transition (Hussey and Smith, 2010). Compared with summative assessment, formative assessment is more effective in nurturing and monitoring students' transition towards desirable results because of the following reasons.

Formative assessment pays attention to the process rather than the results. Transition is a process and, during this process, formative assessment can provide timely and effective feedback for students' transition to autonomous learners. This can be vividly illustrated by the figures of speech used by Biggs(2003) and TKI(2007) demonstrating the difference between these two kinds of assessments. Biggs(2003) thinks that when the chef tastes the sauce it is formative assessment, while when the customer tastes it, it is summative. Another well-known analogy is that of the garden, which takes students as plants.

> Summative assessment of the plants is the process of simply measuring them. It might be interesting to compare and analyse measurements but, in themselves, these do not affect the growth of the plants. Formative assessment, on the other hand, is the equivalent of feeding and watering the plants appropriate to their needs - directly affecting their growth(TKI,2007:15).

It is undeniable that summative assessment may have played a definite role in assisting students' development. However, the problem is that the timing of traditional exams is normally too late for early feedback (Light and Cox, 2001). The results of formative assessment are for feedback during learning, and benefit both teaching and learning(Biggs, 2003).

The other reason to consider formative assessment as a way to nurture students' transition is that formative feedback will enhance students' self-esteem, which is crucial for a successful transition. Traditionally, summative assessment, such as exams and tests, measures student achievement and is intended to be used as a performance indicator(Knight, 2001). It can reduce the self-esteem of lower-achieving students, who will then not believe that they can succeed in other tasks (Assessment Reform Group, 2002). Because the result of summative assessment can affect the students' future in some way, and the greater the impact, the higher the stake, it is always linked to the concept of high-stakes assessment (Trotter, 2006). Therefore, high-stakes summative assessment should be used 'rigorously but sparingly rather than as the main driver for learning' (McDowell *et al.*, 2006: 3).

Teaching methods may also be restricted to what is necessary for passing the examinations. Hussey and Smith (2010: 162) argue for a flexible, personal and individual tailored system that respects transitions, and which assesses students when they are ready, rather than when it suits the academic calendar. In the transition in higher education, students are expected to take more responsibility for managing their learning. Formative assessment practices are expected to empower these students and develop their self-study abilities. The above arguments offer a premise to propose a hypothesis that adopting formative assessment in teaching can facilitate students' intercultural transition in higher education, on the condition that students actively use formative feedback to improve their learning.

3.6 Intercultural Transition—Group Oriented

In this research, due to the unique feature of the Articulation Programme, the participants will study abroad as a group. When they come to the UK, they will meet another group of students, primarily home students, who have studied in the host university for a whole year. The interaction experience between these two groups will unavoidably influence their intercultural transition experiences. Therefore, a discussion on the literature in this area is necessary.

3.6.1 Intergroup Contact

Sherif (1967: 62) defines *group* as 'a social unit that consists of a number of individuals 1) who, at a given time, stand in status and role relationships with one another, stabilized in some degree, and 2) who possess, explicitly or implicitly, a set of norms or values regulating the behaviour of individual members, at least in matters of consequence to the group'. When two people interact they do not merely respond to each other as individuals but as members of their respective groups, and the larger the differences between groups, the greater the tendency will be for the participants to make a distinction between in and outgroup membership (Bochner, 1982: 35). The distinction takes the form of categorising people as belonging either to 'us' or to 'them', through which they acquire the value differentials between these groups (Tajfel, 1981: 254-255). The consequences of group membership is referred by Tajfel (1981: 255) as *social identity* which is 'part of an individual's self-concept which derives from his knowledge of his membership of a social group (or groups) together with the value and emotional significance attached to that membership'. Social identity is based on the motivational assumption that individuals prefer a positive to a negative self-image (Tajfel, 1981: 45).

Turner *et al.* (1987) extended the social identity theory by developing the self-categorisation theory, 'which specified in detail how social categorisation produces prototype-based depersonalisation of self and others and, thus, generates social identity phenomena' (Hogg and Terry, 2000: 123). 'According to self-categorisation theory, group identities arise in context when meaningful differences are perceived to exist between the ingroup and the outgroup, and ingroup members are perceived to share important attributes or experience in common' (Schmitt, Spears and Branscombe, 2003: 8). Social identity theory and self-categorisation theory, which adopt the social categorisation approach, have influenced the social psychological study of intergroup relations since the early 1970s (Brewer, 1996: 291). Brewer (1996: 292) describes the three characteristic features of any social situation possessing a salient ingroup-outgroup categorisation as:

1) The intergroup accentuation principle: ingroup members are considered to be more similar to the self than the outgroup members;

2) The intergroup favouritism principle: positive affects selectively generalised to ingroup members rather than outgroup members;

3) The social competition principle: intergroup social comparison associated with perceived negative interdependence between the ingroup and the outgroup.

Social psychologists tend to understand intergroup relations in three aspects: stereotypes, prejudice and discrimination (Mackie and Smith, 1998: 500). These three aspects are referred to as intergroup bias, which is the tendency to appraise the ingroup (one's own membership group) or its members more favourably over the outgroup (nonmembership group) or its members (Hewstone, Rubin and Willis, 2002: 576). This tendency can take two forms: ingroup favouritism and outgroup derogation (*ibid.*). Bochner (1982: 20) argues that 'individuals are more familiar with ingroup than outgroup behaviour, and the actions of an ingroup member are more likely to be assigned a situational attribution, whereas similar behaviour performed by outgroup members will be attributed to their personalities'. 'This effect may also account for the stability of outgroup stereotypes, since the behaviour of outgroup members would be seen as being determined by their stable personality, racial and national characteristics rather than as a response to changing circumstances' (Bochner, 1982: 20-21). He suggests that 'the better we get to know other people the more do we come to regard them as we regard ourselves, i. e. in situational terms' (*ibid.*).

Sherif (1967: 72) conducted three separate experiments to explore the formation of the groups, intergroup conflict and co-operation. The findings that are related to the present research are 1) the formation of groups influence the choice of friends; 2) the competition for insufficient resources will cause hostility between groups, but will increase the solidarity and cooperativeness within each group; 3) contact as equals does not necessarily reduce conflict between two hostile groups, but contact involving interdependent action toward superordinate goals contributes to cooperation between groups (Sherif, 1967: 75-93). Cooperative interdependence in pursuit of common and superordinate goals is a necessary condition to reduce intergroup conflict and prejudice (Cook, 1985). However, as Sherif has argued, the cooperation toward superordinate goals is not a one-off thing, but a series of activities which has a cumulative effect in reducing intergroup hostility and negative stereotypes. Multiple ways are suggested to reduce intergroup bias, which will be discussed in the following section.

3.6.2 Ways to Reduce Intergroup Bias

3.6.2.1 *Common Ingroup Identity Model*

Dovidio *et al.* (2001:171) support Sherif's argument about cooperative interaction. They believe that it may partially enhance positive evaluations of outgroup members by transforming interactants' representations of the memberships from two groups to one group (*ibid.*). The Common Ingroup Identity Model has been developed as a strategy to reduce intergroup bias and combat aversive racism by redirecting the forces of social categorisation and social identity (Gaertner and Dovidio, 2000). The fundamental idea of the Common Ingroup Identity Model is that 'strategies that expand the inclusiveness of one's ingroup to include people who would otherwise be regarded as outgroup members may have beneficial consequences for promoting more positive intergroup attitudes and behaviours' (Gaertner, Dovidio and Bachman, 1996:273). Thus, the perceptions of the memberships can be transformed from subordinate 'Us' and 'Them' to a more inclusive superordinate 'We' (Gaertner and Dovidio, 2005; Gaertner, Dovidio and Bachman, 1996).

Their arguments are influenced by the Contact Hypothesis (Allport, 1954) which advocates that four distinct conditions are necessary for positive intergroup contact: 'equal status between the groups, cooperative intergroup interactions, opportunities for personal acquaintance between outgroup members, and supportive egalitarian norms' (Gaertner, Dovidio and Bachman, 1996:272). Simple contact between groups is not sufficient to improve intergroup relations. Gaertner and Dovidio's research studies (Gaertner *et al.*, 1999; Gaertner *et al.*, 1994; Gaertner *et al.*, 1990) support the hypothesis in the Common Ingroup Identity Model: the recategorisation of people from members of different groups to members of a common group will significantly influence the intergroup attitudes (prejudice), cognition (stereotypes) and behaviour (discrimination) (Dovidio *et al.*, 2001:171). Developing a common superordinate group identity can diffuse stigmatisation by perceivers and 'produce more productive orientations among the targets of stigmatisation, for example, by enhancing cohesiveness, commitment, and effectiveness' (Dovidio *et al.*, 2001: 172). They argue that developing a common group identity will improve students' satisfaction with and commitment to their institutions, and lessen the effects of factors, such as feelings of racial or ethnic distinctiveness (*ibid.*).

Developing a common ingroup identity does not necessarily require each group to completely abandon their own group identity (Dovidio *et al.*, 2001: 179). Recategorisation can take the form of a dual identity in which superordinate and subgroup identities are both prominent and represented by different groups working together on the same team (*ibid.*). There are four cognitive representations in this model which are based on Berry's (1997) four acculturation strategies: *integration* (different groups on the same team), *separatism* (different groups), *assimilation* (one group) and *marginalization* (separate individuals). The integration model shows a pluralistic integration perspective which recognises a dual identity: one's ethnic group identity and a superordinate identity. A dual identity in the integration model suggests that simultaneous activation of superordinate and subgroup identities has been found effective to reduce intergroup bias and lead to more harmonious group relations (Hornsey and Hogg, 2000: 243). This will not deny the value of culture and traditions of the minority group members, nor threaten their personal and social identity (Dovidio *et al.*, 2001).

Gaertner *et al.*'s (1994) research in a multi-ethnic high school shows that students who perceive themselves both in the superordinate category and subordinate category, different groups working on the same team, have lower degrees of intergroup bias than those who only identify themselves in the subordinate category. In terms of different disciplines at university, Hornsey and Hogg (2000: 242) conducted two studies to examine relations between two groups of students (humanities and maths-science students) who implicitly or explicitly share a common superordinate category (university student). The results show that participants for whom both categories were salient exhibited the lowest levels of bias, whereas bias was strongest when the superordinate category alone was made salient(*ibid.*).

Brewer(1996) proposes that apart from the simultaneous activation of superordinate and subgroup identities, individualisation of members of both subgroups needs to be integrated into the perspective of both groups to enhance intergroup contact. This attempts to depersonalise outgroup members through personalising intergroup interactions to both reduce the salience of category distinctions and increase opportunities to get to know outgroup members as *individuals* (Brewer, 1996: 293). Thus, group members' own personal characteristics are considered as the basis for classification in the interaction rather than the category identity(*ibid.*). This decategorisation will lead to developing cross-group friendships before recategorisation, which will maximise a reduction in prejudice(Pettigrew, 1998). As Gaerter *et al.* (1999: 399) have concluded, decategorisation and recategrorisation can be functionally related, a complementary process to reduce intergroup biases.

3.6.2.2 *Intercultural Competence*

To improve the integration between groups, intercultural competence of the students in the international classroom needs to be enhanced. This ability of communicating across cultures and difference is of fundamental importance to the global citizen(Brockington and Wiedenhoeft, 2009: 121). Byram(1997) develops an influential model of intercultural competence(see Table 3-3).

Table 3-3 Factors in Intercultural Communication

	Skills interpret and relate (*savoir comprendre*)	
Knowledge of self and other; of interaction: individual and societal(*savoirs*)	**Education** political education critical cultural awareness (*savoir s' engager*)	**Attitudes** relativising self valuing other (*savoir être*)
	Skills discover and/or interact (*savoir apprendre/faire*)	

(Source: Byram, 1997: 34)

Byram (1997: 70-71) explains that Intercultural Competence as the process whereby 'individuals have the ability to interact in their own language with people from another country and culture, drawing upon their knowledge about intercultural communication, their attitudes of interest in otherness and their skills in interpreting, relating and discovering, i. e. of overcoming cultural difference and enjoying intercultural contact'.

Furthermore, intercultural competence is not gained purely by exposure to intercultural experience (Deardorff, 2009). We must intentionally develop learners' intercultural competence through 'adequate preparation, substantive intercultural interactions, and relationship building' (Deardorff, 2009: xiii). The crucial way in the cultural learning process is to build authentic relationships through 'observing, listening, and asking those who are from different backgrounds to teach, to share, to enter into dialogue together about relevant needs and issues' (*ibid.*). Berdrow (2009) presents a model for international education programmes that includes pre-departure preparation, on-site structures for interaction, and post-experience debriefing, all focused on learning about the self and other. Brockington and Wiedenhoeft (2009: 123) argue that curricular intervention or programme structure should lead students past superficial contact with the host culture into a deeper, more meaningful cultural experience.

In fact, the success of interaction being dependent on both interlocutors, and the notion of intercultural communicative competence, can be used to describe the capacities of a host (home student), as much as a guest (international student) (Byram, 1997: 41-42).

> Although the host will often speak in their native language they need the same kinds of knowledge, attitudes and skills as their guest to understand and maintain relationships between meanings in the two cultures. They need the ability to decentre and take up the other perspective on their own culture, anticipating and where possible resolving dysfunctions in

communication and behaviour(*ibid.*).

Home students, the other side of interlocutors on campus, seem not to have prepared for intercultural interaction as much as international students have. 'There is the possibility that local students' investment in English monolingualism may work to structure their marginalisation in the transnational labour market' (Singh, 2005:28).

3.6.3 The Intercultural Contact Experiences of International Students and Home Students

International students have been studied as individuals moving independently to study in another country. These students have high expectations towards their study abroad, not only to accomplish their study task, but to integrate with the people in the host country, especially making friends with home students on campus. Therefore, despite the issues they experienced to adapt to their study in the host countries, such as 'culture shock' (Brown, 2009; Ryan, 2005; Oberg, 1960), 'language shock' (Sovic, 2008; Ryan, 2005) and 'academic shock' (Gu and Maley, 2008; Turner, 2006), international students strive hard to participate in their overseas activities to maximise their intercultural experience. Their presence creates international campuses which provide ideal social forums to develop the intercultural competence, skills and confidence for both international students and home students (Summers and Volet, 2008; Volet and Ang, 1998).

Positive evidence has been identified to portray this ideal picture and the optimistic effects. In academic settings, culturally mixed group assignments can be a medium for intercultural contact and an effective means to enhance students' intercultural competence (Smart, Volet and Ang, 2000), which can produce a positive effect on the individual average mark of all students, and generate synergistic effects (De Vita, 2002). Diversified experiences have been proved to positively influence students' problem-solving and team-working abilities, as well as their appreciation of and respect for diversity

(Denson and Zhang,2010). Outside the class,structured contact between host and international students, such as peer-pairing programs, can benefit international students' experience (Quintrell and Westwood, 1994). Through multicultural intervention programmes, such as bus excursions, international students developed a greater number of new friends, especially local Australian friends, and maintained their interests in local culture (Sakurai, McCall-Wolf and Kashima, 2010).

The above positive outcomes are generated mainly through structured interventions. In natural settings, more research projects report negative results and show that the potential of creating an ideal international social forum is often not well developed on many campuses. During their adaptation to a new culture, international students experience isolation and difficulties in integrating with home students (Gu, Schweisfurth and Day, 2010; Montgomery, 2010; Walsh, 2010; Brown, 2009; Middlehurst and Woodfield, 2007; Volet and Ang, 1998). Some research shows that international students do benefit from studying in an international context but this is more to do with interaction with other international students than by integrating with home student cohorts (Montgomery and McDowell, 2004). Home students' general lack of language awareness and unchallenged conceptions of privileged knowledge are contributing factors to the isolation of international students (Sovic, 2009; Ippolito, 2007). Majority of them display 'passive xenophobia' towards their international peers, which was typified by 'a reluctance to interact voluntarily with international students at anything beyond the most surface level', and active avoidance in some extreme cases when worrying about their academic marks (Harrison and Peacock, 2010: 894). In fact, both groups are more likely to work in homogeneous groups to avoid uncertainty and anxiety (Strauss, U and Young, 2011).

The integration between international students and home students deserves a great concern because it will benefit both sides. For home students, intercultural contact with international students will benefit them in terms of intercultural learning, intercultural communication skills, intercultural competence, alternative perspectives, future employment prospects around the world, as well as a sense of global citizenship, agency and responsibilities (Harrison and Peacock, 2010; Sovic, 2009). For international students, peer support is a buffer against acculturative stress (Duru and Poyrazli, 2007; Ye, 2006; Lee, Koeske and Sales, 2004; Yeh and Inose, 2003; Tsang, 2001; Searle and Ward, 1990; Berry *et al.*, 1987). It can help sojourners to cope with uncertainty and enhance perceived mastery and control (Adelman, 1988). International students' bicultural network which consists of bonds with host nationals will facilitate their academic and professional aspirations (Bochner, 1982). Appropriate host culture friends will help sojourners learn the skills of a host culture more easily than those whose friends are all compatriots (Furnham and Bochner, 1982: 174). Sojourners with strong host national identification experienced less sociocultural adjustment difficulties (Ward and Kennedy, 1994). Furthermore, conational groups can limit the heritage worldviews of the individuals (Kosic *et al.*, 2004), and the difficulty to make friends on campus has negative impact on international students' academic literacy practices (Sheridan, 2011).

3.7 Conclusions

Review of the models and theories of intercultural transition leads to the conclusion that existing literature presumes a happy-ending of the sojourners' intercultural transition experience. However, the complexities of the transition process cannot be covered by any of the existing models. To avoid simplification of the individual complexities and an over-optimistic attitude towards the transition process, a microscope perspective focusing on individual factors, such as motivations for studying abroad, attitudes towards pre-departure preparation, language competency and autonomy, is argued to be necessary. This perspective is believed to be able to escape the pitfalls of overgeneralisations of international students' transition experience based on their nationalities and cultural values. It highlights the diversity of each student as an individual and their active agency in the transition process. Meanwhile, from the contextual perspective, the support students receive during the transition, such as social support and formative assessment practices, deserves great concern. Social support has been argued to be a facilitator for sojourners' intercultural transition, while there is still a lack of empirical studies to support the tentative argument that formative assessment can be a way to nurture their transition. To extend it could help the participants' intercultural transition deserves great attention in the current study.

Review of social identity theory finds that ingroup favouritism and outgroup derogation are two tendencies in the intergroup interaction, leading to intergroup bias strengthened by competition for insufficient resources. Therefore, developing a Common Ingroup Identity Model taking the form of a dual identity, and enhancing all students' intercultural competence, is possibly an effective way to reduce intergroup bias. Meanwhile, most of the research on intergroup integration on campus is based on studies whose participants are international students studying abroad individually. The Articulation Programme Students are studying abroad as a group. The size of the group has resulted in Chinese students forming the majority in the Engineering course. This might lead to a somewhat different experience compared to that reported in many other studies. For instance, Denson and Zhang (2010) report that international students, as the minority group, have more chances to be exposed to diverse perspectives and engage with diverse others than those of home students. In a research setting where Chinese students were the dominant group, the interaction experience between them and the home students may be different. Furthermore, certain barriers hindering the integration between home students and international students have been identified, such as language skills, cultural-emotional connectedness, stereotypes on both groups, fear about lower group work marks, work and family commitments, age difference, different 'centre of gravity' in social lives, as well as different expectations and motivations (Montgomery, 2010; Harrison and Peacock, 2010; Sovic, 2009;

Ippolito, 2007; Volet and Ang, 1998). However, to what extent the size of a group of international students could influence the multicultural interaction in class has not been explored.

It has been recognised that the experience of international students must be viewed alongside that of home students and teachers to gain a full picture. As Brown (2009) suggests, this research encompasses the staff and student host perspective to counterbalance studies that document the international student perspective. Research on the interaction between Chinese students and home students in the Chinese-dominated classroom on a British campus has not been extensively explored to date. Yet, with the increasing number of Chinese Articulation Programme Students, this phenomenon will become a common feature in many British universities. This study triangulates the perspectives of the international students with the host views, which will add a new dimension to studies in this area.

Chapter 4 Methodology

4.1 Introduction

This chapter first presents my philosophical assumptions, which consist of ontological orientation, my epistemological consideration, and my intention to be an inside learner with a balance to be an outside expert in understanding my participants' social world. It then moves on to a discussion of the rationale of my choice of a qualitative research strategy: ethnography. My data collection methods, including participant observation, in-depth interviews and document analysis, are described and followed by an explanation of the data analysis process. My ethical concerns and critical reflexivity on the research process are also discussed.

4.2 My Philosophical Position

This section explains my philosophical position in this research, which consists of my understanding of the nature of social reality and how I know what I know (Blaikie, 2007: 13-14). The aim of this research is to understand the transition experience of the Articulation Programme Students from China to the UK. I embrace the idea of multiple realities (Creswell, 2007: 16) which 'are continually being accomplished by social actors', rather than existing independently (Bryman, 2008: 19). There is no objective fact or truth in social construction and people view the world from different perspectives (Burr, 2003: 152). The plurality of truths is associated with different constructions of reality (Blaikie, 2007: 24-25). My role is not to discover the meaning that already resides in the phenomena I research, nor to impose meanings on it (Blaikie, 2007: 18-19). On the contrary, I believe that meaning is constructed and as a researcher I participate in the construction actively (Blaikie, 2007: 19). My participants, as social actors, 'socially construct their reality' by conceptualising and interpreting 'their own actions and experiences, the actions of others and social situations', while I, as a researcher, socially construct my knowledge of their realities, and the 'conceptions and interpretations of the actions of social actors and of social situations' (Blaikie, 2007: 22-23). These two levels of construction demonstrate that this research is a cooperation between me and my participants (Burr, 2003: 152). This collaborative relationship gives voice to the participants (Burr, 2003: 153). The process of their interactions with each other, and with other actors in the new learning environment, is a focus of this research. Taking a critical stance toward taken-for-granted knowledge, I recognise that knowledge is relative (Blaikie, 2007: 24), historically and culturally specific which is sustained by social processes and related to a different kind of social action (Burr, 2003: 2-5).

My participants are human beings who are different from the objects of natural sciences (Bryman, 2008: 16). The social reality 'has a meaning for them and they act on the basis of the meanings that they attribute to their acts and to the acts of others' (*ibid.*). In this research, to understand the participants' transition experience, and their inhabited social world, I need to go 'inside' to build up a close relationship with them and to learn how the participants understand their social world (Blaikie, 2007: 11). I, as a researcher, become the main instrument in data collection (Burgess, 1982, cited in Brewer, 2000: 59). The inside learner position enables me to understand my participants' behaviour. It is my job to gain access to people's 'common-sense thinking' and hence to 'interpret their actions and their social world from their point of view' (Bryman, 2008: 16). According to Bryman (2008: 17), there are three levels of interpretation going on: my interpretation of my participants' interpretation of the world around them and my interpretation furthered by the interpretation using the disciplinary literature, concepts and theories. This epistemological orientation of interpretivism includes a theoretical commitment to constructionism in social research (Bryman, 2008: 22).

I reject the standpoint of a pure outside expert who stands back from the participants and observes them with existing social scientific knowledge (Blaikie, 2007: 11). I agree with Brewer's (2000: 59-60) argument that researchers in the field should maintain the balance between 'insider' and 'outsider' status in order to 'identify with the people under study and get close to them, but maintaining a professional distance which permits adequate observation and data collection'. The outside observer position allows me to reflect critically on what is observed and gathered while doing so (Brewer, 2000: 60). It also prevents me from losing the sense of being a stranger, thus losing the critical, analytic perspective (Hammersley and Atkinson, 2007: 90).

The logic of enquiry to answer research questions in this research is abductive research strategy. The process sees 'a weaving back and forth between data and theory' which is called 'iterative strategy' (Bryman, 2008: 12) or Abductive Research Strategy (Blaikie, 2007: 99). 'Once the phase of theoretical reflection on a set of data has been carried out, the researcher may want to collect further data in order to establish the conditions in which a theory will and will not hold' (Bryman, 2008: 11-12). This is based on a spiral process rather than linear logic (Blaikie, 2007: 57).

The aim of this section is to outline my ontological orientation, my epistemological consideration, and my aspiration to be both an inside learner with a balance to be an outside expert in understanding my participants' social world. My above philosophical position has led me to adopt a qualitative research strategy to answer my research question. This will be explained in the following section.

4.3 My Choice of Research Strategy

Three research strategies have dominated the current research world: quantitative, qualitative and mixed methods. The quantitative paradigm is based on positivism, which believes that the reality is single, objective and independent of human perception (Sale, Lohfeld and Brazil, 2002: 44) Quantitative researchers believe that only objective authentic knowledge is scientific knowledge and define 'science' in terms of measurement and experimental or statistical procedure (Hammersley, 2001). Researchers, as outsiders to the research, attempt to neutralise their influence on the researched and endeavour to achieve objectivity in their research (Sarantakos, 1998, cited in Robson, 2002). They treat the respondents as objects and producers of data (*ibid.*). By contrast, constructivism, often combined with interpretivism, is the basis for the qualitative paradigm (Creswell, 2009). Qualitative researchers embrace the idea of multiple realities by using multiple quotes based on the actual words of different participants and presenting different perspectives from these individuals (Creswell, 2007: 17-18). Researchers conduct their studies in the field, acknowledging their influence on the context. They try to minimise the distance from the participants and make explicit the values they bring to a study, as well as their biases (*ibid.*). Realising that all methods have limitations, researchers may feel that biases generated in any method could 'neutralise or cancel the biases of other methods' (Creswell, 2003: 15). Triangulating data sources, which seeks convergence between qualitative and quantitative methods was thus born (Jick, 1979). One method can be embedded in another in order to probe into different levels or units of analysis (Tashakkori and Teddlie, 1998).

The aim of this research is to understand the transition experience of Chinese Articulation Programme Students from China to the UK. Their motivations for studying abroad, attitudes towards pre-departure preparation, and interaction with the new learning environment are unlikely to be explained by the experimental or statistical procedure followed by quantitative research strategy. Furthermore, Sale, Lohfeld and Brazil(2002) criticise mixed-methods research adopted uncritically by some researchers who have neglected the conflict between the quantitative paradigm and the qualitative paradigm. They argue that these two approaches cannot be combined for triangulation purposes when the two paradigms do not study the same phenomena. Therefore, this research has not adopted the mixed-methods research strategy, either.

Only by going inside the natural setting was I able to be close to my participants and explore their perceptions, behaviours and the dynamic process of their transition. As I discussed in the previous section, I embrace multi-realities in the researched phenomena. The realities cannot be objective or value free. Meanings are constructed through constant interaction between my participants and me. Any knowledge contributed by this study is relative, as well as contextually, culturally, and historically specific. Articulation Programme Students' transition experience is a complex issue which enquires a detailed understanding. A qualitative research strategy enables me to pursue this detail(Creswell, 2007:40).

By participating in their daily activities in the natural setting, I gain closeness with my participants. They are empowered by being given multiple voices. The power relationship between the participants and me is minimised. In contrast, as I have mentioned in the previous section, we are cooperating in this research. Participant observations, in-depth interviews, and document analysis are the ethnographic research approaches I adopted in the data collection, which will be explained in the following section.

4.4 My Choice of Methodology

Methodology is 'the strategy, plan of action, process of design lying behind the choice and use of particular methods and linking the choice and use of methods to the desired outcomes' (Crotty, 1998:3). This research was guided by the principles derived from the set of theoretical and philosophical premises of ethnography (Brewer, 2000: 18). The history, definition and features of ethnography are discussed in this section.

Ethnography originated in western anthropology of the 19th century and became central to anthropology in the early 20th century (Hammersley and Atkinson, 2007: 1). It has two intellectual pillars (Brewer, 2000). In Britain, social anthropologists carried out ethnographic studies to understand the cultures and groups ruled by the British Empire (Brewer, 2000: 11). These anthropologists, such as Malinowski, Boas, Radcliffe-Brown and Evans-Pritchard, closely observed and immersed themselves into those preindustrial groups and cultures (*ibid.*). At the same time in the United States, sociologists at the University of Chicago created the Chicago School of ethnography, in which 'the everyday life, communities and symbolic interactions characteristic of a specific group' were analysed (Deegan, 2007: 11). Led by Park and Burgess, these sociologists studied marginal groups of the urban industrial society via first-hand observations and active participation in the settings (Deegan, 2007; Brewer, 2000). 'Ethnography is about telling a credible, rigorous, and authentic story', through 'the eyes of local people as they pursue their daily lives in their own communities' (Fetterman, 2010: 1). Brewer (2000) defines ethnography as

> the study of people in naturally occurring settings or 'fields' by means of methods which capture their social meanings and ordinary activities, involving the researcher participating directly in the setting, if not also the activities, in order to collect data in a systematic manner but without meaning being imposed on them externally (Brewer, 2000: 10).

As a social science researcher, I am keen on understanding what my participants do and how they experience the world, and this can only be obtained from 'intimate familarity' with daily practice and the meanings of the action (Brewer, 2000: 11). This 'intimate familiarity' is an essential feature of ethnography, which enables me to participate in the field with my participants through closely working with them (*ibid.*). As Feng (2009: 78) has pointed out, 'adopting an ethnographic approach to examine the perceptions and behaviours of individuals or social groups and to study their engagement in a third space is more likely to reveal the dynamics and multifacetedness of the cultures in contact, leading perhaps to a new culture in the forming'. Therefore, ethnography is appropriate to this research.

The naturally occurring setting, the field, is where my participants live and form their community. It is also the place where I directly participated in their activities in order to 'explore the meanings of this setting and its behaviour and activities from the inside' (Brewer, 2000: 27). In this research, the members of the particular cultural group were in the same age group (20-22) and had gone through the education system in Mainland China in their first 20 years. They all passed the National Higher Education Entrance Examination and achieved the academic standard required by the Chinese partner university. Before I entered into the field, these students had been studying on the same campus for one and half years and were going to finish another half a year study in China before moving on to their final two years' study in the UK. The settings, where they experienced their transition from China to the UK, were not deliberately set up for this research. Students' pursuit of education abroad would not be influenced by the study.

'Emic' and 'etic' originated from the linguistic technical terms *phonemic* and *phonetic* (Wolcott, 2008: 142). Ethnographers were required to identify their positions as an 'emic anthropologist' or an 'etic anthropologist' in 1960s (*ibid.*). Currently, the divide is blurred and it is questionable for an ethnographer to conduct a research from a singular viewpoint, i. e. from a pure emic perspective or a pure etic perspective (*ibid.*). These two perspectives are now considered as the insider's view and the outsider's view respectively (Wolcott, 2008: 144). As I discussed in Section 4. 2 on my philosophic assumptions, I intend to be an inside learner with a balance to be an outside expert in understanding my participants' social world. In this research, I shared a similar education background with the participants. All of us went through the 12-year Chinese education system from primary school to high school. I went to university in China in 1994 and spent four years there to achieve my first degree. Familiar language, teaching, learning, cultural and institutional environment had provided me with insider perspectives. However, it had been 10 years since I left university, and this was a fast developing stage for Chinese universities(see Section 2.3.2). Meanwhile, I was nearly 12 years older than most of the participants. My later experience as a lecturer, a PhD student, and a researcher helped me maintain a professional distance from the participants.

Participant observation is the primary data collection technique(Pickard, 2007). It is a way to collect data in a systematic manner but without meaning being imposed on them externally (Brewer, 2000). Apart from that, I also adopted in-depth interviewing and documentary analysis to collect data. The following section will discuss my way of collecting data.

4.5 My Way of Collecting Data

4.5.1 Locating the Natural Setting

This research was designed to understand the Chinese Articulation Programme students' transition experience from China to the UK. Fieldwork needed to be conducted at both partner universities. This required a stable cooperation which had a sustainable number of students moving on to their secondary study stage in the UK. As discussed in Chapter 2, the situation of cooperative programmes in China is very complicated. Many programmes are fragile and less likely to recruit any students. To avoid this risk, I carried out an investigation on the cooperation links that North Britain University had with Chinese universities. Five schools were operating articulation programmes with Chinese universities. Some were newly developed and had not brought in any cohort. Some long-standing cooperation was shrinking due to political, economic and technical factors. After consulting with staff at the International

Office, I located the programme run by the School of Computing, Engineering & Information Sciences and its Chinese partner, the School of Electric & Automation Engineering at Southeast China University. Compared with other programmes, this programme was more stable and less risky. It was officially approved by the Chinese Ministry of Education. By the time I started my PhD course, there had been four cohorts of about 200 students enrolled in the programme. The number increased from 11 in 2004 to 80 in 2007. Two cohorts were studying at North Britain University and the other two cohorts were still at Southeast China University. Cohort 2006 had 50 students① who were officially enrolled in the programme through the National Higher Education Entrance Examination at second tier standard (540 score in that province) and about to study in the UK. These students were at their last semester in China. It was an ideal setting and a suitable time to start my research.

4.5.2 Negotiating to Get the Permission into the Field

The located setting was closed and non-public. There were several *gatekeepers* to get into the field. The agents who had set up the links between two universities were in charge of the communication issues in the programme. They had devoted great effort and money to nurturing the programme. Any unintentional mistake might harm their business, which was not wanted by the Deans of both partner schools. I exchanged emails with the agents and organised face-to-face meetings to inform them of the nature of this research. With the help of my principle supervisor, the Director of China

① About 60 students were enrolled in the programme, but some transferred to non-programme course in the first year and one decided to stay in China in the second year. Some were auditors who could not have the degree from Southeast China University. They could only get the degree from North Britain University after successfully finish all the four years study in China and the UK. They were not Articulation Programme Students in a restricted way. Therefore, my research did not recruit them as participants.

Region Office and the Director of International Business at the School, I finally overcame their suspicions and gained their trust. The agents helped greatly with my fieldwork, not only assisting me to set up links with both Schools, but providing many insightful opinions about the programme, government policy and students' development issues. In early 2008, the Deans of both Schools signed organisational consent forms and hoped that my research might help them to improve the cooperation and students' learning experience. Staff at the International Offices of both Universities were also informed.

4.5.3 Getting into the Field

On my arrival at the Chinese campus, the agents introduced me to the students' personal tutor, Tao. As I will explain in Chapter 5, personal tutors (*Ban Zhu Ren*) in the Chinese education system are authoritative figures, who have the power from the School, parents and the role as teachers. Tao had close ties with the group and their parents. In this research, he became my *facilitator* and eased my access into the field. He set aside time before his teaching and introduced me to the students. I did not disguise my role as a researcher. Covert study would be impractical as well as unethical for this research. In agreement with Pickard (2007), I believe that all research should be overt as research participants have the right to choose to join in or not join in the research on the premise that they are fully informed about the nature, purpose and process of that research.

Seeing students' curious and doubtful eyes, I explained the nature of my research and gave them consent forms with information sheets which were written in Chinese. Worried that they might sign the consent forms due to the pressure from their personal tutor, I made it clear that their participation in this research was completely voluntary and would not affect their study in China and the UK. When I gave them time to ask questions about the research, I expected them to ask questions about 'data collection', 'confidentialities' or 'anonymities'. However, they were very curious about my study abroad. Meeting a student from a university in the UK, these students quickly bombarded me with various questions about my life abroad. Students at this stage considered me as a PhD student and a researcher from a British university. They were very happy to have contact with me before their study abroad and started to call me *Xue Jie*(senior student at school) or *Hou Lao Shi*(Miss Hou), which are two respectful addresses in Chinese culture. As will be explained in the following section, students gradually accepted me as a member of the group, although not completely. My way of getting access into the field has verified the argument of Hammersley and Atkinson (2007:4) that 'access cannot be assumed to be available automatically, relations will have to be established, and identities co-constructed' (p. 4). The process of my role co-construction and data collection are described in the following sections.

4.5.4 Participant Observation

4.5.4.1 *Locating the Self in the Field Work*

In the following sections, I present how I constantly reflected on my own position as an observer in the field and the potential influence I might have given to the research. I did not perceive myself as a total stranger in an alien culture attempting to make sense of that culture from an outsider's perspective, or a complete member in the researched group (Coffey, 1999). It was a constant back and forth process between strangeness and familiarity (*ibid.*). As I mentioned in the above section, my own identity as an international student in the UK eased my access to the field. It shortened the distance between me and my participants immediately. With the help of Tao, I was allocated a room in the students' accommodation, which was next to 16 girls in the group. Four girls stayed in one dormitory and had formed four groups naturally. This was also the case with the boys. These small dormitory groups normally did activities together. Those two groups who were opposite or next to my room were the first to get to know me. They took turns to show me around the campus and shared with me the detailed information of every student in the class. This enabled me to develop familiarity with the setting in a short time. I was new in the setting, and through 'watching, listening, asking questions, formulating hypotheses, and making blunders' to 'acquire a good sense of the social structure of the setting and begin to understand the culture(s) of participants' (Hammersley and Atkinson, 2007:79).

However, I was worried that the perspectives gained from a small group of students might be biased and fail to provide me with a holistic picture of the whole group. Therefore, I deliberately went to talk more with girls in the other two dormitories and boys after class. I also tried my best to remember every student's name and sought opportunities to talk with them. Within one week, I became familiar with their time schedules and daily activities. Meanwhile, I was constantly reminding myself to keep a sense of strangeness (estrangement) in order to keep my critical stance as an observer, which was crucial for fieldwork in familiar settings (Coffey, 1999).

To conduct the observation systematically and effectively, I then started to select times, people and contexts in a sampling manner that agrees with Hammersley and Atkinson's (2007:37) suggestions that both routine activities and extraordinary events should be included in observation, with the aim to ensure a full and representative range of coverage. I woke at 7:00am when I heard girls starting to wash their faces and brush their teeth, and then went to buy my breakfast from the caretaker downstairs as the other students did. Classes started at 8:00am and ran through till lunch time with ten minutes' break between each class. With my participants, I had lunch at the two canteens on campus or snack bars outside the campus. While students were having a nap after lunch, I wrote field notes documenting the observations of the morning. From about 2:00pm, I started my observations with different groups on various out-class activities. After dinner, I went to observe students in the self-study rooms or the library, where I was also able to read books and take down notes. I spared one or two hours to chat with the girls in their dormitory before going to bed. Reflective notes and memos were written on the same day or every other day.

My participant observation consists of two main stages: observation on the

Chinese Campus and observation on the British Campus. These were conducted in three main contexts: classroom activities, out-class activities, and online activities. I was not in the field all the time in these 15 months' fieldwork, especially when participants started their study in the UK. It mingled with my own progress in the PhD course, such as preparing for the Mid-Point Progression and attending research modules. However, I was in the field in a couple of weeks at the beginning and the end of each of their three terms. During the term, I organised visits to the site constantly and conducted more observations online.

4.5.4.2 *Participant Observation in the Class on the Chinese Campus*

In their last semester in China, students took part in two core modules imported from North Britain University: *Electronics* and *Power & Machines*, as well as three compulsory modules required by the Chinese Ministry of Education: *English*, *Physical Education*, and *Mao Zedong Thought*, *Deng Xiaoping Theory & Three Represents*. To facilitate students' intercultural transition abroad, the School invited native speakers to teach students *Oral English*. Consent forms were signed by the lecturers of all these modules before I sat in on their class.

In the class, I was a student as well as an observer. I took notes in the core modules, sometimes worked out exercises, joined in their discussion in the English class, and played *Tai Ji* in the PE class. Students and the staff gradually overlooked my attendance as a researcher. This student role was not complete. I did not take part in the activities in the laboratories as they were too complicated for me. On these occasions, I pursued my role as a complete observer. Meanwhile, I was constantly aware of the danger of 'going native', losing my critical faculties to become an ordinary member of the field (Brewer, 2000: 60). As an observer, my focus in the class was on teaching practices, students' behaviour, staff-student interactions and interactions among students. As the dormitory groups normally sat together, I deliberately sat with different groups, listening, watching and interacting with them. During breaks, I chatted with students beside me about their study and current preparation for studying abroad. When students asked questions after class, I went to observe their interactions with their teachers. I intended to video some of the scenes in the class at the beginning of the research. However, I found this was too intrusive. Although the staff and students had agreed to be videoed, I discontinued it after several days' trying.

4.5.4.3 *Participant Observation outside the Class on the Chinese Campus*

Outside the class, students carried out different activities. This required my observation to be more selective and systematic. I followed one dormitory group for a couple of days to see their behaviour patterns before joining another group. Not all groups gave me opportunities to do so. Girls' groups were much closer to me as we lived together. Many activities, like window shopping, getting hot water from the station, taking showers in the public bathroom and girls' talking at night, can only be shared with the girls. To have a better understanding of the boys, I increased the time to watch them playing basketball and football on the playground and chat with them during breaks.

4.5.4.4 *Participant Observation in the Class on the British Campus*

When students came to the UK, they joined an existing cohort of home students and other international students from different countries. Also included were students who repeated the year and part-time students, so the class became multi-national and multi-aged. Consent forms were obtained before I sat in on the class. Their programme leader became my *facilitator* to access the field in the UK. My strategy here was more or less the same as in the Chinese class, but more effort was allocated to the observation of the interaction between my participants and other students and staff in the class. My role in the class was less as a student than I was in the Chinese class, which was partly due to the harder professional knowledge of Engineering, and partly due to the academic English glossaries. For instance, the topic of a module I observed was Transmission Lines. As I wrote in the diary, '*I know* ***transmission****. I know* ***line****. But I don't know what* ***transmission line*** *is. I can understand every word, but don't understand the contents*'. At this moment, I felt a strong sense of incompetence (Hammersley and Atkinson, 2007). My lack of professional knowledge had become an obstacle to my understanding of the teaching in the class. Meanwhile the staff seldom had a break between two teaching hours. I was unable to chat with students nor to observe their interaction with teachers. When some of the participants complained about the difficulties they came across in the study, such as academic language or being unable to ask questions after class, I understood how they felt owing to my own experience in the class.

When I was curious why my participants always sat together in the front, leaving other students sat at the back, I found some similar phenomena in my own class. During the fieldwork in the UK, I attended some PhD training sessions. When I entered the class, my Chinese friends would wave to me and let me sit beside them. It was rare for me to sit next to someone I barely knew except when some lecturers asked us to. Until then, I realised that it was a common problem for international students. When I re-entered their class, seeing the strange but understandable phenomenon, I had an idea that structured introduction at the beginning of the course, or even before the course, might break the polarised situation in the class. This was echoed by some home students in the interviews later.

4.5.4.5 *Participant Observation Outside the Class on the British Campus*

The observation started immediately from meeting my participants at the airport. Seeing them was like seeing old friends at another country. We were very excited. The university sent 'Meet and Greet' staff to the airport to take them to their chosen accommodation. I took a taxi with one of the dormitory groups to their accommodation building. In the following weeks, I accompanied them to get familiar with the city just as they did for me in China. I was invited to different flats for dinner. I was surprised by their creativity and enthusiasm in reforming Chinese and Western cuisines. We shopped, cooked and chatted together. Students started to address me *Xiao Hou Jie* (elder sister Hou) instead of *Xue Jie* (senior student at school) or *Hou Lao Shi* (Miss Hou). *Xiao Hou Jie* is more intimate than *Xue Jie* and *Hou Lao Shi*, which showed that they had become closer to me and accepted me more as a member of their group. While enjoying the pleasure of the reunion, I suddenly noticed that I had become the information source for these students. I needed to minimise my influence on their experiences in the UK. Meanwhile, this kind of over-rapport relationship with my participants was likely to lead to a skewed perspective of a cultural setting (Coffey, 1999). This was not easy for me emotionally and culturally. They helped me a lot when I stayed on their campus. When they came here, I felt I should help them in return. Furthermore, coming from China where respect for the elderly and care for the young is a traditional virtue, I found it really hard to say 'no' to them, and even felt guilty for doing so. I tried my best to answer their questions by directing them to the university information service system. For instance, I suggested they check the university website, go to Student Services, or write to their personal tutors.

My own identity as a Chinese international student in the UK overlapped with my role in the field. Many activities I did in the field were the same as I did outside the field. For example, I was given a ticket to watch the Chinese New Year performance organised by the Chinese Students' Community. A group of my participants were coincidently there too and sat behind me. Xiao Hua was with his football team members, and this was the first occasion in my observation where my participants were with members outside the group. There were also breaks where students moved out of their own circle and refused to 'stick together'. Although I was reluctant to take down any notes while enjoying my precious holiday, I still could not resist the temptation to write a reflective diary when I got back home.

4.5.4.6 *Participant Observation Online*

Diary writing was designed to collect data from participants in China. However, except for one participant who wrote several diaries, they were reluctant to keep these due to their heavy workloads. Instead, they were very active online. On the internet, students conducted activities such as writing blogs, posting pictures, conducting group discussions to share shopping tips, exchanging mobile numbers, organising ball games, announcing meeting notices or asking for help.

Xiaonei, QQ, MSN and Facebook were the most popular websites or tools students used. Xiaonei, a Chinese website where students linked their own webpage with their friends', was mostly used for students to write blogs or post their instant feelings. On arriving in the UK, some of the students started to use the western website, Facebook, which had more links with students from different countries. However, Xiaonei was still the most active website for communication within their own group and former classmates in China. MSN, a chatting tool, was used by some of the students when they moved to the UK. However, every participant had an account and formed a chat group on QQ, the most popular online chatting tool in China. Students used it extensively for community learning instead of the E-learning Portal. In Module EN0213, a group of students formed their own learning group to exchange information in the chat room. The team leader encouraged students when they came across difficulties. When some students could not go to class, their classmates uploaded the seminar questions and answers for them to download. As will be explained in Chapter 5, this kind of peer support became a double-edged factor in the students' transition experience.

Students signed a consent form to give me the permission to use their web information as data. They added me on their friends' list and allowed me to observe online. This compensated for the loss of diary writing. Furthermore, the data was more naturalistic and did not sound contrived. These tools became my main methods of communication with the participants while I was on holiday.

4.5.5 In-depth Interviews

Interviews are an important means for ethnographers to 'classify and organize an individual's perception of reality (Fetterman, 2010: 42). The formal interviews I carried out were non-standardised, open-ended and in-depth (Robson, 2002: 278). It is an essential way for ethnographers to 'access life on the "inside" and represent it accurately' (Brewer, 2000: 67). In the 15-

month fieldwork, I carriedout three rounds of interviews with 16 Articulation Programme Students, covering their preparation stage in China, initial arrival in the UK and post-final-assessment stage at the end of the first year on the British campus. Interviews were conducted in their native language, Chinese, to enable them to talk freely without the obstacles of language. So were the interviews with two parents and ten Chinese academic and administrative staff members. I also interviewed five home students, two international students and eight British academic and administrative staff members, all in English. In the interviews, I tried to avoid closed-ended questions, long questions, double-barrelled questions, leading questions, biased questions and questions involving jargon (Robson, 2002: 275). Fully informed consent forms were signed before interviews were tape-recorded. Notes were taken down in case of the failure of the tape-recorder. The length of interviews varied from 40 minutes to two hours. Altogether, over 80 hours of interviews were taken. The interview processes and issues will be discussed in the following sections.

4.5.5.1 *Interviews with* 16 *Key Informants*

Sampling

I adopted a purposive sampling strategy. The sample aimed to enable me to satisfy my specific needs in my research (Robson, 2002: 265). By participating in the group for a month, I gradually became familiar with their background information, academic performance and individual personalities. To seek out varying individuals in the characteristics mentioned above, I deliberately invited 16 participants to join the interviews based on a voluntary principle. The stratified sample aimed to achieve representativeness in a group of 50 students (Hammersley and Atkinson, 2007: 106). As the ratio of boys to girls in the group was about 2 : 1, I intended to invite ten boys and six girls to reflect the relative numbers in the group population (Robson, 2002: 262). However, as I mentioned in Section 4.5.4.3, the girls were much closer to me. Comparatively speaking, they were more active in my research, while some boys felt reluctant to be interviewed and declined my invitation. I finally recruited eight girls and eight boys as the interviewees, whose demographic information is shown in Table 4-1. When our relationship developed further, especially after their arrival in the UK, the boys were more willing to talk to me. Although they did not become key informants as the other 16 students did, their information was also very important for me to get a holistic picture of the whole group.

Table 4-1 Demographical Profiles of 16 Key Chinese Participants

Name Code	Anonym	Gender	Age Group	Course①
M01	Xiao Ming	Male	20-22	EEE
M02	Xiao Dong	Male	20-22	EEE
M03	Xiao Qiang	Male	20-22	EEE
M04	Xiao Yu	Male	20-22	EEE
M05	Xiao Jie	Male	20-22	EEE
M06	Xiao Hua	Male	20-22	EEE
M07	Xiao Yong	Male	20-22	EEE
M08	Xiao Feng	Male	20-22	EEE
F01	Ling Ling	Female	20-22	CEE
F02	Ping Ping	Female	20-22	EEE
F03	Yan Yan	Female	20-22	EEE
F04	Juan Juan	Female	20-22	EEE
F05	Min Min	Female	20-22	EEE
F06	Li Li	Female	20-22	EEE
F07	Ying Ying	Female	20-22	CEE
F08	Fang Fang	Female	20-22	CEE

First Round of Interviews

The first round of interviews was taken one month before my participants finished their last semester in Southeast China University. They were conducted in dormitories, gardens outside the classroom, the playground or any

① EEE: BEng(Hons) Electrical and Electronic Engineering; CEE: BEng(Hons) Communication and Electronic Engineering.

other places where my participants felt comfortable. However, as it was the first interview for some students, many of them were a little nervous. Some of the boys were not very familiar with me and were very cautious. I tried to conduct in-depth interviews starting with 'how is everything going on', but found they did not talk much. Therefore, I asked more specific questions. These questions were not listed down before the interviews, but formed in the process. I did not follow the exact order, but proposed one when I felt the opportunity was appropriate. As a result, they were more like semi-structured interviews. This round of interviews focused on the participants' past learning experience, reasons for choosing the programme, learning experience at Southeast China University, expectations and preparation for studying abroad, prediction of difficulties in studying abroad, and preconceptions of teaching and learning in the UK. The interviews were transcribed and analysed before participants' coming to the UK.

Second Round of Interviews

The second round of interviews took place two months after the participants' arrival in the UK. They had undergone the induction week and several weeks' study in a new learning environment. As explained in Section 4.5.4.5, my participants were much closer to me at this stage. They felt they had more to tell me about their exciting yet frustrating experiences. Therefore, the unstructured interviews went on very well and turned out to be friendly and emotional conversations. We shared laughs as well as tears. The interviews lasted longer than the first round with an average length of over an hour. Before each interview, I reread the transcript of their first interviews in China and my observation notes, and took down the points I intended to follow up in this round of interviews.

The first half of the interviews were led by the interviewees discussing whatever they wanted and the things they were interested in. Coincidently, all the participants made comparisons of their new learning experience with what they experienced in China, as well as the differences between their actual experiences with what they had expected in China. However, their attitudes towards these differences and their ways of coping with them were different. For example, facing difficulties in communicating with British staff, some took the difficulties as opportunities and tried to discuss their course work by drawing pictures or listing down formulas. Others would wait until their classmates understood and told them the answers. A small portion of them felt frustrated and shrank into their 'self-believed safe circle' (see Section 5.4.2). It was at this time that I started to feel that the intercultural transition experience was an individual process depending on the level of their autonomy more than their language ability.

In the second half of the interviews I prompted follow-up questions either to solve the puzzles I had in my observations or to check how their understanding on a topic progressed. For example, the participants mentioned in China that studying abroad as a group was a big advantage for the Articulation Programme Students. However, when we discussed the topic again, only two of them insisted on that idea. Most of them considered it as a disadvantage in hindering their integration with other students in the class. In this round of interviews, there was more self-reflection and discussion. This was partly because my participants used the interview as an opportunity to discuss their concerns with me. My role at this stage had many facets. Being an 'elder sister' in the group, I could not ignore these students' asking for help even if it was in an interview. I admit that my participation in the group unavoidably influenced their experience to some extent (see Section 4.9). However, their eagerness for help triggered my questioning of the current personal tutor system and the international students' support system at North Britain University. Why did these students rarely use the system? What was more suitable for this large group of Articulation Programme Students? The questions I proposed in the reports written for the School led the Deans to make the decision to hire a special Chinese tutor for the over 100 Articulation Programme Students at their school.

Third Round of Interviews

The last round of interviews was conducted in the month after they finished their final examinations of the first academic year. The strategy I took at this round of interviews was similar to the second round. The follow-up questions of the first-round and second-round of interviews were discussed. Participants were more concerned about their assessment at this stage. Rich data about participants' assessment experience were collected. At this stage, I asked students to check the credibility of the transcripts of their previous interviews and my interpretation of their individual transition experience. They checked my data analysis tables and diagrammes, pointing out missing points and adding what they thought was appropriate. They all mentioned what they would have done over the last 15 months if they could have gone back to their last semester in China. So did I. We were like old friends reminiscing about our past together.

4.5.5.2 *Interviews with Non-key Informants*

To understand the transition experience of the Articulation Programme Students, I need to know the perspectives of other stakeholders. For example, I found many questions I had during the data analysis required consultation with the Chinese staff. Without the perspectives of the staff, I could not get a holistic picture of the classroom interaction. Students said, since high school, they had been seldom asked to answer questions in the class. After interviewing the Chinese staff, I was informed how tense their schedules were in each module. To compare the two teaching teams, I interviewed English staff in the UK as well. Their programme leader was interviewed twice, at the beginning and the end of the academic year. We also arranged monthly informal meetings at the staff bar for the discussion of the performance of the participants. In the second round of data analysis, I found the participants were frustrated by the divided situation with home-based students in the class. Other students, especially the home students' views on this group of Chinese students, were essential for this research. However, it was not easy to find interviewees. I sent emails to all home students in the class asking for an interview, but did not get a response.

A snowball sampling strategy was adopted then. One staff member in the interview knew my situation and recommended that I talk to their course reps. After his introduction, I emailed this home student and interviewed him in the first term. A girl from Kuwait, recommended by a participant, happened to sit next to me whilst observing the class. A boy from Nigeria was a friend of another participant. At the third round of data analysis, I felt the data from home students was too narrow as only one was interviewed. I had a chat with a group of home students at a workshop and followed this up by emailing them information sheets. The comparison of these two groups of students helped me to triangulate the data. Two parents were interviewed when they came to the UK for their children's graduation ceremony. One interview was tape-recorded. The other was not. Three other parents were informally interviewed at the celebration party. Unstructured interviews were carried out with five home students and two international students (See Table 4-2 for details), as well as ten Chinese staff, eight English staff, and two parents whose demographic information is shown in Table 4-3. The sample strategy I took is theoretical sampling, another form of purposive sampling (Bryman, 2008: 414). This happened during the process of my data collection (Glaser and Strauss, 1967: 45). The aim of taking theoretical sampling was to develop my emerging theory via developing the properties of the categories by seeking relevant data until the categories were saturated (Charmaz, 2006: 96).

Table 4-2 Demographical Profiles of British and International Student Participants in the Interview

Name Code	Anonym	Gender	Age Group	Nationality	Course
H01	Jim	Male	23-25	British	EEE
H02	Joe	Male	23-25	Nigerian	EEE
H03	Nina	Female	23-25	Kuwaiti	EEE
H04	William	Male	20-22	British	CEE
H05	Charlie	Male	20-22	British	CEE
H06	Max	Male	23-25	British	CEE

(contd.)

Name Code	Anonym	Gender	Age Group	Nationality	Course
H07	Jacky	Male	23-25	British	CEE

Table 4-3 Demographical Profiles of Staff and Parent Participants in the Interview

Name Code	Anonym	Gender	Nationality	Job Title
CS01	Tao	Male	Chinese	Academic staff & Personal tutor
CS02	Lin	Female	Chinese	Academic staff
CS03	Sheng	Male	Chinese	Academic staff
CS04	Qing	Female	Chinese	Academic staff
CS05	Bin	Male	Chinese	Academic staff
CS06	Zheng	Male	Chinese	Academic staff
CS07	Xin	Female	Chinese	Academic staff
CS08	Mei	Female	Chinese	Academic staff
CS09	David	Male	Australian	Academic staff
CS10	Ming	Male	Chinese	Administrative staff
BS01	Frank	Male	British	Academic staff & Personal tutor
BS02	Simon	Male	British	Academic staff
BS03	Eric	Male	British	Academic staff
BS04	Tom	Male	British	Academic staff
BS05	Colin	Male	British	Academic staff
BS06	Louise	Male	British	Academic staff
BS07	Ben	Male	British	Academic staff
BS08	John	Male	British	Administrative staff
CP01	Mr. Wang	Male	Chinese	Xiao Feng's father
CP02	Mr. Li	Male	Chinese	Juan Juan's father

4.5.6 Document Analysis

Apart from data collected from participant observation and interviews, some documentary sources had also generated rich data. These included three main facets. First, the official documents from both universities, such as enrolment brochures for Articulation Programme Students, government certification of the programme, programme application to the Chinese Ministry of Education, student regulations and assessment regulations. These documents enhanced my understanding of the programme at the policy level. The second source was about participants' academic activities. Their module guidance book, laboratory reports, examination papers, hand-outs, group reports, presentation slides, and staff feedback on the E-learning Portal which allowed me to make comparisons of the different teaching and learning practices at these universities. The last source was the students' diaries (only one student wrote on the diary book I gave, while others published many on the websites). This source, including pictures and friends' comments, vividly demonstrated the dynamic change of my participants.

4.5.7 Leaving the Field

I officially left the field when my participants finished their first academic year in the UK. In the last round of the interviews, I told them I was going to concentrate on my course and could not join their activities. They showed their understanding, but asked whether they could keep in touch with me when they wanted to talk. I agreed. Therefore, in their final year at North Britain University, I was still invited to have dinner at their flats or China Town, chat at the coffee bar, or help them to solve various problems including settling quarrels between lovers. In July 2010, I received an invitation for their graduation ceremony. Sitting next to their parents and seeing them receiving the blessing from the Chancellor on the stage, I could not hold back tears. As a witness who had seen their ups and downs in the past two and half years, I felt so proud of them. The pictures taken with them afterwards are kept in my album, and will be there forever. Many of them became life-long friends and they encouraged me often while I was writing up my PhD thesis.

4.6 My Way of Analysing the Data

Data was analysed using the data analysis principles advocated in grounded theory(Glaser and Strauss, 1967) to identify the directions for the on-going observations and the following round of interviews. The following procedure was modified from the analytic instruction of Charmaz(2006). This study carried out three stages of data collection: students' last semester in China, within two months after their arrival in the UK and at the end of the academic year. Data was analysed at each stage to identify the direction of the following rounds of data collection, as shown in Figure 4-1. After the first stage of data collection in China, the interviews were transcribed and read through carefully. Open coding was conducted to identify concepts and discover the properties and dimensions in data. Memos were written to capture fleeting ideas. Constant comparisons were carried out to compare the interview data with the data in the observation notes, research diary, and memos. Some categories were identified and served as the foundation for future comparisons. The second stage of data collection was not confined within these categories, but gave an open consideration to the holistic picture of the participants' intercultural transition experience. After the second stage of data collection, data were open coded and compared with the first stage's data and categories. Focused coding was then conducted to concentrate on the most significant codes which had been grouped into tentative categories. Conceptual categories were developed at this stage. These categories had become the focus of the next round of data collection. After the third stage of data collection, new data were open coded and focused coded as well. The conceptual categories developed at the second and the third stages were related to each other through the process of theoretical coding, aiming to tell a coherent analytic story. Constant comparison had been conducted extensively at this stage, intimately linking the three stages of data, codes, categories and memos. Theoretical sampling had been conducted at three stages to collect relevant data to refine the categories in the emerging theory. Thus, the categories were saturated, sorted and diagrammed (Charmaz, 2006). They were finally integrated into the emerging theory.

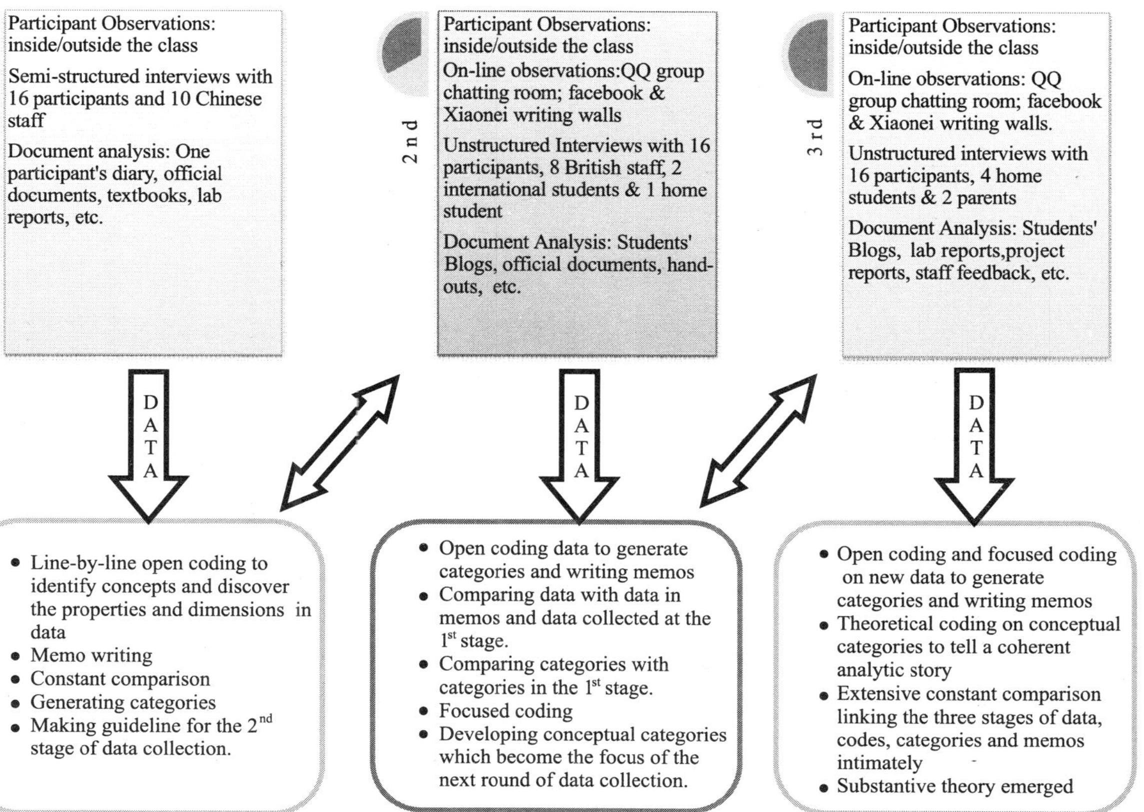

Figure 4-1 Three Stages of Data Collection and Analysis

4.7 Rigour and Trustworthiness of the Research

In the data analysis, it was fully acknowledged that as an instrument of data collection my personal knowledge and cultural background might influence the research. The suggestion given by Strauss and Corbin (1998:43) had been followed that qualitative research should be open and willing to listen and 'give voice' to informants, which means 'hearing what others have to say, seeing what others do, and representing them as accurately as possible'. Meanwhile, the following steps had been taken to ensure the rigour and trustworthiness of the research and to provide authentic and credible findings. First, multiple data sources had been adopted. Data collected from participant observations, in-depth interviews, and document analysis were crosschecked to see if there were any inconsistencies. Field notes were kept while concurrently observing or carrying out interviews. At the end of the day, research diaries were written to reflect and analyse the data in the notes. The field notes and research diaries were also crosschecked at the stage of analysing data. Member checking (Guba and Lincoln, 1989) was conducted to establish credibility in the research: data collected from the observations was double checked with the students during the second and third rounds of interviews. At the end of the second round of interviews, main themes generated from the first round of interviews were restated and negotiated with the interviewees. After the third round of interviews, participants were shown the typescripts, interpretations and analysis of the data to get their views. To some extent, the trustworthiness of the data was safeguarded through these negotiations.

4.8 My Concerns of Ethical Issues

This research took ethnography as the strategy and shared an intense interest in personal views and circumstances. It involved moderate risks and some ethical issues. Before data collection, this research underwent internal review and obtained formal ethical approval from the School Research Ethics Committee. This research is an academic analysis of a learning context rather than an evaluation intended to feedback into a specific programme or institution. Although sensitive personal data were not involved, there was a risk that their identities might be recognised by someone else through the data collected from them. As the researcher, I had the duty to hold the data in confidence and protect the participants from the exposure of identities in processing personal data (Oliver, 2003). I conducted this research abiding by the University's Policy on Ethics in Research and Consultancy and other ethical legislations with full consideration of the Data Protection Act 1998.

In this research, I did not disguise my identity as a researcher in the fieldwork. Participants were safeguarded from any harm. They were fully aware of the purpose of the research and understood their rights. I sent each participant an invitation letter with an information sheet about the nature of this research. The information sheet was written without any difficult terms and coercive wording. It gave the potential participants my contact information as well as my supervisors', the title and purpose of the study, the sponsor, and the way of data processing including data collection, recording, storage and dissemination. The potential benefits to future students resulting from the research were also listed. Voluntary participation was clearly stated, informing participants that they could withdraw at any stage and refuse to answer any questions that they were reluctant to answer. The information sheet helped potential participants to make a judgement whether they wanted to join the project or not. Details of the complaint procedure were provided to protect the participants' rights including the name, address, email, and telephone number of the person to contact. Considering their language problem, the invitation letter, information sheet and consent form sent to the director, academic staff and students in China were written in Chinese. All of the documents were printed on university letterhead paper. Because Chinese staff and students might not be familiar with the Data Protection Act 1998 and the terms of anonymity and confidentiality, the information sheet also had an explanation of those items. In the process of writing the thesis and other academic papers, anonymity and confidentiality assured to the participants were strictly considered. Pseudonyms for persons and settings were used.

In this research, I gave the information of a participant to the University International Student Service under the circumstance of an emergency. This participant locked herself in the dormitory for a month and missed all examinations. When another participant came to tell me about her situation, I was extremely worried. I tried to persuade her to open the door, but she refused. She knocked weakly on the door from inside to let me know that she was still there. She passed me a note under the door with only several words saying that she did not want to see anybody then. After consulting the supervision team, I went to see the staff at International Student Services for help. I intended to get some suggestions, and then went to see her myself. But staff there were worried that she might hurt herself (the University had some similar cases previously). They said I must give them the name of the girl and the address. They also told me that as a PhD student sponsored by the University, I was considered as a member of staff. I had an obligation to give them information under emergency. I went back to her flat and told her that I had to give her name and address to the University considering the priority of her safety. They sent a counsellor to see her and helped her solve her problems. She came to see me the following day and asked me to go to see her programme leader together. At dinner before her leaving for China, she expressed her thanks to me. So did her mother via telephone from China.

4.9 Reflexivity

Reflexivity, consciously looking back at myself in the processes of research 'as inquirer and respondent, as teacher and learner, as the one coming to know the self', concerns quality in qualitative research (Guba and Lincoln, 2008: 278). In the research focusing on the transitional learning experience of overseas students, I was an overseas student myself. Meanwhile, my previous teaching experience as a lecturer in China and a visiting lecturer in the UK had influenced my understanding of the teaching practices in the programme. Conducting this qualitative research project, I need to look critically towards myself, my 'social background, assumptions, positioning and behaviour impact on the research process', as well as the way I constructed my research findings (Finlay and Gough, 2003: xi). This is because scrutinising 'how the researcher and inter-subjective elements impact on and transform research' is a vital part in demonstrating the trustworthiness of the findings in qualitative research (Finlay, 2003: 4). Researchers' individuality is not invisible and their motivations, interests and attitudes may have an impact on any stage from choosing the research topic to interview questions (Gough, 2003). Subjectivity is inevitable in the research process (Maso, 2003). The recognition of this individual dimension to research is considered as enriching and informative by qualitative researchers. There are two main aspects of influence of my own experience on this research.

4.9.1 My Personal Experience on the Interpretation of the Data

My first three years' learning experience in the UK was very positive. The staff in my Masters and PhD courses were supportive. They gave me tutorials whenever I had queries. I was awarded an MA in Education Studies with Distinction in 2007 and started my PhD course with full studentship on the following day. I also joined the University Student Community Action group and won awards for my outstanding volunteer work. I made friends with students from different countries. I often organised parties at home. It seemed that most of the difficulties that other Chinese students might come across did not exist for me. Therefore, when I heard my participants complain about this or that, subconsciously I doubted it. This might be because that they had not tried their best. For instance, one participant, Fang Fang, was depressed, locked herself in her room and missed all examinations. I interpreted her 'failure' as simply as lacking motivation. Why did not she study as hard as others? Why did she watch cartoons all day? Why did not she go to Student Services for help? To me at that time, it was mostly her fault.

However, in my last two-year's study in the UK, my life changed dramatically. This had affected my interpretation of Fang Fang's case. My husband got his MSc in Business Information Technology in the UK. As a former manager with 10 years' working experience in China, he found it was not easy to find a professional job in the UK which was undergoing an economic recession. After one-year's trying, he decided to go back to China where he was appointed as the deputy-chief manager in a software company. I had to stay abroad to finish my course. After he left, I suddenly realised that my 'real' learning experience as an international student just started. I was used to having my husband looking after me. He took care of everything from shopping to cooking, from moving house to changing bulbs. I told him everything when I finished a whole-day study at university, happy or unhappy. He always listened to my long stories patiently. He was also the first audience for my small pieces of writing. His leaving was a big loss to me. I started to skip meals as it was too troublesome to cook. On a rainy day, I could stay in bed for a whole day watching Chinese soap operas. It was a way to escape the pressure of the course. At that time, I moved on to the writing-up stage, which was the most challenging part to me. The tremendous work, on-coming deadline and loneliness gave me huge pressure. I became sensitive, emotional and irritable. Whenever I heard someone kindly asking 'How's your PhD going?", I started to have tears in eyes. I gradually understood the participant and all her troubles. Before things became worse, other PhD students noticed my unstable mood. Rung and Jo chatted with me over lunch very often. Sarah dragged me to have a half-an-hour walk in the afternoon. Gillian invited me to dinner. At her house, I felt at home when running after her lovely son, Max. My supervisors also gave me strong support at this time. They gave me the 'PhD tissue' while I was crying in the supervision. I realised that I was not alone at this difficult stage. Their voluntary help supported me to calm down and carry on.

When I reread the data, I had more insight into those troubles my participants had encountered. Moreover, I had further questions about the current student services and school administrative system. There could have been alternative endings in my participant's case. If someone noticed her trouble earlier, went to talk to her, encouraged her, and gave her the voluntary help just as I received, would she have failed the year? 'Someone' here could be her peers, monitors (course reps), *Ban Zhu Ren* (personal tutor) or student services. Most often, we take for granted that international students should go to ask for help themselves. Under some circumstances, we need go to them to offer our help. I know some people might argue that these students are adults and should take full responsibility themselves. However, sometimes it is really hard to open the door when you lock yourself inside. My personal experience made me realise that. I became more aware of the need for student support systems.

4.9.2 My Participation in the Field on My Participants' Transition Experience

As I mentioned in Section 4.5.4, my participants were very happy to have me, a senior 'sister' from a university in the UK, join their group. They asked me various questions about the life abroad. When they arrived in the UK, I had unavoidably become a source of information. Rather than finding informants for my research, I found I became an informant to their study in the UK. Although I had been trying to avoid becoming the information source, this unavoidably continued being the situation for the rest of the year. With my research questions progressively refined, their questions changed at different stages of transition. When they first arrived in the UK, they were eager to know how to enlarge their social circle and make friends with other international students. Starting their course, they asked me to share tips about communicating with some 'unfriendly' staff. Before their final examination, they worried about how to meet the standards of assessment. Even after I officially finished the fieldwork in their final year at North Britain University, they still often contacted me asking questions about the Masters course and studentship. Here, on one hand, my participants and I had become close friends. They left notes on my webpage, encouraging me to go through the thorny process of my PhD course. On the other hand, the unavoidable consequence was that my participants and I had developed dual roles. I: officially a researcher for my study and an informal informant; my participants: official informants and informal 'researchers' for their 'study'.

While observing their online chatting, I felt guilty that I could not give the answers which I knew. For instance, they were going to attend their first meeting with their personal tutor in the office which was close to my own. I intended to tell them, but had to wait to see how they would find the answer. When I started to sit in their class for observations, the struggle became stronger, as shown in my research diary:

> Fang Fang and Xiao Jie didn't come this morning. I really wanted to call them. I was a lecturer in China. Each time, students didn't show in my class, I asked the monitor what happened. Are they sick? Something wrong? Need my help? In China, Tao, their personal tutor called them directly to ask where they were. Here, my colleagues told me that the lecturers won't ask in the first couple of weeks ... As a researcher, I must minimise my influence on the setting as much as possible.

I thought for a long time about how to help them. In the second round of interviews, I went through their first interviews in China as I did with other participants. I deliberately emphasised the future plans they had told me. Both Fang Fang and Xiao Jie realised that they had gone back to their old habits unconsciously when they arrived in the UK. I really did not know whether what I had done was right or not, especially when the end was not positive. Both of them failed the year (see Chapter 5 for details).

4.9.3 Rethinking the Research Methodology

4.9.3.1 *Lessons Learned in the Field*

When I entered into the field, I was very excited. I believed everything that happened there was valuable and could become important data for the research project. Thus, I followed students everywhere. This was possible in class when the whole group were in one classroom. However, I lost my focus after class. Students took part in different activities. I did not know which student to follow or which activity I should be involved in. I always worried that I might miss some key information that I would regret later. This is a potential problem with ethnographic studies described by Charmaz (2006) as they see data everywhere and nowhere, gathering everything and nothing.

Another problem is when and how to deal with the data. After only one week's observation, I had collected piles of data through informal chatting and participant observation. Students were very happy to tell me about their past learning experiences, current concerns and future expectations. Furthermore, students' transition learning experience is a process rather than a static setting which I could have plenty of time to describe and examine. The mobility of the process and timeliness of data collection opportunities required me to be very organised, focused, efficient and flexible. If I left the data undigested until the end of data collection process, I might lose focus and consistency for the following two stages of data collection.

Through my reading, I found I could use the principles advocated in grounded theory (Glaser and Strauss, 1967) to identify the directions for the on-going observations and following round of interviews. Charmaz and Mitchell (2001) claim that because of the flexibility of data collecting and analysing strategies, grounded theory methods are able to assist ethnographers to conduct 'efficient fieldwork' and create 'astute analyses'.

Grounded theory strategy is to 'seek data, describe observed events, answer fundamental questions about what is happening, and then develop theoretical categories to understand it' (Charmaz, 2006: 25). This approach increased my involvement in the research inquiry. It helped me to select the scenes and direct the gaze within them (Charmaz, 2006: 23). I made connections between events by using grounded theory to study processes through comparative methods. I compared data with data from the beginning of the research; compared data with emerging categories and demonstrated relations between concepts and categories (*ibid.*). 'Grounded theory methods provide systematic guidelines for probing beneath the surface and digging into the scene' (*ibid.*). This prevented my analysis becoming a superficial description as in journalism. It helped me to carry out theoretical interpretations, which involved 'taking data apart, conceptualizing it, and developing those concepts in terms of their properties and dimensions in order to determine what the parts tell us about the whole' (Corbin and Strauss, 2008:64). Therefore, grounded theory enabled me to take a fresh look and created novel categories and concepts instead of relying on stock disciplinary categories. This made my fieldwork more efficient and moved the research toward theoretical interpretation (Charmaz and Mitchell, 2001: 160). Therefore, grounded theory methods were able to help me to carry out a focused, structured and organised project which kept the research within control. As a new researcher, this was very important. Meantime, adopting the grounded theory analytical approach made me realise how much work I need to do to generate the skills and commitment to produce a piece of sound ethnographic work (Timmermans and Tavory, 2007).

4.9.3.2 *Things Could be Done Differently*

This research could be done differently. A case study (Yin, 2003) methodology might be an option. The sampling size can be decreased to six key informants. Multiple data sources will also be adopted, in which in-depth interviews will become the primary data collection approach. Five rounds of interviews could be carried out at the time before their leaving in China, first arrival, and at the end of each term in the first academic year in the UK. This might give me a more dynamic insight on their progress. The presentation of the findings can be their individual transition stories. This can give a clearer profile of each of the key informants than the current style.

4. 9. 3. 3 *Generalisability of the Findings?*

Ethnographic research is very time consuming and breadth is always sacrificed for depth (Brewer, 2000). Findings produced from one or two settings are limited in generalisation (*ibid.*). The intention of this abductive research is to develop theory grounded in the data, rather than generalise the conclusions to a larger population. Although I have tried my best to stratify my participants in the sampling to show the differences within the group, I still cannot say they are representatives of the Articulation Programme Students in other similar cases. Therefore, the findings cannot be applied to other settings directly. However, in the future when similar studies conducted in different fields can be compared across the cases, a body of cumulative knowledge can be built up and generalisations are feasible(Brewer, 2000). Currently, policy makers and other stake holders in Transnational Higher Education can draw some practical implications from my research findings, which will be presented in Section 7. 5.

4. 9. 3. 4 *Limitations of the Study*

There are some limitations in this study. First, I was not very confident in discussing the teaching practices with the staff at the interviews because of my lack of professional knowledge in Engineering. This also hindered me from understanding some specific subject problems, especially in the observation in the laboratory. Second, I should interview more male students as they took up over two-thirds of the participants. Third, I was much closer to my 16 key informants, and might have neglected some of the other participants. I was not able to observe them carefully. Some distinctive incidents might not be noticed.

4.10 Conclusions

This chapter has given the rationale of my choice of ethnography as the research methodology in answering the research questions and reported the procedures of research process. My philosophical position in constructionism and multi realities led me to adopt a qualitative research strategy to explore students' transition experiences in a China-UK articulation programme. Guided by the principles derived from the set of theoretical and philosophical premises of ethnography, data was collected by multiple ethnographic research approaches. My research had become a way for me to participate actively in my participants' meaning construction. Meaningful closeness and critical professional reflexivity were interwoven in the meaning construction as I was trying to keep a balance between an inside learner and an outside expert. In the process, I gave power to my participants by considering them as collaborators in the research and presenting different perspectives and voices from individuals. Data were analysed by using the data analysis principles advocated in grounded theory. Multiple data sources were triangulated and member checks were conducted to safe guard the rigour and trustworthiness of the findings. In the research, I tried my best to safe guard my participants from any harm. Anonymity and confidentiality were guaranteed. Their participation was fully informed and voluntary. Being a qualitative researcher, I was fully aware of the influence of my personal experience on my construction of the findings. Therefore, constant reflexivity was conducted to demonstrate the trustworthiness of the results.

Chapter 5 Individual Transition

5.1 Introduction

This Chapter focuses on the individual transition experience across two universities. Although the students on the programme came from the same country and had similar educational experiences, there were a lot of factors which made individuals' transition experiences and their response to those experiences very different. We should not overgeneralise their experiences based on their nationality and 'culture of learning'. However, there were some significant patterns. Three broad response categories were identified which represented the key types of experience found within the group. They encompassed different motivations for studying abroad and strategies and attitudes towards the pre-departure preparation which particularly influenced their interaction with the new learning environment and their outcomes of academic performance. Three patterns of interaction with the new learning environment were identified and presented in terms of Direct Interaction, Indirect Interaction and Avoiding Interaction. These patterns show, how in the new learning environment, some factors can be 'double-edged' in that they may have negative or positive impacts depending upon the student's transition response. Examples are: 'internet', 'privacy' and 'peer support'.

5.2 Motivation for Studying Abroad

The participants went through the same education journey following the

Chinese education system: a 9-year compulsory education and 3-year secondary education in senior middle school. The senior middle schools that the participants went to were the top schools in their cities, which had good reputations for the proportion of students entering universities. Teaching then aimed to prepare students to achieve a high score in the National Higher Education Entrance Examination, which was 'tough', 'tense', 'terrible', 'very competitive', and something that the participants would 'never want to experience again'. The 16 interviewees did not intend to choose the Articulation Programme when they took the Examination. Most of these students aimed to get into the first-tier universities. Unexpectedly, their score could only let them go to the second-tier universities. The Articulation Programme between Southeast China University and North Britain University was a second-tier programme. Along with their parents, students thought that going abroad to study could be a kind of compensation. In addition, the Engineering courses of the programme enjoyed a comparatively high reputation for employability. Most importantly, on successfully finishing their studies in China and in the UK, students were able to be awarded two degrees, one from each university.

Parents worried more about their children's safety. The first concern was the authenticity of the studying-abroad programmes. Taking the Articulation Programme could reduce risks in three ways. First, the Chinese partner is one of China's key universities. Parents thus felt confident about sending their children abroad through a programme guaranteed by a distinguished Chinese university. Second, the programme was approved by the Chinese Ministry of Education and had a licence which parents were able to check on the Internet. Finally, after two years' study in China, students could go abroad with a group of classmates who knew each other very well, which reassured their parents about their children's safety. Compared with receiving the whole undergraduate education abroad, the '2 + 2' programmes cost less. Parents also believed that their children would be more mature psychologically after two years' university study in China in comparison with going abroad directly after high school.

After two years' study in China, this group of 50 students moved onto the second stage of study at North Britain University. However, their attitudes towards studying abroad were different. Three kinds of motivations were identified in the data: 1) own decision supported by parents; 2) decision out of respect for parents' opinion; and 3) parents' decision, neglecting students' interest.

5.2.1 It is My Decision Supported by My Parents

Participants in this category had high intrinsic motivation (Ryan and Deci, 2000) for their study abroad. They had been viewing studying abroad as an enjoyable journey which they looked forward to for a long time. This journey would enable them to realise their personal goals, such as exposure to British culture, fulfilling their dreams, experiencing different education systems, connecting more to the society, making friends, enjoying more freedom, widening their views, and participating in more colourful activities.

Juan Juan had been interested in English since she was a little girl. Her obsession with the language was one of the main reasons why she chose the programme.

> My father went to America and asked me what gifts I wanted. I asked for English movies and music. He bought me many American DVDs without Chinese transcripts. I listened to them while doing the homework. I could understand them all without looking at the screens. Later I got some British DVDs as well. Sometimes I repeated after the actors and imitated their intonations. My listening and speaking have been improved. I'm fascinated by the language and gradually the countries and cultures behind it. For instance, I like Britain. It might be out of the influence of Harry Porter. I bought an English version of the seventh book and finished it in three days! I'm looking forward

to the study in the UK next semester(Juan Juan, Female Chinese Student, 1st Interview).

Juan Juan's interest in language and literature cultivated her love of British culture. Studying abroad was going to be a journey in which she could experience British culture, which she had been looking forward to since she was a little girl. Her decision was supported by her parents.

> She likes English very much. Going abroad is her dream. As parents, her mum and I tried our best to support her. I've visited many countries around the world and found there is still some distance between the higher education in our country and that in the western countries. We still need to learn more from them. So I hope she can learn the essence of knowledge (Mr. Li, Juan Juan's Father, Interview after the Congregation).

Xiao Hua was another example of how interests led him to choose studying abroad in the third year.

> I have been interested in making four-wheel cars since I was a kid. My parents didn't force me to join different kinds of training courses. Instead, they gave me money to buy spare parts for four-wheel cars. Very expensive. I always want to be an engineer and build my own 'Iron Man'. I always ask my teachers to give me extra experiment tasks. I was told that they will divide us into groups to design a project [in the UK]. The lab will keep open late. I feel excited about that(Xiao Hua, Male Chinese Student, 1st Interview).

Xiao Hua's interests in Engineering gave him the passion to choose the course. He was expecting that the course in North Britain University could help him to fulfil his dream—becoming an engineer and building his own

'Iron Man'. He was enjoying his study in the programme. Experiencing a different education system was his and many other participants' expectation. This was strengthened by the negative feeling of their past learning experience, which was shown in the following case:

> I didn't think highly of Chinese education. I didn't do well only once in the National Higher Education Entrance Examination and I lost the chance to go to my ideal university. Studying abroad is a good opportunity. I hope I can experience a different education system. The senior students abroad tell us that teaching will be more practical. There will be more experiments. Sometimes, they have to stay up till 3 o' clock in the morning. Very intense, but very exciting as well. I don't want to waste my time (Ying Ying, Female Chinese Student, 1st Interview).

Ying Ying, who was very disappointed with the education system in China, hoped she could experience a different education system in the UK. Apart from that, students also believed that studying abroad could bring them some other benefits, as Xiao Ming put it:

> The programme cuts our university life into halves. I'm looking forward to the second half. Here [in China], we don't have many opportunities to know the society. I hope I can find a part-time job in the UK. Not for the money, but to know more about their culture. Hope I can make friends with British students. I'll talk to them first definitely. I'm very independent since I was a child. But this time, I'll be totally separated from my parents. More freedom. Very excited (Xiao Ming, Male Chinese Student, 1st Interview).

Xiao Ming hoped his study in the UK, the second half of the programme, could offer him more opportunities to know the society and understand British culture. Being apart from his parents was going to give him more freedom. Coming from a well-off family, Xiao Ming did not need a part-time job. It was just a way for him to experience the culture. He was also looking forward to making friends with British students. He had made up his mind to take the initiative to talk to them. Ping Ping and Li Li had the same expectations. They were eager to make friends with British students and know more about the society outside the campus.

> I have been planning to study board since I joined the programme two years ago. It hasn't changed. I hope I can make friends with other students, stretch my thinking and broaden my horizons (Ping Ping, Female Chinese Student, 1st Interview).

> Our after-class activity is a little bit boring. Because we're leaving soon, the Student Union didn't invite us for their activities. I hope my university life will be more colourful in the UK. Hope there will be more clubs and organisations to join (Li Li, Female Chinese Student, 1st Interview).

Students in this group made the decision to study abroad because they believed that it was going to be an enjoyable journey. Their decision was supported by their parents. The motivations of studying abroad in the next group were slightly different.

5.2.2 Decision Largely out of Respect for Parents' Opinion

Participants in this group decided to study abroad largely out of respect for their parents' opinion. At the same time, their willingness reflected 'an inner acceptance of the value or utility of a task' (Ryan and Deci, 2000:55). Xiao Dong's example demonstrated how his learning had been influenced by the will power of his parents.

> In high school, my parents wanted me to get a high score, so I worked hard to get a high score. In university, my parents wanted me to be an overseas student, I agreed without thinking too much. I trust them and I know it'll be good for me. Hope it can improve my English and help me to find a good job in an international company (Xiao Dong, Male Chinese Student, 1st Interview).

Xiao Dong trusted his parents' decision to send him abroad. Studying abroad did not conflict with his interest. On the contrary, it could help him to improve his English and find a job in an international company. His parents' decision represented his own personally endorsed needs and goals (Ryan and Deci, 2002). Therefore, he accepted the arrangement willingly. This was the same with Min Min and Yan Yan:

> My parents didn't say anything, but I could feel about it from the way they looked at me. I'm their hope ... Each semester, I brought them the scholarship certificate. Not for the money, but the honour. I bought my mum a ring using my first scholarship, ¥1000. She showed it to everybody. Other parents were jealous. She was happy, which made me feel happy. To me, I want to get a Masters degree after this. It's also what my parents want me to do. I'll try to apply for the best university in the UK (Min Min, Female Chinese Student, 1st Interview).
>
> My parents told me that this course has a high reputation for employment. It's a lot of money, but they said they will give me all their savings to support my study abroad ... I got scholarship every semester to make my parents happy. My cousin studied abroad and found a very good job in Shanghai. Hope I could get a good job too when I come back from the UK (Yan Yan, Female Chinese Student, 1st Interview).

Min Min and Yan Yan worked hard to be the top students and to get a scholarship, which they believed could honour their parents. Their parents' devotion to education and high expectations for their future in the UK gave them pressure to study hard. Moreover, studying abroad in the third year could be a spring board for them to either get a Masters offer from a top university in the UK, or to find a good job after graduation. These were in line with their interests as well as their parents'.

Parents of the students in this group were more autonomy-supportive than those in the next group (see Section 5. 2. 3 for details). For instance, Xiao Qiang stated:

> The reason why I study hard is that my parents have done so much for me. My dad said this course will enable me to go abroad and have a bright employment future. I didn't have an idea then. After the first year, I told my parents I wanted to quit because I failed two modules. Teaching was half in English, half in Chinese. I couldn't understand. I asked them to transfer me to a non-programme course because I didn't want to go abroad. They didn't say anything but asked me to talk to senior students who were in the UK then. I called a student [in cohort 2005] via MSN. we were from the same city. We chatted for three hours! He told me a lot about his study in the UK ... After that, I decided to continue. In the second year, I understood better and passed the exams without difficulties. Now, I like this course, especially it gives me a chance to go abroad. I can experience some part of the university life in China first and get prepared for going abroad. I need to think about my future. I'm going to find a part-time job to improve my English. Hope I could find a one-year placement in the UK to highlight my CV and then apply for a Masters degree offer in America (Xiao Qiang, Male Chinese Student, 1st Interview).

In the above quotation, Xiao Qiang illustrated how his attitude had changed from resistance to willingness towards study abroad, assisted by his parents' support and feedback from senior students in the UK. He gradually took the first two years' study in the programme as a transition from high school to university life abroad, where he could develop professional knowledge and improve his English. The second part of the study in the UK could also be a springboard for his postgraduate study in America. He gradually built up a conscious value of the goal of studying abroad and accepted this behaviour as personally important(Ryan and Deci,2002).

Students in this group appreciated support from their family and acted to please their parents and meet their expectations. Meanwhile, studying abroad was in line with their personal needs and goals. They were willing to accept the decision. They agreed with their parents' view that studying abroad could benefit their future career. This entailsed personal endorsement and a feeling of choice(Ryan and Deci,2000:60),which was not the case in the following group.

5.2.3 Parents'Decision Neglecting Students' Interest

In this group,participants' studying abroad decision was made under their parents' pressure. Xiao Feng's experience was a clear example. His father did not go to university because of the Culture Revolution(1966-1976) 'which closed the entire higher education system,sent many professors and students to rural areas to work,and destroyed a generation of academics' (Altbach,2009: 182). As one of the young people going to the countryside, his father was eager to get into universities to study. After the Culture Revolution, he came back to the city and became a worker in a research institute, where he met many experts and professors.

> They all have been to university and very knowledgeable. I didn't want to be a worker for the rest of my life. I wanted to be

> one of them. So I went to night school after work and attended the National Higher Education Entrance Examination. When I got the offer, I almost cried (Mr. Wang, Xiao Feng's Father, Interview after the Congregation).

After several years of hard work, Mr. Wang became a senior engineer in the institution. Because of his hard and dreadful education experience, he pushed Xiao Feng very hard in his study:

> I didn't want to push him, but the pressure outside pushed me to give him pressure. Without a degree from a good university, he can't get a respectable job. The Entrance Examination is so competitive. Most of the parents are pushing their children, sending them to the top high school and hiring private tutors. The big environment is there. How can I be an exception? You asked me whether I wanted to make a change. I think it's the Chinese education system should change first (Mr. Wang, Xiao Feng's Father, Interview after the Congregation).

The pressure from the competition in the country drove Xiao Feng's father to make the decision to send his son abroad.

> My dad really wanted me to go abroad to avoid the competition. Many of his colleagues had done that. He always compared me with his colleagues' children. He didn't encourage me to do anything except study. I was fond of making small things, such as earphone exemplifiers. But my dad said it wasn't a kind of study. In fact, in his eyes, nothing is useful except study. He always criticizes me and gives me a lot of instructions. You must do this. You mustn't do that. ... He never praised me for anything. I was in top 3 in primary school. In junior school, if I drop to 8th or 9th, he would take it seriously. ... At night, he sat

> beside me watching me doing the homework. Can you imagine how stressed I was? Each time I didn't do well in my exam, he watched me like that. He was very critical: 'why do you write so fast' or' how can you remember?' I was very upset. If my mum wanted to talk to me, he would say 'no'. He didn't want my mum to disturb me while I was working on my homework. I was disgusted with what he was doing, but on the other hand I became reliant on his enforcement. He forced me and I worked efficiently. If he didn't, I could easily idle away my time (Xiao Feng, Male Chinese Student, 1st Interview).

Xiao Feng's quotation demonstrated that on one hand he was very upset and unsatisfied with his father' compulsion in his study, but on the other hand he became reliant on this kind of compulsion. Studying abroad was his father's decision to keep up with other colleagues. Xiao Feng's own interests, such as making an earphone exemplifier, were despised by his father, who thought' it wasn't a kind of study'. In this group, participants' interests were neglected by their parents. Xiao Yong was another example. As the only child in the family, he was given high expectations. In high school, he was transferred to the best school, where he was under great pressure by the competition of class rankings. One day, he knocked out the glass of the classroom window. 'My hand was bleeding. My teacher sent me to hospital. She didn't blame me as she knew how stressed we were'. At that time, he was pushed hard by his parents to go to university.

> I wanted to be a car racer, but my dad thought I was crazy. After the Examination, he chose this course for me. He talked a lot about the benefits of going abroad and how good this course is. He said after I get the degree, my English will be very good. I can go to international companies. I don't think it's a big deal. If I can't be a car racer, I can be a business man like him and

> have my own business. But he thinks his career is too tough and doesn't want me to take the same road. My English is very poor. I didn't know I could go until this term when my father was told that they could accept me as long as I go to take a summer language course at North Britain University. To tell you the truth. I really don't want to go (Xiao Yong, Male Chinese Student, 1st Interview).

Right before his leaving for the UK, Xiao Yong fell in love with a girl. Thinking of parting with his girlfriend increased his reluctance to study abroad. Studying abroad was simply his parents' decision and in conflict with his interests. Furthermore, when students were not confident in their ability of coping with studying abroad, they showed great reluctance in their action. Xiao Yong's lack of language competence strengthened his resistance to studying abroad. This was also the case with Xiao Yu:

> To tell you the truth I'm not that keen on studying abroad. It's just because my parents think highly of western education. My dad hopes I can improve my English and have an easier life in the future. I'm OK with other subjects except English. I don't know why. No matter how hard I work on it, I have never got a good result. That'll be a big problem for me (Xiao Yu, Male Chinese Student, 1st Interview).

Xiao Yu's language deficiency was, as he predicted, the biggest obstacle to his study abroad (see Section 5. 4. 2. 2). Apart from the language, self-management skills were other concerns. Fang and Xiao Jie were two examples:

> In high school I wanted to be a chemist or biologist, but my mum said, 'Do you want to stay in the laboratory for the rest of your life?!' She asked me to take this course. But there's a lot of physics which is my most headache subject. Gradually, I'm like a

> cattle eating the grass and prefer to stay in the dormitory watching cartoon. But because of the roll-call I have to attend the class. Mr. Yang(Tao) would phone my mum if I was absent too much from the class. The other girls in my dormitory also ask me to go to class with them. I won't become serious about the study till the examination. I'm not ambitious to become very rich in the future. I prefer to use the minimum effort to get the maximum achievement ... Not sure what will happen there [in the UK] ... I think the biggest obstacle abroad is myself. I don't know how to manage myself(Fang Fang, Female Chinese Student, 1st Interview).

Because of the pressure from her mother, Fang Fang had to give up her dream of becoming a chemist or biologist. The engineering course was not what she wanted, nor what she was good at. She worried that the biggest obstacle of studying abroad was herself. Xiao Jie was another student who had the same concern. He used to be a top student in high school and was forced by his parents to study hard. When he entered university, he felt life there was 'easy'. He started to become obsessed with PC games.

> My parents woke me up at 5am and asked me to read and memorise. I got to school at 6am and studied until 10pm. When I got back home, I was not allowed to go to bed. They forced me to study until midnight. I only had less than 5 hours to sleep every day. At that time [in middle school], I thought life was miserable. Life at the university is very relaxed. I spend a lot of time in the internet bar. If it is not the roll-call system and the phone calls from Mr. Yang(Tao), I'll just stay in the bar. I don't know whether I can manage myself or not in the UK. Mr. Yang has told us that nobody there will discipline us. It's more relying on us (Xiao Jie, Male Chinese Student, 1st Interview).

Mr. Yang(Tao), mentioned in Fang Fang's and Xiao Jie's quotations, was students' *Ban Zhu Ren*, their personal tutor. *Ban Zhu Ren*, a staff member who is in charge of a class, plays an important role at different stages in the Chinese education system. It is similar to a personal tutor in the UK universities, but has more power and responsibilities. In primary school and middle school, they work closely with the parents to administrate students. They are normally the teachers of core modules. Therefore, they have power from the students' parents, the school, and their roles as teachers. They are the authoritative figures in the students' study life. Tao appointed two monitors to help him manage the whole class. They carried out a roll-call at the beginning of each class, wrote down the names of those who were absent from the class, and reported to Tao afterwards. Tao would phone these students to see why they were absent from the class. He sometimes phoned their parents to discuss the students' performance at school. He believed that:

> These students graduated from senior middle school where they were strictly disciplined by teachers. The university life is free and open. Students need to be more independent. However, without teachers' instruction, some of them don't know what to do. They are like candles. They won't light themselves until you light them. So I am strict with them especially in the first year. I couldn't remember how many long-distance calls I've given to their parents(Tao, Chinese Staff Member).

Tao worked closely with the parents. After the examinations each semester, he texted students' parents the results and rank. If students displayed bad behaviour and were reluctant to change, he would also contact their parents. He hoped their parents could spend more time educating their children. Some students' parents also took the initiative to phone him when they wanted to know their children's performance in the university. If a serious problem happened, he would ask the parents to come to the university.

> The reason why I keep a close contact with their parents is that they sent their children to my class. If these students have some problems and I don't inform their parents, I will be blamed when the situation becomes very serious. For example, if students couldn't go abroad or had to drop out, parents would blame me, 'I sent my children to you. Why didn't you tell us earlier?' It's my responsibility to let them know (Tao, Chinese Staff Member).

Tao organised a Parent Meeting at the end of the first year. He considered it as a middle-point report of students' learning on the Chinese campus. He gave every student an individual comment on their behaviour: hoping parents could help him to manage their children's study and life. He inspected students' accommodation regularly to check the state of hygiene and to see whether they were playing cards. Under this kind of disciplined environment, students were seldom absent from class.

Compared with students in the previous group, this group of students were overly controlled by their parents. Their motivation to study abroad was nonautonomous, and an action to avoid parents' sanction (Ryan and Deci, 2000). The most important point was that studying abroad was either in conflict with their interests or largely what their skills or competency could not cope with. Various motivations of studying abroad influenced students' attitude towards their pre-departure preparation which will be illustrated in the following section.

5.3 Pre-departure Preparation

5.3.1 Preparation from the Programme and Schools

The first two years' teaching and learning at Southeast China University aimed to prepare students to study abroad academically, linguistically, culturally and psychologically. This was to increase the predictability of the new situation and their anticipatory familiarity, which could reduce the uncertainty facing international students(Tsang,2001:352-353). It could also enhance sojourners' readiness and ability to be open and flexible in the new learning environment (Alred, 2003: 18). The following section demonstrates the efforts that both sending and receiving universities contributed to the pre-departure preparation.

5. 3. 1. 1 *Bilingual Education*

The curriculum was designed by educators from both sides. Apart from the compulsory modules required by the Chinese Ministry of Education, students spent the rest of their time learning the first year core modules of North Britain University. The British staff sent their Chinese counterparts the syllabus and also suggested English reference books. The core modules were delivered bilingually by Chinese staff. Each student was given an English textbook as well as a Chinese one for each module. Their choice of which book to read depended on the lecturers' preference. Some lecturers' teaching was based on the English textbook, while using the Chinese one as a useful supplement, and vice versa. The practices had been conducted unevenly due to the language level of the lecturers, attitudes towards bilingual education and contents of the subjects. However, lecturers were trying their best to use English in their teaching. Some made slides in English; some embedded English terminology in the lines; some lecturers, like Lin, whose English was competent enough, taught students in English. Lin had been in the UK for 15 months and stayed in America for seven and half years as part of her PhD. She also taught a demonstration course of bilingual education in the university. She was appointed to teach the module of Engineering Physics and EM Fields.

> In the first class, everybody brought the Chinese textbook instead of the English one. I put my slides up which was in English and started to speak English to them. They all burst into laughter. I knew what that was for, even if they didn't say it out. They were thinking ' Hey Miss, you are really flattering us. Your

> expectations on us are unrealistic. We won't understand. ' But I didn't stop my teaching. Soon they became quiet. After a while, I asked them how they felt. Some said OK. Some said they couldn't understand. In fact, what they didn't understand was the overwhelming English, not Physics. The formula's there. The theory's there. I didn't worry about that at all (Lin, Chinese Staff Member).

Learning a new subject in a second language gave students a taste of the learning environment in the UK. Lin discussed the benefits of bilingual education.

> Encouraging students to read English textbook is to let them enter into the English environment. Teaching in English and Chinese is to build up a bridge between English terminology and Chinese concepts. When teaching new material where students haven't got any concept, we use Chinese to help them understand the theory and get some basic understanding of the concepts. Then we use English to assist them to build some models. Students feel easy about that. If we teach them new area in English directly, they will feel very difficult (Lin, Chinese Staff Member).

In Lin's class, students were encouraged to read the English textbook. Homework questions were from the English textbooks and the examinations were in English as well. After a semester's teaching, students felt their English had been improved. '*All the links are in English, so you started to think the subject in English*' (Xiao Hua). Having been exposed to English teaching predominantly in a module like Physics, they mastered the knowledge of the discipline and improved their language skills.

5.3.1.2 *Early Interventions*

North Britain University valued the cooperation with Southeast China

University greatly, not only because of the revenue made from the high tuition fees paid by the Articulation Programme Students, but also the international atmosphere created by their participation in the School. Therefore, they expanded the visit from management level to academic level. British staff were sent to lecture in China. This was designed to help Chinese students become familiar with teaching and learning practices in the UK. As Xiao Hua commented:

> We have several lecturers from the UK to teach us in the first two years. Before I attended their lectures, I thought it would be very hard. But after that, I felt their teaching was not as difficult as I thought. I think the crucial point is that I did pre-class study. My learning approach works. I'll continue to use it in England. Maxwell [a British staff] said my English was OK for daily activities, but I need to improve my academic English. He suggested that we remember all the glossaries at the back of the English text book. I'm working on that now (Xiao Hua, Male Chinese Student, 1st Interview).

Through the interaction with British staff in China, students assessed their own academic level, built up confidence and worked out things they need to improve. Thus, they were better prepared for their learning abroad. Staff, on the other hand, became familiar with students' previous learning experience. As Frank, one of the British staff members, mentioned:

> I give them some information about the city, university and the programme they are going to be studying, in terms of the content and how much time they have to spend on their studies, how they are assessed, and I also give them a lecture because I know the Chinese approach is different from ours. I do that to give them an idea of what our approach is. From what I gathered in China, their delivery is a bit more one-way and students sit and

> write and the lecturer or academic, delivers. Ours is a bit more two-way. I try to be more interactive to try and get the students more involved in what I'm doing and ask questions all the time. So that's what I did when I was in China (Frank, British Staff Member).

As the programme had only been set up for four years, the early intervention was still at the initial stage. British staff could not spend much time in China. Students hoped the teaching could be longer and more systematic.

> The teaching was too short. Normally one person one session. There's no connection between their teaching sessions. Only a way to help us to adapt. Not systematic teaching. Now after their teaching, our teachers will tutor us in Chinese. We need to see how we can understand their teaching for a period of time without Chinese tutoring (Xiao Ming, Male Chinese Student, 1st Interview).

The early intervention did not cover the assessment part. Students had not experienced the real assessment procedures. The situation was changing. Some Chinese staff started to integrate the assessment practices, which will be presented in the following section.

5.3.1.3 *Academic Exchange and New Assessment Practice*

How successfully the teaching contexts in the two universities could integrate will affect students' transition to a great extent. Every year, North Britain University invited an academic staff member from Southeast China University for a nine-month visit. They attended lectures, workshops and seminars with students. They also exchanged teaching and research experience with British counterparts. Their overseas life had enhanced their understanding of the teaching and learning context in the UK and the challenges their students might be confronted with in the transition.

Sheng lectured on Electronic Machinery in China. He spent about nine months at North Britain University in the academic year of 2007/2008. He was interviewed twice, one month before he left the UK and seven months after he went back to China.

> The participation in the lectures, seminars and laboratories gave me some ideas about how they delivered the module. I also gave the English staff a lecture in English. They asked questions after my teaching. This is a very good opportunity for two staff teams to understand each other better (Sheng, Chinese Staff Member).

When Sheng went back to China, he made some changes in his teaching.

> Now, I'm trying to teach my students in English and make the class more interactive. I also encourage them to ask and answer questions in English as well. Although they felt reluctant to do that at the moment, it's still worth trying. After all, it will benefit their study in the UK and I know that very well (Sheng, Chinese Staff Member).

Tao, the Electronics lecturer, introduced 'Course Design' into his module. He asked students to conduct a two-week design project in pairs in their last semester in China. Students were asked to design an audible and visual alarm. Tao explained why he made the innovations in his modules:

> Through my visit to the UK, I found our experiments are mostly asking students to test out a result, while their experiments are research based. They ask students to work into groups to design a project (Tao, Chinese Staff Member).

In the first three semesters, there were more verification experiments. Students followed the guidance step by step to verify the results. Tao believed that this kind of experiments might not improve students' practical skills and innovative ability.

> We gave students the circuits in the verification experiments and told them what appliances to use. We did demonstration first showing them what parameters to test and how to do it. What they need to do is to follow our instruction and get the results. They don't need to think a lot in the process(Tao, Chinese Staff Member).

Students felt that this kind of experiments did not give them a sense of achievement. As Fang Fang mentioned, '*You can find all the answers in the guidance book. You don't really see the point why you do it. It's easy. Not challenging at all*'. Their passive attitude changed in the new assessment. They needed to find information online, go over text books, discuss with teammates, and use software to draw the circuit, implement it in the lab and write a project report. These practices were similar to the ones in the UK. Getting familiar with these practices was a bridge for their study abroad.

Fang Fang, who previously was not bothered with experiments, became serious this time. She was put into a group with Xiao Hua.

> I picked up the learning points I forgot. I read the two Electronics books from the beginning to the end searching for ideas to design the project. I had never done that before. We kept on changing and changing to implement our design. We realised that theory and practice were totally different. The threads were so hard and hurt my fingers. We were like making cross-stitches [Laughs] (Fang Fang, Female Chinese Student, 1st Interview).

After many attempts, their alarm system was successful. They got 90% for their design course. Looking at the circuit board, Fang Fang was reluctant to take the thread off. It was so valuable and precious to her.

Xiao Jie had spent a lot of time on PC games, but changed his attitudes towards learning and identified his weak points through the design course.

> Before the design course, I thought what we had learned was useless. I couldn't connect the learning points together. Now, I realise that I can apply the knowledge into practice. I also find that there are many areas I need to work on. Otherwise I may fail the study in the UK. I feel regret that I didn't study hard before (Xiao Jie, Male Chinese Student, 1st Interview).

The newly introduced assessment practice helped students link the knowledge they learned in class to real life practice. Their so-called passive and cure-seeking behaviours changed in this assessment. This shows that students' learning behaviours are not fixed as described in the culture of learning theory (Cortazzi and Jin, 1997). They can be changed in the same 'culture' by different teaching practices, which depends largely on the teachers' individual practices. Meanwhile, the learning behaviours are not fixed which change in different contexts based on the information they receive, the tasks they need to finish and the flexibility they may have for their learning.

5.3.1.4 *Culture Learning*

Apart from academic preparation, Southeast China University greatly increased the teaching hours to help students improve their English. Native speakers were appointed as oral English teachers giving weekly classes where students practised their English and learned about UK culture. The lecturer observed in this study was from Australia. He shared the tips of overcoming difficulties abroad based on his own experience as an international student in China.

> One of the topics was 'Culture shock. What is it?' and so I explained to them the five stages that they will go through. And then we actually talked about ways to get over culture shock.

> Doing sports, making friends, QQ and MSN, keeping in contact. Maybe. When I told them about what it was like to study, I taught them what it was like to be a foreign student here. I told them that the food was different. I told them about difficulties I had and I told them about how I got over my difficulties of being in China. ... I said, 'Join clubs, make friends, play sport' and those are good ways to adapt (David, Chinese Staff Member from Australia).

In his teaching, David tried to prepare his students to adapt to the culture they were going into. He introduced students to the features of the city where the North Britain University is located:

> I show them the weather and photographs of the city. I show them photographs of pubs, buildings, and the train station where they will arrive ... I try to give them the prices about how expensive things are in England, so how much is milk and how much is a bottle of water, how much is a bus ticket. ... So they say, 'Oh, the teacher showed us a picture of the train station. I know where I am' and I show them a picture of Chinatown so they know it's not so far away, so it's not so foreign and strange to them (David, Chinese Staff Member from Australia).

Language was taught in a context which aimed to help students understand the environment they were going into and make more sense of the language. Through which, the strangeness these students might feel in their study abroad was likely to be reduced.

> I showed them The Lion, The Witch and The Wardrobe, which was a little bit English related. I explained to them who C. S. Lewis was and explained to them that he went to Oxford and to Cambridge. I explained a little bit about the background history.

> I know one girl who has read all the books in the class; she was very interested in it, so that was good. Because I'm trying to expose them to English literature (David, Chinese Staff Member from Australia).

Students were given topics that they might come across while staying abroad, such as culture shock and goals to go abroad. Ways to cope with problems, such as boarding a plane and losing the passport were also discussed. These made their language learning more relevant and practical.

> Because what I'm doing is, I'm teaching them to think and not just to repeat ... I try to pick topics like going overseas or things that are related to where they are going. Because I think that if you make language practical and they can see the point, they want to learn it because, 'Hey, this would be useful when I'm over in England, I'm going to travel over there' and so if it's more practical then there is a point, rather than learning about fashion or something, or learning about something that's maybe not so related. So I try to make it practical for them (David, Chinese Staff Member from Australia).

Through discussing these topics, students started to think about the culture of the country they were going to, predicting the difficulties they might come across, and preparing for the challenges in the new learning environment. In his teaching, David tried to encourage students to participate in the class. He allocated a mark to students' participation.

> I give them a debate on a topic, 'There is no advantage to going overseas' and then split them into two groups. In that way, they have to talk about it. But with the debate, what I was marking was their participation. I'm looking to see which students actually say something without me asking ... I know from different

> studies that the people that make better speakers in the long run, are the ones that are more extroverted and are the ones that ask questions, are curious, that are more involved, they are the ones whose language will get better and better (David, Chinese Staff Member from Australia).

David's teaching differs from the argument in the literature (Cortazzi and Jin, 1996a) that students' learning in China is teacher-centred and emphasises listener responsibility. When the institutions become more internationalised and various teaching approaches are adopted, students are exposed in a more diverse learning environment. The so-called distinctive divisions in the education practices between Chinese and UK systems are blurred. Being exposed in an internationalised teaching environment, students become familiar with the future academic culture to some extent. However, not all the students have done the same level of preparation. This will be explored in the following section.

5.3.2 Attitudes Towards Pre-departure Preparation

5. 3. 2. 1 *Active Preparation*

Students with intrinsic motivation or internalised extrinsic motivation demonstrated great autonomy in their active attitude towards pre-departure preparation. Going abroad was the main reason why this group of students chose the Articulation Programme. They knew from the start that they were going to the UK for the latter stage of their study. Their attitude resulted in high-quality learning and creativity. They actively collected information about living and studying in the UK from the Internet and they chatted online with students who were studying abroad and read their blogs.

> Studying abroad in the UK is not strange to me. I have relatives and friends who have been abroad. Our lecturers who have visited the North Britain University told us how they felt about

the country(Xiao Dong, Male Chinese Student, 1st Interview).

These students were actively seeking chances to develop their familiarity with the signs or cues that might reduce their anxiety in the new environment abroad. Lecturers, relatives or friends who had been abroad, and the senior students became the sources of knowledge. They predicted the difficulties they were going to come across in the UK, such as food, missing home, self-management, language and making friends with home students, and started to develop the skills to cope with the difficulties. The prediction set up an alert in their mind and pointed out the directions they could take.

> I chat with the seniors who have already been there. They tell me self-study is very important. You have a lot of free time. You must do a lot of self-study. Mr. Yang(Tao) told us that nobody there will ask you to go to class. It's your own responsibility. In England, everything relies on you (Xiao Ming, Male Chinese Student, 1st Interview).

The feedback given by the senior students and their tutor highlighted the importance of autonomous learning. With this kind of alert in mind, students were more likely to work in that direction. They took extra work, more than the teachers had asked. For instance, Ping Ping read both versions of the textbooks to get familiar with the terminologies and definitions in English. She believed that trying to study the subject in English could facilitate her study in the UK.

> From what others told me, a larger academic vocabulary will help me there ... I collect the glossaries from my daily reading, mark them down and will go over them again this summer holiday(Ping Ping, Female Chinese Student, 1st Interview).

Methods to cope with English teaching abroad were tried and practiced in their study in China, as shown by Xiao Ming:

> To understand the class better, you really need to read the English textbook before the class. Look up words in the dictionary. Find the Chinese version and get to know the English meaning. When we are asked to work out the questions in English and submit them as homework, we need to go over the textbook again (Xiao Ming, Male Chinese Student, 1st Interview).

As data shown in Section 5.3.1.2, these students identified their strengths as well as weak points in the interaction with British staff. Xiao Ming's way of learning was effective, which gave him confidence to succeed in studying abroad. The advice offered by British staff pointed out the direction students need to work towards.

These students had been working hard to enhance their language ability. Apart from increasing their academic glossaries, students joined in various language training schools outside the campus to polish their English. To be accepted by the North Britain University, they need to achieve 5.5 in IELTS (International English Language Testing System) or equivalent. They developed the techniques to gain high mark in listening, speaking, reading and writing in IELTS. Xiao Ming got 7.0 in his second year. He shared his experience in preparing for the language test.

> I studied very hard preparing IELTS and I think my English has been greatly improved. Many classmates went to language training school in the summer holiday. I went there in the first year. I bought many reference books and recited a 3000-new-word book. We studied very hard in language school. Two days per week. 5 hours one session. The teachers there encouraged us to talk. I talked a lot in that school. I had an MP3. I listened to BBC every day. I got 7.5 in listening (Xiao Ming, Male Chinese Student, 1st Interview).

Juanjuan got 6.5 in IELTS in her first year. Apart from preparing for the language test, she and her roommates watched TV series and movies shot in English.

> I watched *Gossip Girl*, *Desperate Housewives*, *Hero*, etc. Our English teacher showed us *Little Britain* in the class. I covered the subtitles to practice my listening (Juan Juan, Female Chinese Student, 1st Interview).

> I finished ten seasons of *Friends* as well as 24 *Hours*, *Lost*, *Desperate Housewives* and *Prison Break*. I like *The Princess Diaries* very much. It was hard to understand the British accent at the beginning, but now it's much better (Yan Yan, Female Chinese Student, 1st Interview).

These English movies or TV series not only allowed students to pick up English, but also the customs and cultures of western countries while they were still in China. These students also created opportunities to communicate with native speakers.

> I helped the British lecturers set up multi-media equipment. So I had more opportunities to chat with them and helped them communicate with others (Xiao Ming, Male Chinese Student, 1st Interview).

> I offered to show the UK staff around the campus. I talked a lot that day. They said my English was good. I was very happy about that (Xiao Hua, Male Chinese Student, 1st Interview).

The initiative to communicate with native speakers was also shown in their strong desire to make friends with British students and other international students as well to integrate into the local culture. Before leaving China, they expressed their strong willingness to get to know other students abroad as well as their concerns in the process of integration:

> I'm eager to make friends with British students and will take the initiative to talk to them, but I'm also worried that there might be ethnic conflicts with British students. Hope they won't bully us (Yan Yan, Female Chinese Student, 1st Interview).

> Western media gave a lot of negative reports on China. They blamed many things on Chinese population. For instance, if one country's employment rate dropped, they would say, 'that's because Chinese people come and steal our jobs'. So they will discriminate Chinese or even assault us. I'm just worried this kind of report might influence the public's opinions on Chinese overseas students. But I believe in Yanni's point of view that the world is a family. We should see the common things among us instead of differences. I'll take the initiative to talk to the British students first (Xiao Qiang, Male Chinese Student, 1st Interview).

The willingness to integrate with other students and the concerns of conflicts interwove together and this was shown in their strategies of accommodation application. Apart from one dormitory group who applied to live in the same flat, all the other students applied to live with one roommate (normally their best friend) and asked the Accommodation Office at North Britain University to dispatch foreign flatmates. The reasons were:

> I apply to live with one of my current roommates and hope the rest of the flatmates will be British students. We two could look after each other on one hand. On the other hand, we could communicate with foreign students to practice our English. I don't want to stay with Chinese all the time. It'll be meaningless

> if we only stay with our own group members (Min Min, Female Chinese Student, 1st Interview).

From reading senior students' blogs, students predicted the problems they might come across, such as missing home.

> I know I'll miss home. I'm teaching my parents how to chat online. We could do video chat every week (Ping Ping, Female Chinese Student, 1st Interview).

Ping Ping here worked out a way to cope with her future problem assisted by new technology. Through the test of chatting online, she and her parents had the psychological preparation for their being apart in the next couple of years. As the only child in the family, Xiao Qiang expressed his concern about cooking.

> Cooking will be a problem for me. Last winter vacation, my parents taught me how to cook. It's not as difficult as I thought. I'll learn more dishes this summer holiday (Xiao Qiang, Male Chinese Student, 1st Interview).

Students were working hard to solve the problem. This had been observed on the internet. They shared recipes of Chinese cuisines on the blogs. For example, Xiao Hua made his first two dishes: *Sweet & Sour Ribs* and *Roasted Chicken Wings* in the winter holiday of 2008. He posted the recipes with pictures on his blog (24th January, 2008). His classmates made comments on his webpage:

> You can make a living when you come here [the UK] (Student in 2005, 24-01-2008 22:20).
>
> Professional chef! Mine doesn't look as good as yours. What's the secret? ☺ (Ying Ying, 24-01-2008 22:23).
>
> The secret is to leave them in the source of salt, soya source and

cooking wine ☺(Xiao Hua,25-01-2008 01:40).

The above dialogues between Xiao Hua and his classmates or students who were in the UK demonstrated that this group of students were actively preparing for their future life in the UK. As Xiao Hua predicted:

> I think there will be a run-in period. They said it's hard to get to know English students. I'll take the initiative to talk to them. We're all young people with a lot of common interests. It shouldn't be a problem for me. I'm practicing English, collecting information about England, going over the learning points teachers have covered in the first two years, and will polish my cooking skills this summer. I don't think it'll be very difficult (Xiao Hua, Male Chinese Student, 1st Interview).

Xiao Hua anticipated that there might be a run-in period. He might come across various problems such as how to get along well with home students. However, he believed that the positive attitude he was taking and the preparation he had done in China would enable him to overcome the difficulties. For students who were unwilling to study abroad, their attitude towards the pre-departure preparation was different.

5.3.2.2 *Passive Preparation*

As presented in Section 5.2.3, some participants were unwilling to study abroad. Their parents made the decision for them. These students' attitude towards pre-departure preparation was passive. Evidence showed that the stronger the negative feeling about studying abroad they had, the less autonomous they were in pre-departure preparation. Unlike students in the previous group, who intended to stay longer in the UK either to continue their course or find a job, this group of students were determined to come back to China as soon as they finished the final two-year study at North Britain University. Their studying abroad was a 'return' to their parents' expectation and investment. This might let them underplay the importance of various moderating factors, such as acquiring language competence and establishing interpersonal relationships known to enhance positive adaptation, owing to the temporary nature of their stay and their intention to return home (Berry and Sam, 1997: 306). For these students, the importance of bilingual education was not appreciated. For example, Xiao Yong believed that '*It's weird to see teachers teaching modules in a different language*' and was reluctant to read English textbooks. He commented that:

> Those books are big and thick! They're not as concise as Chinese ones. I think the first two years' teaching should focus on giving us a solid theory foundation. Once we understood the theory, we could just pay attention to the language in the UK. I think Chinese teachers should teach us in Chinese only (Xiao Yong, Male Chinese Student, 1st Interview).

These students went to the letures, attended the examinations, prepared for the IELTS test, and finished the homework and other tasks required by the teachers. Apart from that, they did not do extra work as the students in the previous group had done. Although they expressed their concerns about studying abroad, they did not do much preparation for overcoming the potential challenges.

> I prefer to use the minimum effort to get the maximum achievement. I don't want to work too hard that in the near future I'll be sitting there counting how many grey hairs I've got. I know I need to read English books and recite those technical words. In fact, I make plans at the beginning of each semester, but after two weeks, I'll just be who I am. Maybe when I get there, I'll make some changes. I'll cross the bridge when I get to the river (Fang Fang, Female Chinese Student, 1st Interview).

Fang Fang did not do much preparation due to her attitude of '*using minimum effort to get the maximum achievement*'. She knew what she should do, but she did not do it. Xiao Jie had many friends in the grade above who were in the UK then. They gave him some 'positive' feedback.

> They told me that the passing line is 40%. You can also get the previous examination papers. It's easy for you to pass it as long as you go through those papers. I just want a pass and get the degree (Xiao Jie, Male Chinese Student, 1st Interview).

The tips he had received from the students above gave him a rosy picture of learning in the UK. The passing score (40%) was lower than what they were in China (60%). However, Xiao Jie did not realise that the standard was not lower and the possible effort he should devote was not less, either.

Unlike students in the previous group who applied for accommodation with one Chinese classmate and left three or four vacancies to home students or other international students, students in this group, such as Xiao Yu and Xiao Jie, preferred to stay in the accommodation with their own classmates.

> I didn't apply to live with British students because I don't want to have conflicts with them as our cultures are different. I'll stay with my Chinese classmates. They are *Zi Ji Ren* (people on my side). It is more secure and easy to look after each other. With *Zi Ji Ren*, you can do whatever you want to do. I might have problems with the British students as we can't understand each other. I don't think going abroad is suitable for me. I feel headache to speak English. I really don't know how I will go through those two years abroad (Xiao Yu, Male Chinese Student, 1st Interview).

Zi Ji Ren are people from the same group who will stand beside you when you have problems. They can also give you freedom without worrying about courtesy or conflicts. Xiao Yu's deficiency in English aggravated his reluctance to communicate with British flatmates and increased his negative feelings towards studying abroad. This kind of negative feeling made him become passive towards the pre-departure preparation. Students' motivation towards study abroad and pre-departure knowledge affected their adoption of different strategies in coping with the changes in the new learning environment, which will be discussed in the following section.

5.4 Interaction with the New Learning Environment

5.4.1 New Features in the New Learning Environment

Most of my participants arrived at North Britain University on the 11th of September, 2008. In the following week, the University arranged induction programmes for every new student which talked about health care, bank accounts, Students' Union, the library and other topics relevant to their university study. The participants opened bank accounts, registered for a GP, enrolled at the School, and registered at the police station as required by the British government. Interacting with the new learning environment, the participants identified some differences in the features of two campuses.

5.4.1.1 *General Features*

Coming to North Britain University, students experienced different administrative systems: from being disciplined to discipline themselves. As mentioned in Section 5.2.3, in the first two years in China, *Ban Zhu Ren* worked closely with their parents to discipline students. Things in the UK were different.

> You could ask your friends to tick the box for you. No one will find out nor care. In China, we're 'scared' of our *Ban Zhu Ren*. There isn't a figure in the UK that we're 'scared' of. And I don't think the lecturers here want us to be 'scared'. They treat us as adults (Ping Ping, Female Chinese Student, 2nd Interview).

Although a personal tutor was assigned to these students, he managed them in a different way.

> Under the University regulations, we can't make students come to classes. The only thing the University does is, students are assigned a tutor, and obviously if there is continuous absence, then the tutor will contact a student to find out what is wrong. But there's nothing that the University can actually do to say, 'You must come to class.' But ultimately it's the decision of the student (Colin, British Staff Member).

Staff also expressed their concerns about giving the parents students' information.

> Over here, there is the Data Protection Act. So as soon as they are 18, they are adults. And strictly speaking, you're not allowed to give any information to their parents because they are 18 (Tom, British Staff Member).

Being self-disciplined was considered by some participants as a big challenge. This was exaggerated by some new features on the British campus. These were supposed to be facilitators but became 'double-edged', such as more privacy and easier access to the internet. At Southeast China University, students were asked to pass National Computing Rank Examination (Grade 2) and *Computing* was one of the compulsory modules. However, students did not use computers very offen for their learning. Computing was used in the teaching, but mainly in showing slides. Apart from the report in Course Design, which was done by computers, most of the reports and homework were handwritten. Worrying that students might play PC games, the University allowed the internet to be installed in the students' dormitory under strict conditions (See Table 5.1 for details). At North Britain University, students were able to get access to the internet anywhere on campus. They used the internet extensively for their study. This came along with a problem: distraction. As Ping Ping described:

> Here, it's so easy to just wander on the internet, checking email, chatting on QQ, surfing on facebook or Xiaonei. I found time flying quickly (Ping Ping, Female Chinese Student, 2nd Interview).

Another 'double edged' factor was 'privacy'. As shown in Table 5-1, the participants lived on campus at Southeast China University. Four lived in one room with bunk beds. They slept on the lower bed and put books and luggage on the upper bed. Washrooms were shared by about 50 students on the same floor. There were no kitchens in the building. Students normally attended activities in the form of 'Dormitory Group'. At North Britain University, students were dispatched to several accommodations near the University. They had their own rooms. Compared with their accommodation in China, these students had more privacy. Some students, like Fang Fang, could watch cartoons as late as she wanted without worrying about disturbing others. This had partly led to her failure of the academic year which will be discussed in Section 5.4.2.4.

Table 5-1 Comparison of General Features on Two Campuses

	Southeast China University	North Britain University
Facilities	Walls around the campus with gatekeepers at two entrances	No walls. Open to the city
	Library: Time limit	Library: 24 Hours
Accommodation	Four students live in one room	Every student has an individual room
	Roommates are from the same class	Flatmates can be in different courses
	Boys and girls live in different accommodations. Boys are not allowed to visit girls in their accommodation	Flatmates can be boys or girls
	No kitchen. Students have meals in canteens; sometimes go to restaurants or snack bars near campus	With kitchens. Students normally cook for themselves; sometimes go to canteens on campus or restaurants outside campus

(contd.)

	Southeast China University	North Britain University
Administration	*Ban Zhu Ren* is responsible for most of the administrative work. He also represents the power of the School and is assisted by students' parents	Personal tutor helps students with their academic and personal development. He is not allowed to contact parents without students' permission
	Two monitors help *Ban Zhu Ren* to supervise the class	Course reps support and represent the views of other students in the course through attending meetings with staff to ensure that staff take into account the concerns and needs of students
Internet	Students can have internet in the dormitory, but have strict regulations (eg. All the roommates have to pass the examinations in the first year) They use internet bar outside campus/at home during holidays, but seldom use internet for study, expect the Course Design	They have access to the internet everywhere on campus/dormitory and use internet for the study

5.4.1.2 *Teaching and Learning Practices*

Two weeks after their arrival, students started their study on the new campus. Seven chose the course of *BEng (Hons) Communication and Electronic Engineering (CEE)* and the rest chose to take *BEng (Hons) Electrical and Electronic Engineering (EEE)*. However, except for the module of *Power, Machines and Instrumentation* (EN0215) for CEE students and *Distributed Circuit* (EN0219) for EEE students, this group of students took their other five modules together. These included *Electronic Product Development* (EN0213), *Data Communication & Transmission Systems* (EN0214), *Advanced Engineering Mathematics* (CG0037), *Microprocessor Systems & Digital Signal Processing* (EN0217) and *Analogue & Digital Electronics* (EN0216). To facilitate students' transition to the new learning environment, the school provided the module of *Language Support* (CM0561) specifically for the programme students.

Each module had a lecturing team of two or three staff members. They uploaded their slides to the E-learning Portal before the class. There were no text books, but reading lists with several reference books. Staff compiled their own hand-outs and gave them to students at the beginning of the modules. Assessment tasks, requirements and deadlines were informed in the first lecture. Students were expected to attend lectures, seminars and laboratories. They needed to read lecture notes and suggested reference material after class. Seminars were new to students. They were divided into four or five groups and asked to download and work out the questions from E-learning portal before seminars. Answers to those questions were discussed in seminars facilitated by a staff. Students were constantly comparing the teaching practices of both campuses. Table 5-2 shows the main differences identified by the students.

Table 5-2 Comparison of Teaching and Learning Practices on Two Campuses

	Southeast China University	North Britain University
Teaching Language	English and Chinese	English
Delivery Format	Lectures and laboratories	Lectures, seminars and laboratories
Lectures	Around 50 students; Lecture theatres	Around 120 students; Lecture theatres
Seminars	No	Yes. Four to five groups; Seminar is considered as an important part of the teaching for students to ask questions
Laboratories	Verification experiments; Course Design	Research-based experiments
Learning Format	Direct learning and independent learning	Direct learning and independent learning
Teaching Hours	40 minutes per teaching hour; Two or three teaching hours per lecture; 10-minute break when the bell rings	50 minutes per teaching hour; One or two teaching hours per lecture; No bell (Whether taking a break or not was decided by lecturers)

(contd.)

	Southeast China University	North Britain University
Textbook	One English text book; One Chinese text book; Teaching is based on the textbooks	Reading list; Hand-outs; Professional websites and journals
Teaching Facilities	Computer/Slides/Projector	Computer/Slides/Projector E-learning Portal
E-Learning Portal	No. Lecturers recommend students to read the textbook before their teaching	Yes. Lecturers put the hand-outs on the E-learning Portal before the teaching
Teaching Team	Individual teaching	Co-lecturing

Staff at North Britain University tended to keep the lectures more interactive. They set up slots in the class for questions. They believed that one student's question might be many students' question and '*students don't learn if they are just talked to all the time and they have got to do something to be more likely to get engaged and learn about the subject*' (Eric, British Staff Member). An interactive atmosphere was believed to be able to facilitate the staff's teaching, especially in a large class.

> We'd like them to interrupt, to say, 'Can you just do that again? I didn't understand that bit.' Because if one says it then you know there are probably 30 other people thinking the same thing but don't say it. So as long as one says something then you can stop and say, 'Okay, let's go over this one more time' and then everybody gets the idea again (Simon, British Staff Member).

However, the Articulation Programme Students had their own philosophy for questioning in the class. First, they considered questions as a way for the staff to test knowledge, rather than to promote interaction. They were more interested in 'hard' questions than 'easy' ones. As Yan Yan described:

> Sometimes the questions are too easy. For instance, once a lecturer asked 'what's sin $\frac{\pi}{2}$?' Nobody gave him the answer. He got the cold shoulder and answered himself 'equals to 1' [Laughs]. You see you don't have any sense of achievement (Yan Yan, Female Chinese Student, 2nd Interview).

Answering questions was considered by some students as a way of showing off. As Xiao Yong pointed out:

> A maths teacher asked us questions, I didn't answer. Everybody can answer the question. Why do you stand up to answer it? Show off. Even if I know everything, I won't give the answer. Why should I answer the question? I know how to do it. That's fine (Xiao Yong, Male Chinese Student, 2nd Interview).

In fact, their questioning behaviour was influenced by the teaching practices in the first two years in Southeast China University.

> We think that the time in the class is limited. If we disrupted the lecturer, he might not finish his teaching in time. In addition, it'll be unfair for other students if my question takes up too much time. I'd like to ask questions after the class (Ping Ping, Female Chinese Student, 2nd Interview).

Teaching in the first two years at Southeast China University was very intense. Lecturers were asked to cover the learning points of the syllabus in allocated teaching hours. Because other compulsory classes had taken half of the teaching hours, staff felt that they did not have enough time to deliver the material they had prepared.

> 40 minutes is too tight. I need to finish my teaching task first. So

> I don't encourage them to ask questions in the class. They could ask questions after class(Xin, Chinese Staff Member).

Because of the above concern, staff seldom built up a session in the teaching to interact with students in the class, but encouraged students to ask questions before or after the class. Therefore, in the class observed, students paid attention to the teaching and took down notes. They normally asked questions during the break.

When students had questions about the teaching, they were more likely to continue the listening through which they tried to find the answers. They engaged themselves in active learning. Therefore, not being interactive in the form of questioning in class did not mean they were passively listening to the lecturers' teaching. Students, like Ping Ping and Xiao Ming, found that with questions in mind they became more active in classroom learning.

> When I have a question, I would like to keep it in my mind. Try to find the answers in the teachers' further explanation. I find I am more attentive with questions in mind (Ping Ping, Female Chinese Student, 2nd Interview).

> Many questions could be sorted out by reading after class. With the question in mind, I read more actively. I could also discuss it with my classmates. If we couldn't answer it, we could ask the teachers(Xiao Ming, Male Chinese Student, 2nd Interview).

This questioning behaviour influenced their learning approaches, as illustrated by Xiao Hua:

> I read the textbook before the class and mark down the things I don't understand, which will push me to learn actively in the class as I am trying to find answers from the teaching. If I still couldn't figure them out, I could ask the teachers during the

> break or after the class (Xiao Hua, Male Chinese Student, 2nd Interview).

The impression these Articulation Programme Students gave to the British staff was that they were *quiet*, *shy* and *less interactive*, which was linked to the presumption that '*they seem quite passive in the class, but obedient*' (Frank, British Staff Member). However, as time passed, the staff noticed that these students did interact, but not at the time and place they had expected.

> What I have noticed is that I built in some time for questions and answers, and nobody asked anything. But as soon as the lecture finished, they all came to the front and asked me individually. I don't know if that was a cultural thing or not (Frank, British Staff Member).

It was considered to be time-wasting and courage-lacking by some staff, if not asking questions at the built-in time.

> I do get the odd students that do come up and ask me. They got the notes and what was all this about? But they should really ask me at the time. I would like it if they said, 'Can you do that again?' because if they are asking me then there must be at least 10 or 15 others who would want to ask the same point, but that they haven't got the courage to ask, so they go away and try to learn from friends (Simon, British Staff Member).

In China, when the bell rang, there would be a break. In the UK, there were no bells to stop the class. Staff had their own preferences. Some of them would like to finish the two-hour lecture without a break.

> I never break. I finish early so I usually do an hour and a half, because if you have a break and they go away, they've forgotten what we were talking about and you have to recap, 'This is what

> we're doing, this is where we were ... ' and so I intend to just carry on straight through to about half past (Simon, British Staff Member).

> I think it's part of the language problem. They don't ask too many questions in the class, but they do ask questions after I finish. And I don't mind doing this [having a break] but sometimes it becomes hectic if I have another class to go to (Louise, British Staff Member).

There was a conflict that these students were 'quiet' when staff wanted them to 'ask', but 'ask' when staff expected they should be 'quiet'. As presented before, being 'quiet' in the class did not mean being passive in learning.

Some staff attributed students' asking questions after class to culture (Frank), language problems (Louise) or a lack of courage (Simon). Data collected in this research found that learning and teaching behaviour might be about 'habits' not 'culture'. Students formed the habit of asking questions after class because of the teaching practices at Southeast China University. They also took questions as a way of testing knowledge in class, rather than a way to interact with the staff. When the teaching practices changed in the UK, some students made relevant changes to join in with the new classroom culture. Some were still keeping silent in the class or asking questions after class. Data collected from this research did not show the differences of two kinds of questioning behaviour in affecting students' academic performance.

5.4.1.3 *Assessment Practices on Two Campuses*

The programme was accredited by the Institution of Engineering and Technology in the UK and successful graduates could become Associate Members of the Institution. In their first year at North Britain University, the participants took the modules listed in 5.4.1.2. There were some similarities and differences between the assessment practices at North Britain University and what students had experienced in the first two years at Southeast China University(see Table 5-3 for details).

Table 5-3 Comparison of Assessment Practices on Two Campuses

	Southeast China University	North Britain University
Formative Assessment	Mid-term examination; Homework	Lab reports; MCQs; Seminar Questions
Examination Questions	Compulsory to finish all	With choices(e. g. eight questions and attempt five)
Examination Time Each Year	Four times(two middle-term exams and two final-term exams)	Once (at the end of the academic year)
Previous Assessment Paper Provided	None	Yes(previous five years)
Tutorial before Examinations	Yes	Yes
Marking Criteria	Not provided in paper, but was explained in the tutorial before exams	Yes
Feedback on Assessed Work	Middle-term examination papers were explained in the class; Final examination papers were given the mark only	Group feedback was posted on the E-learning Portal; Individual feedback was given
Confidentiality of Grades	Parents were informed of students' ranking and grades	Confidential
Grade Category	Distinction: over 90%; Commendation: 80-89%; Clear Pass: 70-79%; Pass: 60-69%; Fail: under 60%	Distinction: over 70%; Commendation: 60-69%; Clear Pass: 50-59%; Pass: 40-49%; Fail: under 40%
Scholarship System	Awarded according to the ranking based on the academic score, attendance, extra work done for the collective and award. 1st class scholarship: Top 3; 2nd class scholarship: 4-9; 3rd class scholarship: 10-23	Awarded according to the academic score: 1st class scholarship: over 70%; 2nd class scholarship: over 60%
Degree Classification	Pass: 60% and over; Failed: under 60%	First Class: 70% and over; 2:1: 60-69%; 2:2: 50-59%; 3rd Class: 40-49%

As the participants moved to the 2nd stage of study, the requirements and formats of the assessments were different. Some of the differences in practice were due to the different stages of academic requirements rather than being purely influenced by the 'culture of learning'. Most of the assessments in the first two years were closely connected with the textbook used in each module. Lecturers chose the textbooks for their modules according to the syllabus. Teaching and learning were based on the textbooks. In the class, lecturers used Power Point slides to assist their teaching. Students were asked to take down notes. After theory explanation, they gave examples. Sometimes they asked students to do some questions in the class, and check the answers afterwards. Homework was often the exercises in the textbooks. Students submitted their answers for feedback once or twice a week. The majority of the exam questions were based on the format of the examples in the textbook or homework. The term of 'formative assessment' was not familiar to the Chinese staff. It was not mentioned in the curriculum. However, there were four examinations in one academic year, twice a semester. Feedback was given after the exams. Mid-term examinations, as well as the twice-a-month submitted homework, were considered by staff and students as ways to check the progress. Therefore, they resembled the functions of formative assessment.

At North Britain University, the participants found that the different practices of grade categories, scholarship system, degree classification system, formative assessments, and new requirements of assessment had influenced their learning.

Grade Categories

At Southeast China University, there were two semesters in each academic year. The first semester started from September to January, and the second semester started from February or March (normally two weeks after Chinese New Year) until the end of June. Students had two rounds of examinations in each semester, and these happened in the middle and at the end. The weight of assessment consisted of middle-term exam (20%), final-term exam (50%), laboratories (20%) and homework with attendance (10%). The pass mark was 60%. 80% was commendation and 90% was distinction.

Students expected higher marks than they achieved in the UK. Xiao Hua who always received 90% in China, could not accept the fact that one of his first reports 'only' got 80% which was a high score in the class. '80% *doesn't sound good enough. In my mind, distinction is over* 90% ' (Xiao Hua). He set up a higher standard for himself and worked hard toward it. At the end of the first academic year, his average score for all the modules was 83%.

Xiao Jie had a different opinion:

> The passing line is only 40%. That's easy. We used to have to pass 60% in China (Xiao Jie, Male Chinese Student, 1st Interview).

Here, Xiao Jie did not realise that the lower marking lines did not mean the lowering of the assessment standards. This misunderstanding gave him a kind of false sense of security, which had influenced his attitude towards study. He did not devote enough effort to his study, which led to his failure in his modules (see Section 5.4.2.4).

Scholarship Systems

Scholarship as a kind of honour was important to these students' motivation. At Southeast China University, they were put into a rank according to their academic score at the end of each semester. Parents were updated by texts sent by *Ban Zhu Ren*. Student committee members could get some points for their contribution to class administration. Students absent from a class would be deducted by two points. Students worked hard to get the scholarship.

> My motivation is to get the scholarship. I think all the girls in my dormitory have the same goal. It's not only for the money, but the certificate which will be helpful for my future. My parents were

> very happy each time I showed them the certificates (Yan Yan, Female Chinese Student, 1st Interview).

Scholarships and certificates were evidence of hard work and a reward to parents' high expectation. Meanwhile, students positioned themselves in the group according to the league. They compared their achievement with other classmates.

> I studied very hard in the first semester because I didn't know others' strengths. After the examinations, I was among the top five. I had a sense of security. I knew I couldn't drop to the bottom (Yan Yan, Female Chinese Student, 1st Interview).

Once the group position was set up, students at the top had a sense of security, while students at the bottom felt that it was hard for them to beat the top 3 and win the 1st scholarship. This was different at North Britain University. To award students' academic achievement in study, the School set up the 'Dean's Award' for international students. Students could qualify for the 1st scholarship if they achieved an average of 70% or higher for the year. Theoretically speaking, every student had the chance to win the prize if they achieved the standard.

> In the first two years, we were put into a ranking list. We were constantly competing with each other. Here, we don't have the concept of ranking. You get 70%. You get the Distinction. We all have the chance to win. We're willing to have a discussion with other classmates, because all of us could make progress and get benefit from the discussion. There is less vicious competition (Ping Ping, Female Chinese Student, 3rd Interview).

Ping Ping compared her academic performance with the standard rather than other students. This had greatly enhanced her motivation and collaboration with peers. The other practice which has the same effect is the degree classification system.

Degree Classification System

There is no degree classification system at Southeast China University. Students who successfully graduate from the University will get the same degree.

> The certificates are the same no matter you get 90% or 60%. The employers won't ask to see your grades. So pass is OK (Xiao Yong, Male Chinese Student, 3rd Interview).

To get a postgraduate offer in China, students need to pass the National Postgraduate Entrance Examination which is held once a year.

> 'In China, to get an offer for a master course, you need to pass the National Postgraduate Entrance Examination. So many students focus on the Examination. While here, universities will see all your academic scores in your undergraduate study. To get a first class degree, you need to be excellent in all the modules. So I have to work harder throughout these years' (Ping Ping, Female Chinese Student, 3rd Interview).

> 'Here, they don't have the ranking, but the degree classification. I'm aiming to get a first class for my degree, first scholarship and get an offer from Oxford or Cambridge. My parents will feel proud of me' (Min Min, Female Chinese Student, 2nd Interview).

As Ping Ping and Min Min pointed out, getting a good class degree in the UK might help them to get an offer for their Masters course. The classification was based on their academic performance in every module, which cut the big task (getting first class) into small tasks (getting over 70% in every module). The risk was lowered and the tasks were easier to accomplish. Obtaining a good classification in the degree encouraged them to study hard all through the course.

Formative Assessment Practices

Students experienced different types of assessment practices at North Britain University, which are shown in Table 5-4.

Table 5-4 Assessment Practices in Different Modules

Modules	Assessment Practices
Advanced Engineering Mathematics (CG0037)	Final Examination: 100% (Eight questions, attempt five. Questions are of equal value)
Data Communication & Transmission Systems (EN0214)	Laboratories: 30%; Final Examination: 70% (40 MCQs; seven questions, attempt three. Questions are of equal value) One formative assessment by MCQ test after the 1st semester to highlight the basic knowledge that students should know prior to the formal examination
Microprocessor Systems & Digital Signal Processing (EN0217)	Semester 1: Laboratory 10%; assignment 40%; Semester 2: Examination 40% (Two questions 50% + 25 out of 40 MCQs 50%); assignment: 10% (two laboratory scripts of equal marks)
Analogue & Digital Electronics (EN0216)	Two labworks on Analogue/Digital: formative; Two labworks on Analogue/Digital: 30%; Examination: 70%
Power, Machines and Instrumentation (EN0215)	Two labworks: 30%; Examination: 70% (Eight questions and attempt five with minimum of two from each section)
Distributed Circuit (EN0219)	Laboratories: 30%; Examination: 70% (Eight questions and attempt five)
Electronic Product Development (EN0213)	Preliminary Design Review: 20%; Intermediate Design Review: 45%; Final Design Review: 35% (Report 20%; attendance 5%; presentation 10%)
Language Support (CM0561)	Non-credit. No test

Apart from Language Support (CM0561), which was a non-credit module, five out of the seven key modules assessed students in the form of summative assessment (laboratories assessments, examinations, assignments, group reports and presentation) and formative assessment (laboratories, MCQs and seminar questions). Although examination was still the main assessment tool, some laboratories and Multiple Choice Questions were given during the year to highlight the basic knowledge that students should know prior to the formal examination. The continuous assessment practices in Module EN0219 drove students to identify the deficiencies they had and gave them the direction to improve their learning during the study process. Students could manage their time evenly during the term, rather than 'cramming' for examinations at the end (See Section 5.4.2 for details).

New Requirements of Assessment in the Lab: Being Independent and Critical

The most challenging part in the assessment was being independent in the lab. Staff were there to facilitate research in the workshop. Students could not get solutions from the staff. They were asked to find the answers themselves. This was different from the verification tasks they did in the first two years.

> We were told to make an amplifying circuit. We need to think why to make it, how to make it, the theories we need, the formula for calculating, the components we need, etc. Basically, everything. Most of the experiments in the first two years told us what to do and how to do. We needn't think much, just follow the instruction step by step and note down the results. Course Design was different, but the circuit was given. We only need to calculate the parameters and choose the components. If we couldn't work it out, our teachers would tell us. Here, some of my classmates believe that the teachers are waiting to see us making

> mistakes. It's not easy to adapt to it at the beginning(Xiao Hua, Male Chinese Student, 3rd Interview).

Apart from being independent in learning, being critical in report writing was another challenge. The laboratories students completed were mainly verifying tests in the first two years. In the reports, students wrote down the results and steps of the experiments they had followed without the interpretation of the results. Moving onto the next stage of study, the laboratory tasks became research-based, which required students to be more critical about the results they obtained in the experiments.

> We were asked to reflect more on what we have done. Getting the result is just the first step. We have to interpret it and be critical about it. What are the conclusions from this lab? How is the practical experiment compared with theoretical results? What are the reasons for any differences? Writing a report was not easy, not because of the language, but the critical thinking(Xiao Hua, Male Chinese Student, 3rd Interview).

As Xiao Hua found, critical thinking was more challenging than the language in report writing. Many students did not have a clue at the beginning of the academic year. Lecturers explained the format and requirements of the report writing in the first class.

> I don't want them to write a report which comes in and I just scratch it all off and then they get disillusioned and disheartened. And I tell them at the start, 'This is what I'm expecting' and I also send an email out to all the students when they've had to do their submission, with further instructions as to what they have to do, then hopefully they will follow it ... the next reports are better. And really, It's leading them to their final year thesis(Simon, British Staff Member).

As Simon pointed out, he had tried to give students instruction and feedback on their first report. Students were supposed to use the feedback to improve their next report, gradually leading to a successful final thesis. However, as will be discussed in Section 5. 4. 2, feedback was treated differently by different groups of students.

Apart from the above five practices, some factors also influenced students' transition experiences. For example, attendance and homework were included in the assessment in China, with a weight of 10%. If students were absent for one-third of the class, they would not be allowed to take the final examination. Homework, which was assigned every two weeks, had been marked and registered. However, the attendance and seminar questions were not considered in the students' academic score at North Britain University. Fang Fang and Xiao Jie's failure in their academic year was partly attributed to these factors. This will be discussed in Section 5.4.2.4.

5.4.2 Three Patterns of Students' Interaction with the New Learning Environment

This section will discuss the different responses from students to the changes in the new learning environment. Three patterns of their interaction were identified, which led them to different outcomes at the end of their transition. They are Direct Interaction, Indirect Interaction and Avoiding Interaction. Within each pattern, there were also some varying responses.

5.4.2.1 *Direct Interaction*

Students in this group were willing to interact with the new learning environment directly. They were highly motivated and intended to get a first-class degree and a postgraduate offer from the top universities around the world. They chose to have dialogues with staff. They identified the requirements of the learning and assessments themselves. They sought the feedback from the staff, and sometimes from their peers. They also provided 'tutorials' to their peers. Students who actively prepared for their study abroad were in this group.

Response to the Changes in General Features

As presented in Section 5.4.1.1, the new administrative feature at North Britain University required students to be self-disciplined. Furthermore, easier access to the internet and more privacy brought about more distractions from their study. This was true with this group of students, such as Ping Ping. She realised that surfing the internet had taken her a great amount of time.

> I forced myself to be away from the internet, just focused on the study. While we were in China, our *Ban Zhu Ren* and the students above told us that nobody would discipline us. We have to take the responsibility ourselves, but it's hard. We use computers a lot for our study. So I take one-hour surfing online as a reward after several hours study, and it works (Ping Ping, Female Chinese Student, 3rd Interview).

Ping Ping demonstrated that the 'preventive injection' of self-disciplinary given by their *Ban Zhu Ren* and senior students in China, had some effect. She found a method to avoid the distraction. The strategy she used was to identify the priority of her tasks and set up a time boundary, in which she had improved her time management skills.

For some students, like Xiao Qiang and Min Min, parents' expectation and expensive tuition fees pushed them to become more disciplined.

> I used to idle around during the term in the first two years. My parents and the lecturers always pushed us to study and study. I was not bothered. But when I get here, I find I want to study. My parents have spent so much money. I can't waste their money (Xiao Qiang, Male Chinese Student, 3rd Interview).

> My parents always give me the best education. Although they tell me not to put pressure on myself or worry about the fees, I still

> couldn't help thinking about that. When I think of them working hard, I can't help blaming myself. I didn't realise that last year, but now I understand them more (Min Min, Female Chinese Student, 3rd Interview).

Studying abroad, the annual tuition fee increased from around £2,000 to £7,000. Accommodation and maintenance fees were almost twenty times that of in China. It was unnecessary for them to find a part-time job to pay these fees. They received full financial support from their parents. Their understanding of their parents' expectation developed with growing age and change of the environment. These students learned to take responsibility for themselves. They responded better to being 'free' and 'unwatched'.

Response to the Changes in Teaching and Learning Practices

The prominent change in the teaching and learning practices in the new learning environment was the teaching language. All the modules were delivered in English. Unlike the bilingual education in China, where either students or teachers could go back to Chinese when there were difficulties, English was the only medium in the communication between staff and the students in the UK. Students who actively prepared for their study abroad felt easy in class.

> For most of my classmates, the biggest obstacle is to couple the two versions of the terminology. We know most of the technical parts, but it's hard to set up the connection immediately when you hear the English. So I read the hand-outs before the class and try to remember the English definitions. In fact, I started to build up my academic vocabulary when I was in China. I think this really helps (Ping Ping, Female Chinese Student, 2nd Interview).

Like Ping Ping, Xiao Ming previewed the lesson which gave him more confidence in the class.

> I borrowed books on the reading list and read through the chapters that our teachers were going to cover in the following lecture. I looked up the words I didn't know in the dictionary (Xiao Ming, Male Chinese Student, 2nd Interview).

Xiao Hua, who had adapted to bilingual education very well in China, felt excited after his first class.

> My learning approach works here too! I borrowed books from the library before the class. *Data Communication*. I thought it would be very abstract. But after the reading, I felt it was not that difficult. After the lecture, I understood more. The teachers put the hand-outs on the Blackboard. I went through them before the class. This makes my study in the class more efficient (Xiao Hua, Male Chinese Student, 2nd Interview).

Xiao Hua used the resources provided by the University to improve his learning. The active attitude towards pre-departure preparation also helped his academic transition in the UK.

> I think the two years' study in China provided me with a solid foundation for the main modules, such as *Electronics*, *Electronic Machinery* and *Mathematics*. If I had come here to learn those modules without any previous knowledge, I would have died like a dog (Xiao Hua, Male Chinese Student, 2nd Interview).

Another change was the different practice of asking and answering questions in class. At the initial stage, these students did not realise that they could save questions for the seminar. They still did what they had done in China, asking questions right after the class. As not many lecturers had a break between the classes, students highly valued the time after the whole session. Their classroom behaviours affected the learning experience of the existing cohort in the class, which will be discussed in Chapter 6. In the observation conducted during the second and final terms, some of the students had picked up the requirements of classroom interactions and interacted with the staff more in the class. Xiao Hua and Xiao Ming were two examples.

> I find here students can just sit in their seats and prompt the questions instantly. You don't need to put up your hands. I answer the questions when I know the answers. Sometimes, the teachers can come down to us to have a discussion. I also like seminars where you have smaller groups and better discussion with tutors (Xiao Ming, Male Chinese Student, 2nd Interview).

> I normally sit in the first row and ask questions when I have. Once in *Data Communication*, I didn't agree with the solution given by the teacher and we had a discussion. It turned out that he forgot to give us a parameter which had misled me (Xiao Hua, Male Chinese Student, 2nd Interview).

Other students in this group still remained in their previous habit of asking questions after class. As discussed in Section 5.4.1.2, data collected from this research did not show the differences of two kinds of questioning behaviour in affecting students' academic performance. Students in this group asked their lecturers questions straight away, including Xiao Qiang whose English was not very good.

> My English is poor and I didn't get a good score in the language test. It's very hard for me to organise my words when I have a question. But I believe that apart from getting the degree, improving English is also my aim. I explain my questions slowly to the teachers by pointing to the equations on the blackboard. Some of them are very patient and give me answers clearly. There is only once I felt very uncomfortable. One teacher

> cleaned the blackboard while I was asking him a question. I think he might be in a hurry to go to another class. Anyway, I prefer to ask teachers questions to get the answers while improving my English (Xiao Qiang, Male Chinese Student, 2nd Interview).

Through Direct Interaction, the presence of this large cohort of Chinese students also motivated some of the academic staff to modify their teaching to adjust to the students' learning. Staff found that some Chinese students lacked practical skills in the laboratories, report writing and presentations. Although they were good at line-by-line Mathematics, they were weak in interpreting the results. Thus, in the first couple of weeks staff were trying to help these students make up for their deficiencies. Simon explained the criteria and format of the report step by step; Eric instructed basic practical skills with the equipment used in the laboratories; Tom put a mathematic problem into an Engineering context to encourage students to interpret the results they have got. In assessment practices, they also made great effort to provide more formative feedback. Students appreciated the help from staff.

> Before I came, I was told that it was not easy to find staff. You need to make an appointment. But when I came here, I found the lecturers were willing to help us. They're very patient. I came across a professor on the corridor. I asked him something about the work placement. He spent more than one hour explaining it, which was very helpful (Ping Ping, Female Chinese student, 3rd Interview).

> Getting my first report, I went to see the lecturer to clarify the comments he made on my report. He explained them one by one and told me why he marked me down by one point here or two points there (Xiao Qiang, Male Chinese Student, 3rd Interview).

Through interaction, staff gradually recognised the strength of these students as well. At the end of the term, staff gave very positive evaluation towards this group of students: they were hard working, determined to succeed, and committed to learning with good knowledge of Physics and Maths.

> I'm quite surprised actually, the Chinese group, just for the first report. They are much better than the English students. They had a first report; when was it? I think it was about two weeks ago, and I gave all the students a chance that if they did it two weeks earlier that I could look through it and tell them what they'd done wrong and what's going to help improve it. The Chinese students did that. The English students thought, 'Oh well I don't need it. I'll do it myself (Eric, British Staff Member).

Some lecturers noticed the strengths of the Chinese students and adapted their approaches to teaching accordingly. For example, Tom, a British staff member noted:

> My teaching style changed a little bit when the Chinese students arrived because I would say that I lecture or teach slightly differently, depending on the group of students in front of me. ... If I know there are some good students, which is certainly the case with Chinese students, I will tend to give one or two more difficult problems or do something that will puzzle them, to make them think a bit more (Tom, British Staff Member).

Students' final assessment results showed that the standard of the course had been improved, owing to the Chinese students' participation in it. 45 of the 50 participants gained over 70 per cent in *Advanced Engineering Mathematics* (CG0037) and 14 achieved over 70 per cent in *Electronic Product Development* (EN0213). In terms of the average score for the six modules, 19 students achieved over 70 per cent, which was the standard of a first class award. Staff appreciated their participation:

> This group are committed to learning and to scoring high marks. It's brilliant for the University because we say that the students are scoring top marks, brilliant for staff that they can say, 'Okay, out of my group, all the average is up because of the Chinese students' and that is superb for us as a University and we can be proud of this group. I know for a fact that some of last year's group in the final they scored First Class and they got the top of the project, marks of distinction, so that is superb. So keep sending more students! [Laughs]. We need them; we need good quality students (Ben, British Staff Member).

Through lecturing students who studied the same modules in another university abroad, staff noticed the difference in academic performance between the home students and the Chinese Articulation Programme Students. Some of them started to be more critical of the education system in the UK.

> It's a bit like football. What you don't see when you watch a football match is, all the training that goes on. The Premiership footballers are that good because they train hard all the time, they practise their skills and do things over and over again until they are really good. And then you see them in the match and think, 'Oh, good footballers' but they had to do all this training. ... We've not quite got that right over here at the moment and I think there's not enough training (Tom, British Staff Member).

Response to the Changes in New Assessment Practice

Compared with their first stage of study at Southeast China University, the second stage of study at North Britain University required students to be more independent and critical in lab experiments and report writing. Students, like Xiao Ming, took the challenges as opportunities to enhance their independence in learning and research abilities.

> These circuits have similar structure with different characteristic features. We need to work out their slight difference through experiments and to decide which one to use. We have to try many times before we get it. It's like we're doing research (Xiao Ming, Male Chinese Student, 3rd Interview).

Through independent research-based experiments, students digested and absorbed what they had learnt in the class. After the workshop, students went back to the laboratories, which were open to them anytime during week days. Students in this group finished their reports independently. For instance, Xiao Ming highlighted the requirements and followed them step by step. Xiao Dong and Xiao Hua went to the laboratories whenever they had time. Xiao Qiang asked tutors for feedback.

> Writing the report is not easy; I have to look up the dictionary constantly. This is not the biggest issue. Teachers emphasised many times: be critical, be critical. I didn't have any idea about it. So I asked them many times and showed them my work asking for feedback. Gradually, I think it means never taking your results for granted (Xiao Qiang, Male Chinese Student, 3rd Interview).

Students' first reports were not as good as they had expected. When the report came back, there was not only a summative score on the cover page, but formative feedback given by the lecturers. These students asked the staff to clarify the feedback, and then used it to make an improvement for their next reports. Xiao Hua, who achieved 80% for his report, went to the lecturer to go through the feedback step by step. Xiao Qiang, who asked the lecturers to clarify the requirements, got over 70%. When he got the feedback he went to see the lecturer for further feedback.

> I was thinking how to improve my next report. I wanted to know why here he marked me down by one point, why there he marked me down by two points. I wanted to know the mark standard clearly (Xiao Qiang, Male Chinese Student, 3rd Interview).

Through writing their first report and getting feedback from their tutors, they became familiar with the requirements of being critical. Feedback here was used to improve their next reports. The following case showed another function of feedback. Yan Yan, Ling Ling and Li Li used to 'cram' for examinations. They waited until the last minute, relied on the textbooks, remembered the examples and were able to 'sail' through the examinations. They studied to pass the exams. The assessment task was not challenging, which they could cope with without putting in too much effort during the semester. When they moved on to the next stage of study in the UK, they realised that their ways of learning did not work.

> Lecturers will check our answers in seminars. After several seminars, I found if I didn't review the lesson after class, I couldn't work out the questions (Yan Yan, Female Chinese Student, 3rd Interview).

> I thought MCQs would be a piece of cake. But after the test, I found they were more than A, B, C, D. You need to understand the theory very well before making the choices (Ling Ling, Female Chinese Student, 3rd Interview).

What Yan Yan and Ling Ling referred to were the formative assessment practices encouraged at North Britain University. Different formats of assessment were held along the process of teaching and learning to give ongoing feedback to guide students' learning, such as laboratories and seminars. For instance, Module EN0214 (*Data Communication and Transmission System*) and EN0219 (*Distributed Circuit Theory and Communications Circuits*) gave students formative assessments by MCQ test after the 1st semester to highlight the basic knowledge that students should know prior to the formal examination. Module EN0216(*Analogue and Digital Electronics*) asked students to submit two pieces of lab work to get familiar with report writing. Formative assessment was via tutorial questions given at regular intervals and within the laboratory sessions. In Module EN0217 (*Microprocessor Systems and Digital Signal Processing*), practical exercises and MCQ tests were carried out during seminar sessions to provide instant feedback to students. These practices enabled students to constantly check their performance with the requirements of the module, and helped to manage their time during the term. Students gave positive feedback to these practices, especially the assessment of the group project on Module EN0213.

> We are more interactive with the lecturer at weekly workshop where they give us feedback to our progress. We could use their feedback to improve our next report(Ping Ping, Female Chinese Student, 3rd Interview).

> As a team leader in our group, I have to study harder. Three reports and each builds upon the content of the previous report. It cuts my time into small slots and makes me feel I have task to do every week(Li Li, Female Chinese Student, 3rd Interview).

In the observations, there were more collaborative activities in this module. Students met their group members regularly outside the class. Some groups, like Xiao Ming's, set up online chat group because they lived in different buildings.

> We exchange information instantly. Any useful information I get, I'll forward it to my group members. Our tutor gave some supporting information. But we still need to go to the library to read the books on the reading list. We'll end up with reading other books that are not on the reading list. We have to surf online to identify the market, do a survey on the street and contact a company in China to get some suggestions (Xiao Ming, Male Chinese Student, 3rd Interview).

In coping with the assessment, these students directed their own learning path. They had a great sense of achievement at the end of the module. Xiao Ming had always wanted to be a manager in the future. He became a team leader in his group. He distributed different tasks to his group members according to their strengths. He highlighted each item of the assessment standards and chose a group member to be responsible for it. He believed that this module improved his team management skills.

> I like to learn something about team management, but haven't got a chance. Now I was chosen to be the group leader. I set up an online chat group just for our group project and exchange information there. I motivate my group members that we'll finish the best project in the class. I borrowed books about risk assessment, marketing, engineering, etc., and marked down the part I think they should know. I think the experience will be useful for my future career (Xiao Ming, Male Chinese Student, 3rd Interview).

At the end of the group presentation, one professor asked Xiao Hua's group a question. Xiao Hua gave an answer, but the professor did not agree. Xiao Hua stood up to defend his answer, even if he knew that this professor was going to mark his presentation and final report. In the final interview, he told me proudly that:

> After one year's research, I believe I'm an expert in my area. He [the professor] has his reasons, I have mine. I don't think I'm wrong. I'll do more to convince him (Xiao Hua, Male Chinese Student, 3rd Interview).

Students felt the result of the assessment, not the mark but the designed product and the process to design the product with other students, was useful. '*It's something you can and you want to use in the future*' (Xiao Ming). Some even considered developing their ideas as potential business opportunities in the future.

The design of the assessments had motivated these students. They were attracted by learning itself, as shown by Xiao Hua:

> I used to care more about the ranking. I worked hard to achieve a high score. Now I don't care about the score. My second report of *Electronic Machinery* only weighs 10%, but I spent a whole week in the lab. I don't care how much the core is. The requirement of the reports is very interesting. So I like to spend time on it (Xiao Hua, Male Chinese Student, 3rd Interview).

The purposes of their learning changed from caring about the score to being interested in the learning itself, and from learning for the examination to learning for the future. Their concept on the function of the assessment changed as well

> I study to get a placement and find a job in the future because many companies value the working experience gained in the placement. I used to study just for the examination, but now I think more about my future (Yan Yan, Female Chinese Student, 3rd Interview).

These students also became the 'tutors' for their classmates. As Xiao Hua explained:

> Sometimes, I have to explain the solution to 5 or 6 classmates... I learnt a lot through the teaching. To know something is one case, to teach something well is another case ... I won't give my report to them. I have spent long time on my work, sometimes a whole week. They can ask me questions, but can't copy my work. I know there is a software to check our work (Xiao Hua, Male Chinese Student, 3rd Interview).

Through tutoring his peers, Xiao Hua enhanced his understanding of what he had learnt. He also showed his concern of plagiarism. North Britain University adopted the software, *Turnitin*, to help students avoid plagiarism in their work. As some of the tasks were the same every year, some students could ask the reports from the students above and make slight changes. When students were blamed for plagiarism in learning, they asked why the lecturers did not design new tasks in teaching. If the tasks were different, students might think '*I'll just take this report as a reference to see the format. I need to do it myself*' (Xiao Hua).

In general, participants with intrinsic motivation or internalised extrinsic motivation demonstrated great autonomy in their coping with the challenges brought by the different features and teaching practices on the new campus. However, not all the participants had taken Direct Interaction with the new learning environment. Their different journeys are discussed in the following two sections.

5.4.2.2 *Indirect Interaction*

Facing changes in the new learning environment, students like Xiao Yu and Xiao Yong were reluctant to interact with the new learning environment directly, but prefer Indirect Interaction through their classmates. This was largely because of their language deficiency, passive attitude towards studying abroad and insufficient pre-departure preparation.

Response to the Changes in General Features

As presented in Section 5.2.3, Xiao Yu and Xiao Yong were reluctant to study abroad due to their language deficiency. They applied for accommodation with their own classmates. They spent most of their time hanging around within the circle of their classmates coming from Southeast China University. These students became their intermediaries to communicate with outside world.

> Five of my flatmates are from my own class. It's very convenient. We go shopping together, share the bills, and take turns to cook. I needn't speak much English. Students who came here last year took us to open a bank account and register for the police (Xiao Yu, Male Chinese Student, 2nd Interview).

> I hangout a lot with my classmates. My English is worse than before, because I seldom use it here. You pick up food in the supermarket and pay at the casher. The only thing you need to understand is how much you need to pay (Xiao Yong, Male Chinese Student, 2nd Interview).

Both Xiao Yu and Xiao Yong showed that their language abilities were not improved due to the absence of direct interaction with the new environment. They relied largely on the peer support to interact with the outside world.

> I play PC games a lot in my own room. Time is flying. Xiao Dong asks me to go to class or library together. (Xiao Yu, Male Chinese Student, 2nd Interview).

> I am not absent from class a lot. My friends attend class, so I go with them (Xiao Yong, Male Chinese Student, 2nd Interview).

Unlike students in the previous group who were self-disciplined in the new learning environment, these students' behaviour was influenced by their peers. This was especially evidenced in their strategies to cope with the new challenges in teaching and learning.

Response to the Changes in Teaching and Learning Practices

Unlike students in the previous group who read English books, this group of students preferred to go back to Chinese books they took from China or turn to their peers for help when they were stuck with the learning. As Xiao Yu has noted:

> I still prefer to read the Chinese textbooks. I got *Electronics*, *Electronic Machinery* and *Advanced Mathematics* with me and all the notes I took in China. My head was muddled in the first week. I waited till Xiao Ming understood the teaching, and then asked him to explain it to me. I used to communicate a lot with my teachers when I was in China, but now I prefer to discuss with my classmates. I think it's because of my language (Xiao Yu, Male Chinese Student, 3rd Interview).

His problem in English has hindered his interaction with the staff.

> My language holds me up. I don't know how to organise the words. I don't know how to express many Engineering symbols in English. Xiao Dong and I live in the same flat and he has helped me a lot. Xiao Ming is our team leader and I ask him many times. They read English books and sometimes tell me what they have read. Reading takes me so much time (Xiao Yu, Male Chinese Student, 2nd Interview).

Although students were alerted in China that there was going to be more self-directed learning at North Britain University, Xiao Yu felt that it was not easy to meet the requirements in the UK.

> They [British staff] had taught us several times when we were in China and I know I need to learn more on my own. But I find they always want you to guess. They don't tell you the correct answer. They won't give you the things you need to learn. They didn't teach us as thoroughly as our Chinese teachers did. I miss my teachers in China (Xiao Yu, Male Chinese Student, 2nd Interview).

Xiao Yu's insufficient English language and academic preparation hindered his understanding of the teaching in the UK. His reluctance to participate in bilingual education affected his learning in the UK. He was not confident in English, which hindered his communication with the staff. This was true with Xiao Yong:

> When I found I couldn't understand the teaching, I didn't want to continue. English makes me feel headache. You have to look up dictionary constantly. I wrote in Chinese first, then put it into Google Translate, made some changes and copied the English translation to the report (Xiao Yong, Male Chinese Student, 3rd Interview).

These students' interaction with the staff was rare to see. The deficiency in language pushed them to rely more on their Chinese classmates, which can be noted from the following quotation.

> I think the classmates I hang out with mostly just want to fool around and get the degree. We never ask teachers. When we can't understand the teaching, we ask the good students. (Xiao Yong, Male Chinese Student, 3rd Interview).

In the class, when they could not understand the teaching, they constantly sought help from their peers. This caused more noise in the class and complaints from the existing cohort of students(see Section 6.2.3.3).

Response to the Changes in Assessment Practices

Unlike students in the first group, who coped with the changes in assessment practices independently, students in this group asked for help from their classmates when they had difficulties in working out the experiments or writing up the reports.

> I have more questions here in the lab and sometimes get stuck there for a long time. My classmates who are top students are very helpful. We have discussion and they will help me to detect problems and find the solutions. I know I should work it out on my own, but I don't copy theirs. I get a lot from the discussion (Xiao Yu, Male Chinese Student, 3rd Interview).

When Xiao Yu was not sure whether the results he got were correct or whether his writing was what the tutors wanted, he preferred to have discussion with his classmates, especially those who were independent in the previous group. In a way, seeking help from the peers had become a surviving strategy for these students. However, their habit of 'cramming' for examinations did not change.

> I need to go over everything before the exam. I couldn't sleep last night. I didn't feel very well in the exam. Hope I could pass them all. I don't think I learn a lot this year (Xiao Yu, Male Chinese Student, 3rd Interview).

However, in the Module EN0213, where students were divided into groups to carry out a project together, they behaved differently.

> I learned a lot from the project. Even if I copied something from

> the internet, I still need to understand it to give the presentation and answer the questions from the examiners. Most of us felt that we had learnt a lot. For instance, we didn't use computer software offen in China, but for this project, we used a lot (Xiao Yong, Male Chinese Student, 3rd Interview).

Xiao Yu was a team member of Xiao Ming's group. They got 71%.

> In our group, I'm responsible for information searching. I think Xiao Ming saw me on the internet all the time. Searching for information might be my strong point. It's correct. This is a long and continuous task. The disadvantage of exams is that some of the students won't study during the term, but wait till the deadline and then cram for exams. They only focus on some learning points that the lecturers mentioned in the revision class. They can't learn much. While for this module, we are constantly focusing on the project for a whole year. The most important thing is that we can understand it better (Xiao Yu, Male Chinese Student, 3rd Interview).

Although Xiao Yu and Xiao Yong seemed to be passive in their communication with staff, they were still very active to seek support from their classmates. They chose to avoid direct interaction with staff and the challenges they were confronted with, but instead conducted indirect interaction through their peers. Although they were not as keen as the students in the first group to interact with the learning environment directly, they still sailed through the academic year with the help from their peers and their own effort. However, some other students, who had passively prepared for their study abroad, failed.

5.4.2.4 *Avoiding Interaction*

Students in this group shared some of the common features of the students in the previous group. Their interaction with the new environment relied largely on their peers. However, the indirect interaction was rare to see during the term except the weeks before the examinations. They misinterpreted the information they were given and misjudged the amount of effort they need to devote to achieve their goals. They had a rosy picture based on selected information passed by the students above. They retracted into a 'self-believed safe circle' fostered by the double-edged factor 'peer support'.

Response to the Changes in General Features

Double-edged factors, such as 'Internet' and 'privacy', distracted this group of participants. Students like Xiao Feng, Fang Fang and Xiao Jie found it was hard to stay away from the distraction.

> I didn't go to the library, because I can't use some software on the university computer, such as 'Ping Mu Qu Ci' (instant translation). So I prefer to use my computer in the dormitory. Here we have more privacy, but it might be too much. I mean no one to disturb you. You don't know whether other classmates are studying or not. You can easily idle away your time by clicking on the links of website news one after another. Hours past and you won't notice it. I tried to give it up, but I couldn't (Xiao Feng, Male Chinese Student, 2nd Interview).

As discussed in Section 5.2.3, Xiao Feng's father was very strict with him and used to sit beside him to observe him doing homework. He was reliant on this kind of compulsion, which pushed him to be more efficient. At Southeast China University, his *Ban Zhu Ren* could inform his parents of his performance. This was not the case in the UK.

> If I didn't do well in the exam, my father would ask me to tell him what I had done wrong. Then he would keep an eye on me all the summer holiday and force me to study. But now he can't ring my teachers here to ask about my performance (Xiao Feng, Male Chinese Student, 2nd Interview).

Without his father's and personal tutor's supervision, Xiao Feng felt his life in the UK was more relaxing. At this time, he started to be distracted by the internet.

> There're links one after another. You don't need to think anything when you read the webpages. I could spend hours reading the rubbish news. When I get used to the jumping among websites without thinking, it's hard for me to go deep with the study. I knew I shouldn't do it, but I just couldn't stop. I didn't study well because I didn't sleep well. Feel very tired during the day as I surf online a lot (Xiao Feng, Male Chinese Student, 2nd Interview).

Fang Fang and Xiao Jie also found that self-management became the biggest challenge to their study abroad. Fang Fang would not concentrate on her study until the examination in the first two years. As a cartoon fan, she preferred to watch cartoons in the dormitory. However, if she didn't go to class in China, her monitor would report her name to *Ban Zhu Ren* who would talk to her to see what happened. If things got serious, her parents would be informed. They could also phone her *Ban Zhu Ren* at any time to ask about her performance at the university. Furthermore, three other roommates in her dormitory encouraged her to attend the class and go to the library. When Fang Fang came to the UK, there was no roll-call at the beginning of the class. Students only need to tick the attendance sheet, which she could ask her classmates to do for her.

> Even if I don't go to the class, nobody will notice me. I ask my friend to tick the box [sign the attendance sheet] for me and get the hand-outs. Gradually they got bored and refused to do that. In China, four girls lived together. They asked me to go to the class together. But now, I live in my own room with the door

> shut. They don't know where I am or what I am doing. We don't have a person here like our *Ban Zhu Ren* in China to phone me to go to the class (Fang Fang, Female Chinese Student, 3rd Interview).

> My flat is twenty minutes' walk from the university. The road is slippery in winter. Too cold. I shut myself in the room playing PC games or reading something. No roll-call here, so I needn't worry about the attendance (Xiao Jie, Male Chinese Student, 2nd Interview).

Their former roommates felt it was unfair to help them in such a way. They pointed out:

> We haven't seen her (Fang Fang) for a long time. In the first several weeks, we could sign for her or get the hand-outs for her, but we can't do that all the time. To be frank, I think it's her responsibility for her own study. I think it's unfair for us. We're too busy now (Ni Ni, Female Chinese Student, Informal Chatting at the End of the Academic Year).

The 'nobody-will-notice' system at North Britain University fostered their absence. Few people contacted them when they were absent from the classes for several days. Their parents, 8,000 miles away, were unable to call the tutor. Both Fang Fang and Xiao Jie failed their modules at the end of the academic year and had to repeat their second year. Xiao Feng passed the second year, but failed his final year.

Response to the Changes of Teaching and Learning Practices

This group of students noticed the changes of teaching and learning practices in the new learning environment and their difficulties in coping with the changes. However, they sometimes attributed their difficulties to the teachers' 'laziness' or 'unsupportive attitude'. For example, Xiao Jie found that the British teachers were 'lazy', and did not provide the same support as the Chinese teachers used to do.

> I don't think the teachers teach us a lot. It largely depends on us. Teachers here might be lazy. They won't give us the learning points as our Chinese teachers did. You have to find them out by yourself(Xiao Jie, Male Chinese Student, 3rd Interview).

Fang Fang felt frustrated in her first class too:

> I went there and found I couldn't understand anything. So I stopped going. In China, without study before the class, I was able to understand most of the teaching, but not here. I tried to study by myself in my room. We had text books in China. Each of us got one for each module. It gave you everything in detail. Here we need to borrow books from the library. They're big and thick. Headache. I borrowed some, but it's very hard to find learning points. In China, I could ask my roommates. Now, we don't live in the same building and they are busy. Nobody to talk to here. I'm alone most of the time. (Fang Fang, Female Chinese Student, 3rd Interview).

Frustrated by the teaching in the class, Fang Fang tried to learn by herself. But the language became the obstacle again in her reading. Her former roommates were all busy and lived far away. She understood less and less of the hand-outs. Gradually she hid herself in the room to escape from the pressure.

Evidence found in this research showed that language was not the only obstacle to the interaction. For example, when Xiao Feng did not get on very well with his supervisor, he did not know he could find another supervisor. He did not know that he could make an appointment with staff before going to see them, either. When he could not find the tutor at the office, he just gave up. His unfamiliarity with the academic culture in the UK showed that he was not ready for his study abroad. Furthermore, he did not get enough sleep at night because of surfing the Internet. He always felt tired during the day. He was absent many times from the class. At the end of the final year, Xiao Feng's parents came to the UK for his graduation congregation, but found he failed two modules and could not get the degree. At the request of his father, I arranged for his parents to meet his programme leader. At the meeting, Xiao Feng had a long discussion with the programme leader about the possibility of repeating the final year. He also interpreted for his father in the meeting. English was not a barrier in the communication. As his father explained:

> I sent him to English training school when he was five years old. Three years. Every Sunday, I waited for two hours outside the class. In the National Higher Education Entrance Examination, he got 135 out of 150 score in the English test. I don't think English is a problem for him. He needs somebody to tell him what to do and when to do (Mr. Wang, Xiao Feng's Father, Interview after the Congregation).

In Xiao Feng's case, rather than language deficiency, unfamiliarity with the academic culture on the new campus and a lack of self-management skills contributed to the unhappy ending of his transition.

Response to the Changes of Assessment Practices

As presented above, some of the Articulation Programme Students who were in the final year told these students that the exams in the UK were easy to pass.

> The students above told me the examinations were not difficult. I'm not ambitious now. A pass is OK (Fang Fang, Female Chinese Student, 2nd Interview).

The rosy information from the students above matched with Fang Fang's expectation: a pass was OK. She did not pay attention to the new requirements of the lab reports. She was waiting for the deadline of the examination as she had done in China. One month before the examinations, Fang Fang started to go over the modules. It was at this time that she became serious, but it might be too late.

> There were no textbooks to follow. I need to review all the hand-outs and seminar questions. I was panic and had a try, but gave up finally. It was too late (Fang Fang, Female Chinese Student, 3rd Interview).

After several days' trying, Fang Fang felt exhausted. As she had not been in touch with her peers, she was too embarrassed to ask for help. She shut herself into her room and missed all the examinations.

As presented before, Xiao Jie was very 'optimistic' about the passing level here at North Britain University. The false sense of security he gained based on the misunderstanding of the assessment practices influenced his attitude towards study. He believed what the students above had told him. His aim was to pass the exam. Any 'useless' material did not deserve his effort.

> Some of the students download the hand-outs from the Blackboard (E-learning Portal) and check the words, but I don't. Students above told me that hand-outs were useless for the exam. Why am I bothered? (Xiao Jie, Male Chinese Student, 2nd Interview).

The rosy information passed on by former students strengthened his false sense of security.

> They told me seminars were not important as long as you had a look at the questions and solutions. My classmates published the questions and answers on QQ (online chat room). I downloaded

> them and had a glance ... No need to read books or hand-outs. Just work through the previous papers and remember the steps. The secret is that this year's examination paper will follow the examples of the year before. So this year, 2009, I should focus on the paper of 2007. As long as I remember the steps, it will be a piece of cake (Xiao Jie, Male Chinese Student, 2nd Interview).

Following these instructions, Xiao Jie did not go to seminars very often. He downloaded the answers from the online group files posted by classmates and read through the answers without figuring them out first. However, on leaving the examination hall, Xiao Jie felt puzzled:

> The types have changed. I didn't realise it till I finished the exams. I thought one week would be enough for me to prepare for an exam. The questions were not as easy as they told me (Xiao Jie, Male Chinese Student, 3rd Interview).

Spending too much time on the internet, Xiao Feng found he did not have enough time to prepare for the examination.

> Before the exam, I only had time to look through the hand outs, and tried to remember the solutions to the examples. That's it (Xiao Feng, Male Chinese Student, 3rd Interview).

However, these students had positive feedback to the assessment of group project in Module EN0213.

> I think 213 is more interesting than other modules, as you can design something. We rehearsed twice before our presentation (Xiao Jie, Male Chinese Student, 3rd Interview).

Xiao Feng recommended himself as the team leader.

> I like to make small things since I was a child. But my dad

> always blames me for wasting time. This time, we're going to make a high frequency switching power supply. I told my group members I wanted to be the team leader. They were nice and agreed. Xiao Hua is my team member who is responsible for technology design. He used to be our monitor. He helps me a lot. In fact, all the group members are watching me. They count on me. I can't be lazy any more. The module asks us to write three reports. It kind of helps us to divide our time into three portions. We need to work evenly hard during the whole year (Xiao Feng, Male Chinese Student, 2nd Interview).

Here, Xiao Feng found his interest in the group project and created a chance to improve his skills as a team leader. With team members' 'watching', he did not waste his time on the Internet. The module also helped him to improve his time management skills, which had been a problem without his father's supervision. Their group project received 66% at the end.

Fang Fang listed some reasons why she liked the module.

> In Course Design, I got 90%. I was looking forward to carrying out the group project. In the weekly workshop, our tutor looked at our progress report and told us what was good, what needed to do more. We had three reports. One based on the other. It's less risky. I had to go to all the workshops because the attendance was marked by group. I didn't want to upset my team members. They asked me to design the outlook of the shoes and the cartoon for presentation, which are what I'm interested in and good at (Fang Fang, Female Chinese Student, 3rd Interview).

First, a similar assessment practice, Course Design, was introduced by Chinese staff in their last semester in China as a kind of pre-departure preparation to enhance their practical skills and design abilities. Fang Fang obtained 90% for the assessment and was looking forward to doing the group project in the UK. Second, the assessment assessed students by stages (see 5.4.1.3 for details). Compared with examinations, it was less risky. Third, the assessment gave 10% for students' attendance in the workshop. Fang Fang went to all workshops, as she did not want to let her team down. Last but not least, she was responsible for the design of the outlook of the shoes and the cartoon for their final presentation, which was what she liked and was good at. She achieved 65% in this module.

Out of various reasons, Fang Fang, Xiao Feng, and Xiao Jie chose to 'quit' the interaction with the learning environment in most of the modules. It was a kind of Avoiding Interaction. Their indirect interaction with staff through peers was rare except for some formative assessment activities. They retreated into their own 'self-believed safe circle', where they thought they were secure and certain to achieve their 'unambitious' goal—passing the examination. The boundary of their circle was built up by the information they selected from the students above. They interpreted the information and made judgements on the amount of effort they need to put in to achieve their 'unambitious' goals. Once those two parts matched, they made the conclusion that this amount of effort was enough for them to achieve their goals. They were sure that they were able to sail through their study as well. This judgement misled them to avoid the interaction with the new learning environment. Their retraction was fostered by the 'kind' peer support, which was supposed to be a facilitator to their study. The publication of seminar questions and solutions was used by other students as an additional method for learning, but had become the main way that these students took in their learning. Their classmates 'kindly' signed the attendance sheets for them, which had pushed them to stay away from the class. In addition, the 'nobody-will-notice' system had also fostered their retraction.

5.5 Transition Outcome

At the end of their first academic year in the UK, 48 Articulation Programme Students passed the assessment. Among the 16 interviewees, nine achieved over 70% , two obtained over 60% , three got over 50% and the rest failed the academic year and had to repeat their second year. As presented in this chapter, the participants' transition experiences from Southeast China University to North Britain University were different. As shown in Figure 5 – 1, three significant patterns representing the key types of experiences found within the group were identified and presented in terms of Direct Interaction, Indirect Interaction and Avoiding Interaction. The transition model encompasses different motivations for studying abroad, the attitudes towards the predeparture

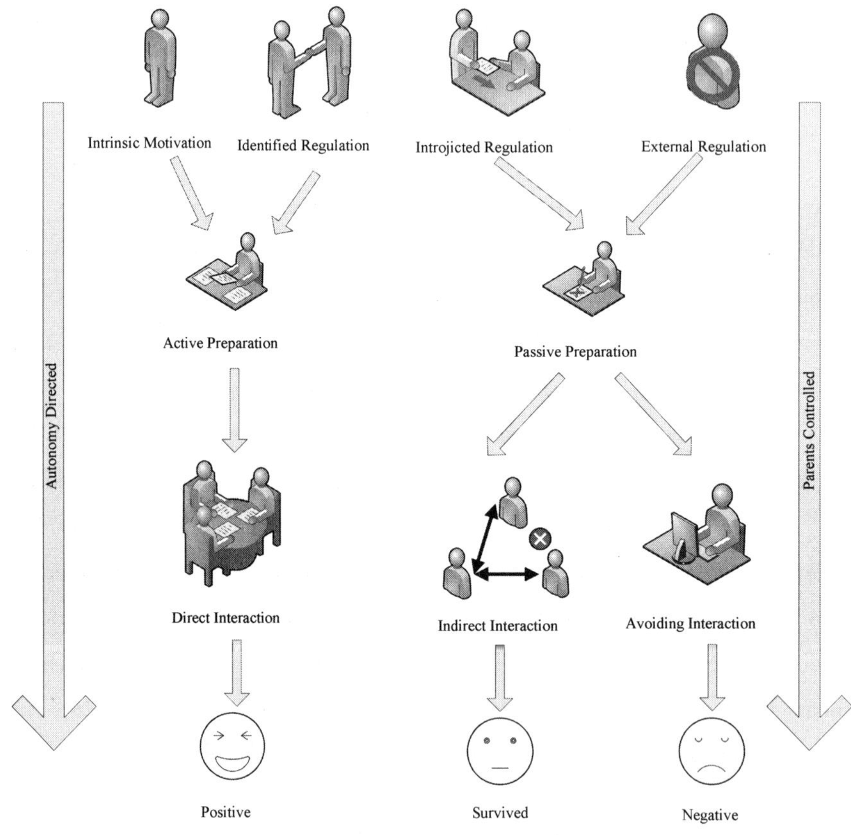

Figure 5-1 Three Patterns of Transition Experiences of Articulation Programme Students

preparation, the strategies in interacting with the new learning environment, and the outcomes of their transition. Participants who had high intrinsic motivation or internalised extrinsic motivation were active in their pre-departure preparation. They demonstrated great autonomy in their direct interaction with the new learning environment and achieved positive outcomes in the transition. Students who exhibited high level of introjected regulation or external regulation were passive in their pre-departure preparation. Some of them chose indirect interaction with the new learning environment through the help of their peers, others retracted into their own ' self-believed safe circle ' to avoid the interaction. The former survived in the transition, while the latter failed.

5.6 Conclusions

This chapter presented the different journeys and outcomes of the participants' individual transition experience from Southeast China University to North Britain University. It showed that each of the Articulation Programme students' transition experience was an individual process. They responded in their own ways to the interaction with the new learning environment. Even within the same typology, the individuals' responses were different.

This chapter first pointed out that their motivations to study abroad affected their attitudes towards pre-departure preparation. For students with intrinsic motivation for studying abroad, they took it as an interesting and enjoyable journey, which resulted in high-quality learning and creativity (Ryan and Deci, 2000). For students who agreed with their parents' view that studying abroad would benefit their future career, they developed the relevant skills and confidence through pre-departure preparation, which facilitated their personal endorsement of the task. This kind of extrinsic motivation internalised by the participants showed the same effect in this research as intrinsic motivation in encouraging the participants to gain autonomy in their transition experience. For students who had a strong negative feeling for studying abroad, they demonstrated low level of autonomy in the pre-departure preparation and their transition process. The chapter also explored the pre-departure preparation activities carried out by sending and receiving universities, such as bilingual education, early intervention, academic exchange, new assessment practices and culture learning, which were useful in general for students' transition. However, the actual usefulness depended on students' attitudes and their responses to what was on offer. The next section of this chapter demonstrated different features on the new campus which brought about new challenges to all the students. Many factors, such as the 'internet', 'privacy' and 'peer support' were 'double-edged' in that they could have negative or positive impacts depending upon the participants' individual responses. Three significant patterns (Direct Interaction, Indirect Interaction and Avoiding Interaction) were identified which represented the key types of experiences in coping with the changes in the new learning environment. Cross-pattern analysis showed that apart from motivation and pre-departure knowledge, language competence and autonomy influenced students' choices of coping strategies, which affected the extent to which they became autonomous learners in their transition and the outcomes of their transition.

Chapter 6 Studying Abroad as a Group

6.1 Introduction

Because of the unique feature of the Articulation Programme, the participants studied abroad as a group of 50 and came across another group of students, primarily home students in the course at North Britain University. The interaction experience between these two groups in the class unavoidably influenced the participants' intercultural transition experiences. Therefore, this chapter focuses on the Articulation Programme Students' interaction with the existing cohort of students and the impact of their participation on the learning environment at both universities. Participants' interaction experiences with their flatmates are also explored. This chapter blends the perspectives of home students, other international students and the staff to provide a holistic view of the Articulation Programme Students' transition experiences. The chapter first analyses how the home-based students and Chinese students in the same class were divided into two social and psychological groups, Us & Them. Then, it moves on to investigate how their own shared group membership influenced their social relations and behaviour in the class. Finally, the current structured interventions to improve students' integration were explored at the university, school, and staff level.

6.2 Formation of Two Groups: Us and Them

6.2.1 Students in Sino-British Class: a *Close* Group on Chinese Campus

Entering into Southeast China University, students found that they were considered as a special group on campus. The Articulation Programme was one of the first programmes in the province. The participants in this study, the 2006 cohort, were the third cohort in the programme. When they were in their last semester in China, the 2004 cohort and the 2005 cohort were studying in the UK for the final year and second year study respectively, and the 2007 cohort were in their first year on the Chinese campus. The participants had close contact with the 2005 cohort, who were one year above them and often gave them information. At the same time, they were an information source for the 2007 cohort. These students were called 'Students in Sino-British Class' on campus.

This community was considered as a special group on the Chinese campus. Southeast China University recruited full-time undergraduates through the National Higher Education Entrance Examination. As one of the key universities in China, it normally required students to pass the first tier of the undergraduate degree admission requirements. However, students on the Articulation Programme were allowed to register at the second tier standard, which was about 30 points lower than the first. The annual tuition fee of the Articulation Programme was about four times that of the non-programme students in 2006. The main differences of the two groups of students are shown in Table 6-1.

Table 6-1 Comparison of Articulation Programme Students and Nonprogramme Students on Chinese Campus

	Articulation Programme Students	Non-programme Students
Admission Requirement (Year 2006)	540 points	570 points

(contd.)

	Articulation Programme Students	Non-programme Students
Tuition Fee (Year 2006)	RMB 19,200	RMB 4,600
Duration of the Degree	4 years (2 years on Chinese campus and 2 years abroad)	4 years on Chinese campus
Course Content	Syllabus of the core modules imported from North Britain University and the compulsory modules required by the Chinese Ministry of Education	Syllabus compiled by Southeast China University and the compulsory modules required by the Chinese Ministry of Education
Language of Core Modules Delivery	Bilingual	Chinese
Text Books	Bilingual	Chinese
Teaching Staff	Chinese staff and foreign teachers	Chinese staff
Overlapping	Students who were not able to go abroad could transfer to the non-programme class	

The higher tuition fees and lower admission requirements influenced non-programme students' opinions on the programme students. As these students only stayed on campus for two years, they were excluded from many of the activities organised by the Student Union. As Min Min explained:

> We are close here [in China] because others consider us as a special group. They do better in the National Higher Education Entrance Examination than us. Our tuition fees in China are more than four times higher than theirs. Everywhere we go, they point to us and whisper, 'Look, students in Sino-British Class'. In their eyes, we are rich people. The Students' Union seldom invite us to take part in their activities, because they think we're leaving soon. Gradually, we only spend time with our own classmates (Min Min, Female Chinese Student, 1st Interview).

Being considered as a group of special students who were undertaking a foreign course, the Articulation Programme Students experienced some kind of discrimination and isolation on campus. This drove them to form a close group.

> I don't have much connection with students outside our group. We're special. Some students spend their first year on the new campus, but we don't. Most of the clubs are on that campus. So we haven't been involved in many activities. They have some social practice activities, but we don't have a chance to join them. In other students' eyes, we are special. Some of my classmates then believe we're special too (Xiao Ming, Male Chinese Student, 1st Interview).

In the observation in China, all the activities my participants undertook were within the group. There was only one activity, roller skating, observed in the research, which featured members from outside the group. However, those two students were Articulation Programme Students in the first year, who transferred to other courses due to financial problems.

6.2.2 'Chinese Students': a *Closed* Group in the Class on British Campus

The class of fifty Chinese students, who moved to North Britain University after two years studying the first part of the programme in China, joined a class of twenty-five who had studied the first part of the programme, over one year in the UK. This class included mainly home (UK) students but also two non-Chinese international students. The Chinese group outnumbered other students on the programme. Within each group, students had got to know their respective classmates well and had formed supportive groups. Jacky, a home student, reflected on the UK class:

> First year, after a few weeks we all started to hang around with each other anyway, then when the assignments came up ... we

> all sort of bounced ideas off each other. And then you started to get group work ... and then you sort of find out that some are better than others and so you tap into their resources and ask them, 'Oh, you're good at this ... ' and then you just always sort of work together (Jacky, British Student).

These relationships were also important within the Chinese group. The observation in this research showed that students acted in accordance with the prevalent Chinese view of friendships with 'classmates' as sincere, uncontaminated by material considerations and a powerful factor that will help students to succeed in their future careers. Classmates were expected to help each other with course work and join in many activities together. Chinese students expected that this would also be true in a British class and many of them were determined to make friends amongst British classmates. They were almost all disappointed.

Although two existing student groups joined together when the Chinese students arrived on North Britain Campus, neither group appeared to have been prepared for this. The existing cohort of home students had not taken on board the impact of a large cohort of Chinese students joining them in their second year:

> I didn't expect it ... I turned up on the first day and there was a whole bunch of Chinese students there and it was a bit of a shock (Charlie, British Student).

In the lectures observed, the Chinese students outnumbered the UK students by a considerable margin. Many Articulation Programme Students felt that they were still in China. For example, Ling Ling questioned:

> Why don't put us in a normal class? We thought there would be many British students to mix with. It's like we move our classroom from China to the UK. That's it (Ling Ling, Female

Chinese Student, 2nd Interview).

Here the real situation of the class was largely different from Ling Ling's expectation of a normal 'class' in a British university. 'Students in Sino-British Class' on the Chinese campus were addressed as 'Chinese students' on the British campus. They addressed the other group in the class 'British students'.

Compared to the number of Chinese Articulation Programme Students, the School of Engineering at North Britain University had fewer home-based students on the course. As Frank mentioned, '*there are numerous different avenues to try to attract more home-based students onto the programme; It's just not popular at the moment*'. Moving from a small class in the first year to a large class, home students felt 'shocked' and 'overwhelmed' by the participation of a 'whole bunch of Chinese' students. They argued that the school should inform them of the change in classroom culture, which has unfortunately not been the case.

> It would be nice to be warned, you know, 'Oh in the second year you are joined by a cohort from South China' just to be told about it and so you expect it. It wasn't exactly off-putting or anything in any way, but I suppose it might have been nice to have been told (William, British Student).

> It's quite overwhelming seeing the Chinese students ... all it does is kind of keeping people grouped into their little individual groups away from the bigger international community group itself (Jim, British Student).

A lack of preparedness for both groups and early structured interventions, such as icebreaking activities, meant the integration of the two groups in the class was hard to realise, leading to separation and bias. The status of separation and bias strengthened the distinction between in and outgroup membership. A new learning group was forming and, as students participated in this new context, it was observed that they focused on differences in behaviour, ways of studying and social interaction between the two constituent parts referred to here as the Chinese student group and the home student group. The following section particularly noted how students used the classroom space, issues of language, classroom behaviour and a lack of integration between the two student groups.

6.2.3 Intergroup Bias

6.2.3.1 *Geographic Division: 'Front-back' Separation in Class & Competition for Insufficient Resources*

Chinese students always came early to class and sat in the front. When the home students came, there were no seats in the front. Home students commented on this, suggesting it could be detrimental to their learning, preventing them from sitting in the front when they *wanted* to.

> I think the Chinese were quite prompt for lectures and they always come in early, so when we came in there were only the back seats left ... If you're at the front you go to the front because you might not understand it so much, and so you're closer to it so that you can see it better and hear better. And maybe if you understood it more, then you make your way back and sit at the back where you understand it and you're just there to sort of pick up anything else that's said, sort of thing. But I think it's kind of in the reverse because we get there on time, not late, but we get there and are forced to go to the back even though we might not understand it (William, British Student).

As William complained, home students were not late but were 'forced' to sit at the back. When they didn't understand the teaching and needed to sit in the front, they found it was impossible as the seats were always occupied by

Chinese students. This kind of loss resulted in fighting for insufficient resources in the class, and caused hostility in the home students (Sherif, 1967). Seats were not the only resource those two groups were fighting for in the large class. Home students felt that they were not able to get enough attention due to the size of the class.

As discussed in Chapter 5, the Articulation Programme Students preferred to ask questions right after the class. This habit made home students felt that staff did not have the time and attention for their questions.

> If I do want to ask one or two questions myself, maybe something like, for example, maybe I've got a 'yes' 'no' question such as 'Are the labs on this week?' whereas the Chinese students, will sit in the front and then will quickly sort of ambush the lecturer and you can't ask the very basic question because the lecturer is too busy dealing with queries (Max, British Student).

Furthermore, some considerations made by the staff to facilitate the initial transition of the Chinese students had caused some complaints from other students in the class.

> Most of the modules are continued from the first year and the Chinese students don't understand what's going on. He has to tell us past information from last year. It's very strange to me. I've got all the notes at home and I understand what's going on, but the Chinese don't, because he just repeats the first year. That's why some English left the class (Nina, International Student from Kuwait).

The existing cohort felt that the repetition of past information was unnecessary for them, which made them lose their interest. Therefore, attendance went down.

Students, who had paid full tuition fees for their university study, complained, and questioned the coherence of the teaching for the programme students.

> We don't mind revising some stuff and then learn some new stuff. It would bother me if we had to put new work on hold and then rush the new work to hurry up and get it finished because the Chinese weren't up to speed. It wouldn't bother me if the tuition was free, but if I'm paying £3,000 a year ... What would be best is if, at the end of the first year, we both learnt exactly the same things, so when the Chinese students come over everything is sort of, you know, we learn all the same things (William, British Student).

William demonstrated the expectation of a full-tuition fee payer of the service quality the University provided. This was the same with the Chinese students. Both sides considered themselves as customers of the University and had high expectations of their education experiences. Both groups were disappointed at the newly immerging classroom features. Competition for insufficient resources in this large class worsened this kind of negative feeling and caused hostility between two groups. The following discussion on different questioning behaviour shows how it became a differential between these groups and invisibly split the class.

6. 2. 3. 2 *Invisible Division: Different Questioning Behaviour in Class*

In the interviews, home students showed their doubts of why Chinese students preferred to 'ambush the lecturers' after class, but seldom answered questions in the class. As discussed in Chapter 5, staff at North Britain University tended to keep the lecture more interactive. They had the impression that Chinese students were 'quiet', 'shy' and 'less interactive', which linked to the presumption that '*they seem quite passive in the class, but obedient*' (Frank, British Staff Member). Home students shared the same opinion:

> I don't know whether they do it in China, a lecturer will say 'Oh, it's one of two things. Who thinks it's this one?' and some of the class put up their hands, and then he'll say, 'Right, who thinks it's the other one?' and the rest will put their hands up. The Chinese don't participate in that. ... I don't know if they are scared to answer or they just don't see the concept. ... I wouldn't worry about that because I give silly answers all the time. They might be afraid (William, British Student).

Meanwhile, Chinese students noticed that British students were 'noisy' and 'high' in the class.

> British students are noisy in the class. It seems that they are always very high. When the teachers ask a question, they shout back the answers quickly without going through their mind (Xiao Yu, Male Chinese Student, 2nd Interview).

Chinese students had another explanation for their tendency not to answer questions. It was not due to shyness nor to worry in answering questions in a second language when the classroom dynamics were poor, as claimed by MacIntyre (1995). Xiao Hua said:

> I normally sit in the first row and answer the questions often. But I won't shout as loudly as the British students. To be frank, some of the questions are not challenging enough. You're like doing a favour to the teachers (Xiao Hua, Male Chinese Student, 3rd Interview).

Although there were some participants who picked up the classroom culture quickly, they interacted with staff in a different way.

> Here, the class atmosphere is relaxed. You can call teachers' names and ask them to come to your seat to answer

> your questions. I do that sometimes. When I know the answer, I say it out. My voice is not very loud. It's OK. You know you're right (Xiao Ming, Male Chinese Student, 3rd Interview).

As discussed in Section 5.4.1.2, Chinese students considered questions as a way for the staff to test knowledge, rather than to promote interaction. However, home students appreciated a more interactive class, with debate and engagement involving every student, so they were disappointed that the Chinese group seemed to be reluctant to be involved. This different questioning behaviour made the classroom dynamic a conflict.

> They pick up really well and they had stuff [understood course material] before we did, working it out. But I think it would help if they interacted in class more. It would be nice to have debates in some of the more interactive classes, with them, and involve everyone. Because it always seems like there's a quiet area and then the lecturer, after a while, tried to incorporate the Chinese people, but then ends up coming over to one side of the classroom and talking to this side because we interact. So I think they could get more out of it if they interacted more. I think it's just confidence (Jacky, British Student).

The different questioning behaviour became a great differential between these two groups within the classroom culture, which split the class invisibly. The new classroom culture was created by the participation of the Articulation Programme Students and the existing cohort as well. Both groups need to adapt to the new culture.

> Definitely in the classroom there always seems to be a split of interactivity. We're kind of a chatty group and we all communicate with the lecturer and staff, but the Chinese I think, I don't know if it's because of the language or if it's because of feeling a

> bit shy, that they don't sort of interact very much, they sort of write everything down but keep to themselves. A few of them have actually progressed to interacting a lot, but some of them stay in the corner and keep to themselves. But we are quite loud and will say anything and we treat the lecturer like a friend really (Jacky, British Student).

Jacky's comments showed that there might be a stark difference of classroom culture with Chinese and home students having different views about questions and their function. These views lead to different ideas about what is appropriate behaviour, rather than suggesting a simple explanation such as 'shyness' on the part of Chinese students. The splitting situation in the class was strengthened by the communication barriers which will be discussed in the following section.

6.2.3.3 *Visible Differential: Double-language Barriers*

As discussed in Chapter 5, if they did not understand the teaching during lectures, some Chinese students would ask their friends sitting beside them. Within the Chinese group, all communication was in Chinese, sometimes even in students' own dialect if they were from the same city, because it was 'comfortable' (Yan Yan), 'natural' (Xiao Yong) and 'just it is' (Xiao Jie). This partly caused more noise in the class and complaints from the students. The problem was exacerbated by the larger class size. Counting the numbers of the Chinese students, the dominant language in the class was Chinese instead of English. The dominant atmosphere of the Chinese language made some of the home students feel 'vulnerable', 'irritated' or 'frustrated'.

> I think if they were speaking in English it wouldn't bother me as much as if they're speaking Chinese. ... Sometimes when they're speaking Chinese you think, 'Are they talking about us?' and you never know. I think people feel vulnerable when they don't know what someone is saying (William, British

Student).

> ... they're just chatting but ... in Chinese, so even if I wanted to listen, I couldn't, because all I could hear was Chinese... it's just a bit irritating that you can't kind of join in, I guess... It can be frustrating in a way, because if you want to ask someone something then you just feel like you can't because you don't speak their language (Charlie, British Student).

In the above quotations, both William and Charlie were annoyed by Chinese students' chatting in Chinese, a language they did not know. William felt vulnerable as he thought people might be talking about him. Being unable to participate in the conversation irritated Charlie and made him frustrated. Meanwhile, Chinese students also felt excluded. Perhaps their use of Chinese allowed home students and lecturers to make less effort to include them in their interactions in English.

> The home students at the back are chatting. Don't know what they're doing. I never cut in. Sometimes the staff tell jokes. I don't understand. How do I know it's a joke? The English students will laugh loudly. Then they tell jokes back and the teacher laughs as well (Xiao Dong, Male Chinese Student, 2nd Interview).

The double language barrier contributed to a divided atmosphere blocking interactions between home and Chinese students. As Byram (2008) argues, the presence of another language is one indicator of group difference, which accentuates the presence of group characteristics. The size of the Chinese group in the class resulted in two competing languages: Chinese and English. Not knowing the strangers' language and their perspectives caused anxiety and uncertainty (Gudykunst, 2005). It was hard to say which language was more powerful in this setting. Home students described their feeling as being intimidated when surrounded by the Chinese language within their own country. Some lecturers felt disempowered:

> In my workshop class, all of them are Chinese and that is one of my concerns ... I don't understand what they are talking about because they are discussing in Chinese, all the time, during the two hours, unless I am speaking to them (Ben, British Staff Member).

This double-language barrier hindered the peer learning in class. As Joe, an international student from Nigeria, mentioned:

> I really don't get on well, because half of the class really don't understand me. The majority of the class are Chinese. When you don't know something and you keep studying over and over and you still don't get it, you need someone to pull you through. And if you can't get your hands on the teacher then you need to find a student who can help you, and there the language barriers comes up again (Joe, International Student from Nigeria).

English is the official language in Nigeria. Joe did not have a problem with English. The majority of the class were Chinese and they preferred to communicate in Chinese. This made Joe felt that he was outside the circle. The participation of this large cohort of Chinese students influenced the learning context in the class.

6.2.3.4 *Division Between 'Us' and 'Them' and the Impact on Learning*

Gradually, both of the groups found that there was a great divide in the class.

> In the class, British students didn't talk to us and we didn't talk to them. It's weird as we are like two separated parts but sitting in the same class (Xiao Ming, Male Chinese Student, 2nd

Interview).

> There is quite a large divide in the class. There was a lot more of them than there was of us. And there wasn't much integration . . . It is a bit 'us and them' and it's very separate. There are a lot of Chinese students on the course and I don't know a single person(Max, British Student).

Both Xiao Ming and Max described the separation between the home cohort and the Chinese cohort. After eighteen months of study in the same class, Max still did not know anyone from the Chinese group. Xiao Ming was not happy with the division in class. It was in conflict with his concept of a normal class, where peers could integrate and help each other. His English was competent enough but his direct interaction with fellow students was blocked by the divide in the class. This was the same case with Yan Yan, who said: '*Whenever I come across a problem, I'll ask my classmates from Southeast China University*'. She put a question to me at the interview:

> Have *you* noticed anybody talking to them [home students] in the class? (Yan Yan, Female Chinese Student, 2nd interview).

The separation in the class was driving the two groups closer within themselves.

> The situation has probably brought together the home students who we were with in the first year; we're all sort of quite a close group now (Jacky, British Student).

Charlie, William, Jacky and Max were interviewed in the second term of their final year, at which point they had studied with Chinese students for 18 months. There was some mixing, but the integration was still not optimistic.

> Now it's like a bit more mixed, but not to the extent where you could say it was completely mixed. It's still like a group of home students and a group of Chinese students ... It still feels like there's a divide but it's not like an unapproachable divide. Whereas before, in the second year it would be like, especially at the start, it would be a direct split between the two (Charlie, British Student).

The separation in the class disappointed the Chinese students who expected to make friends with home students when they were in China. Integration with the home students was what they had pictured in their minds. Home students on the other hand did not have the same expectations or such a strong desire as the Chinese students did. They had their own life, friends, and family members in their own country, often nearby. Many of them took the engineering course to find a job in the near future. Students, like Jim and Max, had to take out a loan to cover their tuition fees. They need to get a part-time job to support themselves financially. In contrast, all the Articulation Programme Students received full financial support from their parents. It was unnecessary for them to find a part-time job. They could spend most of their spare time on their study, while home students could not.

> It's all right for them, they'll come into the lecture and don't understand anything, go home and read a book, while we English students, we finish University and basically most of us have got jobs. So we go home, get changed and go to work. I don't know many of the international students that have got jobs here ... The English students, we need to worry about the financial side. ... Coming to University, a lot of students need to get part-time jobs (Jim, British student).

The financial pressure made Jim concentrate as much as possible on his study during his hours at university, as he had to go to work after school.

There was no extra time for him to make friends with a new group of Chinese students. They were not as disappointed as the Chinese students with the divide in the class.

The consequence of this segregation was not only forming into two groups, but affecting students' learning in the class. At North Britain University it was usual to require students to undertake some of their learning in groups. This was seen as a contribution to graduate skills needed by engineers. However, the ' us & them ' separation made the group hearning difficult. William, who wanted help from the Chinese students, felt it was difficult to break the ice.

> I mean, there are groups ... we're doing a project. You have to write a code and programme this little box, and some Chinese students have it working, and we don't at the minute. For some reason, we can't figure out way, but it seems awkward to sort of ask if theirs is working and what they did about that, because we've never spoken to them before (William, British Student).

William felt awkward about asking for help from students who were still strangers, even though they had studied together for a whole year by this time. Peer learning was constrained within groups. Chinese/UK peer learning was seldom observed in the study. Intergroup bias, the tendency to appraise the ingroup members more favourably over the outgroup (Hewstone, Rubin and Willis, 2002), was generated in this separated class.

Group work provided further evidence of the impact of the separation between the two groups. For the module EN0213, Project Design, students were asked to form groups of five to six to conduct group work. Students chose their own group members. Apart from one group with Joe, all the Chinese students were with their previous classmates, and so were the home students.

> Our project supervisor told us to organise ourselves in a group of four ... we all worked together for the first year so there was

> five of us together and we just stuck together. So we basically chose our friends (Max, British Student).

Max chose his group members within the existing cohort. Through working in the first year, they knew each other very well. The unbalanced number of the two groups and the language barrier made the home students worry that they might be left out in the group discussion. As William and Max explained:

> Because there're more Chinese. If they said 'Right, we're going to have groups of three, two Chinese and one English', and then straight away the English person is in the minority, and they would possibly speak Chinese and the English person would be left out, and things like that (William, British Students).

> If I was the only English person and the rest were all Chinese, then I would feel intimidated because I know they all speak Chinese to each other and I have got a strong accent and they might struggle to understand me. I feel that they would probably speak Chinese to each other a lot and I wouldn't be able to get as much out of a group who are speaking a language that I can't understand ... I wouldn't be able to participate as much (Max, British Student).

This difficulty was verified by the past experience of the staff.

> I know in the past as well, sometimes when a UK student has been by himself in a group of Chinese students, they found it difficult because the Chinese students speak Chinese to each other and the UK student feels a bit excluded. Unfortunately, there are numerous different avenues to try to attract more home based students onto the programme, it's just not popular at the

> moment. For the Chinese students, it's a bit unfortunate because there aren't sufficient home based students for them to be able to mix with (Frank, British Staff Member).

As Frank mentioned, the imbalance in class made the group project difficult. He was concerned that if UK students and Chinese students were assigned to the same group by staff, it might make the former group feel excluded. On one hand staff welcomed the enrolment of more Chinese students on the course as it made a great contribution to the finances of the school and the strong academic background of Chinese students could benefit the learning and teaching in the class. On the other hand, staff were concerned over the current segregation in the class. Ben, another staff member, expressed his concern of the divide and the importance of integration between the groups of students in class.

> I don't think the class has much mixing. We have to, as a University and the School, start to address this. Somehow, we need to break that barrier. It's very important because we want British students to know about other countries. And also, I find that some of the Chinese students have a very strong understanding of technical topics. Some of the home students are possibly slightly weak on these. So, if we can mix them, hopefully that creates a result in benefiting both [groups] to have a better result and better group at the end of the year. I am really concerned about this because we should break the barriers between backgrounds, religion, colour and everything, and start to learn in the organisation that everyone could actually participate to work together for the benefit of everyone, somehow (Ben, British Staff Member).

Both Chinese and home students were worried about a possible negative effect on their academic performance if they worked with students from the other group. Home students worried that language limitation would prevent Chinese students from working effectively with UK students and might pull down their grade. Chinese students did not know how well individual UK students performed and so had no idea whether their group grade would be affected if they worked with them.

> We choose our own groups. So if the lecturer says 'Choose your own groups', then the Chinese choose their own and the English choose theirs, and you might argue that's bad because it prevents integration, but if ... obviously some of the Chinese speak really good English but some of them are very limited. So if I was put with someone who barely spoke English and had that little translator that they have all the time for every word they are saying, and I wasn't able to work effectively and got a lower grade then that would be mad (William, British Student).

> It's fine if we could have a British student member, but we won't cry for it. And we really don't know who studies well, who doesn't. We have to consider our score. We know our classmates very well after two years (Xiao Hua, Male Chinese Student, 2nd Interview).

This unfamiliarity hindered the possibility of facilitating intergroup integration through academic group work. No structured intervention was carried out to enhance the understanding. Both the Chinese students and the home students expressed a willingness to get to know each other. Both said that more integration could have a positive effect on their learning experience and future career. However, they still stayed in their own groups and felt that there were barriers to acting in a different way. In the final year, Jacky, wanted to join the Chinese students for group work, but he did not know how to break the by-now-established patterns of working in separate groups. He found they were too close and made it hard for him to join in.

> I think it would be better to mix the groups up though. For instance, this year, I wouldn't have minded working with one or two of the Chinese people. But, I didn't get a chance to. We had a group of four, and the assignment came out for three. So it was either going to be three and one or two and two, but the workload was for three. And so in the end there was a three and a one, so I said I didn't mind going and working with someone else, so I was going to work with a Chinese person just to sort of bridge the gap. But we ended up working two and two. So even though we had more work, we decided to do that. But for other group work, I was willing to work with any of the Chinese people. I thought they were all in groups themselves though so I didn't know how to go up and be like, 'Can I work with you'? (Jacky, British Student).

Jacky's group ended up working in two groups of two, instead of three. They chose to work in smaller groups thus taking on more work individually, rather than opting to form groups which included UK and Chinese students together. Jacky himself was willing to work with some Chinese students, but found they were too close and made it hard for him to join in. He did not know how to go up and ask to break into the circle.

Some Chinese students worried about being criticised by their friends if they approached the other group, as Xiao Qiang illustrated:

> It's impossible for you to keep on talking to home students, because my previous classmates will think I'm strange. You have studied and lived with the [Chinese] group for two years. How can you break away from them and sit with white people? Even

> white people might think, 'what's wrong with this guy? Why doesn't he get along well with his group?' So I seldom talk to them (Xiao Qiang, Male Chinese Student, 2nd Interview).

Jacky and Xiao Qiang were dragged back to their own groups, in spite of their tentative motivations to work or talk together. In addition, the separation in the class also influenced the Chinese students' opinions towards the Articulation Programme, which will be presented in the following section.

6.2.3.5 *Studying Abroad as a Group: Advantage or Disadvantage?*

The separation in the class failed to meet the Articulation Programme Students' expectation to mix with home students and make friends with them. This disappointment triggered their questioning of the unique feature of the programme: studying abroad as a large group. In the interviews in China, the participants believed that studying abroad with a group of classmates who knew each other very well was a big advantage of the programme. A representative comment is shown below:

> It's safer to join in this course. Going abroad alone will be lonely, with no one to look after me. We will help each other (Xiao Qiang, Male Chinese Student, 1st Interview).

The difficulties in integration they predicted were mainly from the outside of the group, such as race discrimination, bullying and untruthful reports on China. None of them predicted that their close relationship, a kind of bond, could affect their integration with British people and the culture. Classmates, parents, friends and lecturers were the four sources to whom they would turn for help when they came across problems in China. Their classmates, part of their support network, came with them to the UK and this greatly facilitated their transition at the early stage.

> I thought I might not adapt to a strange environment. But these two months past, I find everything is OK. I didn't feel there were

> many things that were inconvenient. After all, I have so many classmates around me. Things I don't understand, I can ask my classmates in Chinese. I haven't started missing home, but I can't imagine what I would do if I had come alone (Ling Ling, Female Chinese Student, 2nd Interview).

Initially, students talked about the benefits of helping each other in daily life, discussing academic problems in their native language, overcoming loneliness, and providing a familiar and trustable circle they could rely on. These were seen as the main advantages of coming as a group. Later on, their views changed when they found that the *close* group had become a *closed* group and it was very hard to break out of the circle as shown in the above sections. Xiao Qiang, who believed coming as a group was an advantage for his study abroad, changed his views after the first academic year of study in the UK.

> I chose the programme because our parents believed that it was safe coming as a group. Before I left China, I thought we could make English friends when we arrived in the UK as you could see English people everywhere. But, It's not the case. Wherever we go, we're a group, a small collective group. We are wired in. In the class, the majority are Chinese. The majority are from our own class in China. We come earlier and sit in the front, while other students come later and sit at the back with their first year classmates. We are two different groups. I think it is the Chinese who isolate the home students (Xiao Qiang, Male Chinese Student, 3rd Interview).

The large number of the group gave them the power and influence to make impact on other groups. The imbalanced number of Chinese students over home students partly led to the separation in the class and hindered the establishment of friendship networks.

> Coming as a group was very helpful at the beginning. I could turn to my classmates whenever I had problems. But, gradually, I found it was hard for us to make friends with home students or students from other countries. We isolate ourselves. It seems that other students think we are a closed group. For instance, home students have got to know those Indian students, but not us. I guess they are scared because we are such a large group (Ling Ling, Female Chinese Student, 3rd Interview).

Ling Ling noticed that it was easier for students who came to the UK individually to make friends with home students. The size of their group made the home students feel 'scared' about making friends with them. This was verified by home students:

> It's probably the size of the group; it would probably be easier if there were less. I think that's probably one of the main reasons (William, British Student).

> It's not that Chinese people I wouldn't approach, or I would hope that they didn't feel that they couldn't approach me, It's just that when, say, Mo came from Bahrain and he came on his own so he doesn't speak Arabic to anyone except for Hassan who he met in the second year, and now a few more who have come from individual places, whereas ... Because obviously, he wouldn't just want to sit there on his own, so he has to speak English to you, and you can't speak his language so you have to speak back (Charlie, British Student).

The example given by Charlie showed that international students who came individually spoke English to integrate with other students in the class. The space around them gave home students the chances to go to talk with them on one hand, while on the other hand they could also go towards home students when they wanted friends. However, the Articulation Programme Students had already had their own friends to rely on.

> When there's only one, say, Indian student, then they are more likely to talk, whereas when you do have a group that already knows each other and maybe even for two years, then they don't need to speak to other people because they've got their own friends (William, British Student).

Other international students in class integrated with home students both within the class and outside the university, as shown by Max:

> Other international students have integrated very easily with the home students. Some of them we've known from the first year and some we've met since then, and they have integrated very well with us and we're good friends and we socialise outside of university, whereas there's been no outside of university integration between the English and the Chinese, whereas we have integrated with people from Greece and Bahrain (Max, British Student).

International students who came individually expressed their worries about the Chinese students. It was hard for them to mix with the Chinese group as well.

> They are into themselves. I know they are so scared about mixing up. They want to be together; you don't get them alone or you can't get in between them. It's always safer to be with people you know. In a foreign country, you have to accept you can socialise and that's the point. You can't come to England and leave England and not make any friends (Joe, International Student from Nigeria).

A lack of friendship with home students and other international students in class made Chinese students gradually confine themselves to a closed circle. Some students were trying to escape from the group. Ying Ying was a distinctive example. She had a high expectation to make English friends and improve her English when she was in China. The separation in class had greatly disappointed her. Although she applied for accommodation to live with home students, she was dispatched to a flat shared with three other Chinese classmates. They went everywhere together. Ying Ying found her English had not been improved as they spoke Chinese together.

> We four go everywhere together and speak Chinese all the day! I feel I'm still in China in the class. All the people surrounding you are your classmates in China! My English hasn't been improved! What about two years later when I go back to China? I can't speak proper English. I will be embarrassed to tell people I have been studying in the UK. I also feel embarrassed now to go out socialising with English students without taking my flatmates with me. We tell each other where we are and what we are doing all the time' (Ying Ying, Female Chinese Student, 2nd Interview).

Ying Ying was reluctant to confine herself in the Chinese circle and intended to make friends with local students. However, she felt embarrassed to act individually. Her own closed group culture blocked her direct interaction with the home students. She did not want to hurt the feelings of her Chinese flatmates and let them feel she was not getting along well with her group. It was hard for her to leave the monoculture group to join the large international group.

For students who had indirect interaction with the new learning environment was also disappointed with the divide in the class. As Xiao Yong argued:

> I think the disadvantage of this programme is coming as a large group. Except for some very good students, most of us are still in

> this group. We don't have much contact with students outside the group. It's better to come here individually or in a group of five or six in this respect. I have a friend who came here himself. I found he had integrated himself into the English society very well. He doesn't have many Chinese around him, which has forced him to get along with English people. I have a cousin who wants to join the programme. I told him not to. He'd better apply for a university himself rather than coming as a group (Xiao Yong, Male Chinese Student, 3rd Interview).

The existing cohort at this point was more multicultural because some of the international students had joined them, while the Chinese students group was still monocultural (seven Chinese students from another Chinese university joined them). The advantage changed into a disadvantage.

> It is very hard for such a large group to mix with other British students. I think this is the biggest disadvantage of this kind of programme. I wouldn't choose it if I knew it. My overseas study lacks something (Xiao Qiang, Male Chinese Student, 3rd Interview).

The Articulation Programme Students were very disappointed with the divide in the class and felt something was missing in their overseas study. How to create an integrated multinational class deserves attention from all the stake-holders aiming to run a successful programme. The current practices encouraging the integration at North Britain University are presented in the following section.

6.3 Current Practices of Intergroup Contact

North Britain University organised some activities to encourage international students to integrate into the community. For example, to facilitate international students' settling down in the UK, Student Services set up a team of international advisers to give students advice on visa, jobs, study, safety, culture and other issues. They also organised social activities to engage international students on campus, such as 'Friends International' which recruited volunteers with at least one-year learning experience at the University to provide training on cultural awareness, communication and interpersonal skills. These volunteers became 'buddies' with one or two international students who newly arrived in the UK. This was an opportunity for new international students to make friends with students from all over the world and adjust to the new environment. However, there were no participants took part in the activities in this study.

The Students' Union also organised 'Student Community Action' activities to encourage students to make a difference in the local community through student-led volunteer projects. Min Min, Ling Ling and Li Li joined in the Student Community Action group and undertook some voluntary work, such as cleaning the beaches, telling stories to children and organising parties for disabled people. They won the University Award for their contribution in volunteer work. Li Li was appointed to be a team leader in a student-led volunteer project.

> The group members were from different courses. We learned a lot from each other. We went to clean the beaches and farms. I really enjoyed it. Our team organised a Christmas party for children. I sent emails to others. So I have to force myself to practise English and get to know other people (Li Li, Female Chinese Student, 3rd Interview).

Through actively participating in volunteer work, some students started to enlarge their friendship circle, improve their English and learn from other students. Another practice was trying to create culturally mixed accommodation. Some students, such as Xiao Hua and Li Li, made friends with and through their flatmates.

> My flatmates are from America, France and Ukraine. They ask me a lot about Chinese culture. I feel a sense of achievement. Sometimes they help me to dice the meat. We're getting on well with each other now (Li Li, Female Chinese Student, 3rd Interview).

Li Li's flatmates were international students from other countries, who were interested in Chinese culture. This gave them a common topic. Li Li gained a sense of achievement through introducing her own national culture which was valued by the flatmates. The integration with her flatmates became an important channel for her to integrate with other students outside the group.

Xiao Hua's experience was clearly outstanding. He became friends with his flatmates, with whom he went to pubs, parties and played football. He was also invited to a flatmate's home and spent the Christmas holiday with his family. Through these flatmates, he made more friends. He attributed his success to the international accommodation.

> Those days were wonderful. I didn't meet any Chinese. At the Christmas dinner, all his family members, his grandparents, uncles, aunties were all there. They were very warm to me. I brought some Chinese gifts. His grandpa had a company in Thailand. They had many arts from Thailand and China. He asked me to explain the meaning of the Chinese idiom 'Da Peng Zhan Chi' [A roc spreads its wings]. I explained it to him word by word. This experience is very precious. I can proudly say that nobody else has the same experience ... No matter how much money you give me, I won't trade my accommodation (Xiao Hua, Male Chinese Student, 3rd Interview).

Culturally mixed accommodation enabled Xiao Hua to experience more English culture than other students. Another important reason was his active attitude. He shared tips on getting along well with his flatmates.

> At the start, we didn't talk much. Just 'hello' or 'bye'. One day, I said, 'We, Chinese, invite you to dinner'. After our first dinner, we became familiar immediately. They might think that we are very easy going as we invite them to dinner. We clean the kitchen up each time we use it. They said, 'You Chinese are very polite'. Now they often cook pasta and make pizza for me. When their friends come, they will introduce me to them. I get to know more friends in this way ... We watch TV or play PC games after dinner ... When there is some problem, we always say, 'That's all right. It's OK.' Every problem will be solved ... We play football together, where I get to know many other guys ... They asked me to go to pub and I did! At the Halloween Party, I put on hair wax, pulled the hair up, painted my face white and drew a large red scar. I was very uncomfortable at the beginning as I was the only Chinese there. Later, I got used to it. People saw me and said, 'Chinese, cool' (Xiao Hua, Male Chinese Student, 3rd Interview).

There were some reasons for his successful integration with his flatmates in the culturally mixed accommodation. First, he took the initiative to talk to home students, which made them feel he was not shy, but very easy going. Second, he used some strategies, such as cooking Chinese food for his flatmates. In a nice and friendly atmosphere, their distance was shortened. Last but not least, he and his flatmates shared the same hobbies, such as watching TV, playing PC games and playing football. Similar to Li Li's experience, these gave them a common ground or a reason to talk.

Once the friendship was built up, it would be easier for Xiao Hua to overcome the language barrier.

> They were very warm and encouraged me constantly, 'keep talking, keep talking'. My flat mates studied French, Spanish or Latin at school. They know it's not easy to learn a foreign language. They told me learning a language need practising all the time. They told me, 'we will help you'. ... don't care too much about your face. Sometimes you feel this word might be wrong. Don't worry, say it out. British students will say, 'pardon?' Then you could say, 'I don't quite understand this. Maybe I can spell it to you'. Sometimes, I spell it on the electronic dictionary on my mobile and show it to them. They will say, 'oh, it is this'. Then they will tell me the meaning of the word ... They are very friendly. They won't think you're a trouble ... Gradually, you'll learn more words. Don't be shy. Once shy, you'll be shy next time. I speak it out every time. Don't be afraid. Say it out and you won't feel it's a barrier next time (Xiao Hua, Male Chinese Student, 3rd Interview).

Here, Xiao Hua demonstrated how encouragement, empathy and friendship from the home students helped him to overcome the 'face' problem and language issue. These factors were essential in Xiao Hua's successful direct interaction with the local students. Without them, integration was unlikely to take place. For example, Xiao Ming and one of his classmates stayed with three British flatmates. They tried to approach these home students, but felt very frustrated by their 'cold' reaction.

> We suggested going out for dinner or having a party. British students refused our invitation. They said they were busy. We cooked Chinese dish for them, but they didn't eat. Those dishes are what we're good at and very clean. Not Chicken feet. But they didn't accept. We gave them some pretty Chinese gifts, but

> they just had a look and put them aside carelessly. Our passion was damped. One of them likes watching movie, so we want to invite her to watch 007 or High School Music, but there won't be any chance, because they're very cold. They three are a close group (Xiao Ming, Male Chinese Student, 3rd Interview).

Some people may attribute the failure of the integration to the language barrier. However, Xiao Ming achieved 7.0 in IELTS before he came to the UK and 8.0 in the final year. If IELTS is under the criticism that it cannot represent international students' language competence, then his academic achievement (first-class degree, 'ADM Prize for Best Final Year Project' and 'IET Prize for Best Overall Student Performance'), and his employment at Hilton Hotel might show how competent he was in English.

Xiao Ming had some similar factors as what had contributed to Xiao Hua's successful integration with British flatmates: he stayed in a culturally mixed accommodation; he took the initiative to talk to his flatmates; he adopted some strategies, such as giving Chinese gifts and cooking Chinese food (clean and culturally accepted), and they shared the same hobby (watching movies). However, his flatmates gave 'cold' and 'careless' responses to his active gesture. The communication was not successful. His intention to interact with the home students was given up because of the negative attitude of the interlocutors. Those three home students formed a close group in the dormitory. There was no 'encouragement, sympathy and friendship'. Xiao Ming's experience showed that some of the home students were not ready for intercultural communication, due to the lack of preparation for developing intercultural competence. Therefore, simply being exposed to a culturally mixed environment, such as accommodation, does not definitely lead to cross-cultural communication or intergroup integration. More structured interventions need to be carry out to build a culturally competent campus.

Xiao Jie, who avoided the interaction with the new learning environment made some friends on internet through playing PC games:

> I don't have many chances to practise English during the day. But I play Warcraft, a PC game developed by an American company, Blizzard. I chat with the group member in English. Most of the other group members are foreigners. I made some friends there. They are from different countries. We use English to communicate. To tell you the truth, most of my English is learnt in this way (Xiao Jie, Male Chinese Student, 3rd Interview).

Outside the class, students like Xiao Hua and Li Li made friends in volunteer activities or their accommodation. However, both of them complained that there were not many opportunities to integrate with their British classmates at school. At school level, no particular effort was devoted to facilitate the integration in the class, except a football match which was held in the middle of the first term. This took place when some staff realised that the divide in this multinational class was having a negative effect on peer learning. They organised the football match.

> I play quite a lot of football so I arranged a few games of football against the students last year and they seemed to mix quite well. Half Chinese and half English students (Eric, British Staff Member).

This kind of structured contact between host and international students can benefit international students' experience (Quintrell and Westwood, 1994) and the mutual contact will also benefit the home students (Montgomery and McDowell, 2004). As Jim, the English student suggested:

> That's when the ice started to break, and a lot of the students started talking and things like that. With those three turning up, they will realise that we're not evil devils that are going to kill them and we are just a group of lads. The lad that came to the

> match last year, Lee, his English name, I still talk to him when I see him around the university (Jim, British Student).

The integration facilitated peer learning in the class.

> In my group lab, all of them are Chinese, so when you do the labs together, someone asks me and I ask someone and it makes it easier (Nina, International Student from Kuwait).

> I played football with some of them. They know me and always say hello to me. Last time in the lab, some students didn't know how to do the experiment. I showed them how to do it. Then we got to know each other. Although I could not name them, we do say hello to each other (Xiao Hua, Male Chinese Student, 3rd Interview).

Jim's course had a high failure rate. Studying with Chinese students, Jim reflected on his past learning experiences and highlighted a gap in Engineering education between high school and university, a potential obstacle to young people studying Engineering.

> Without going too much into it, there's a gap between university, college, and school. From school to college, there's a gap in what people should be learning, and then from college to university there is a gap ... there is such a big gap between what they learn in college for Maths to what they learn at university for Maths. There is a big, huge jump and that big jump puts a lot of people off, and unless they want to actually push themselves (Jim, British Student).

Only a few students went to the football match. Because of the heavy workload, staff did not have enough time to organise more activities. At the end of the first academic year, there was still not much integration. Home students gave some suggestions. First, the icebreaking activities should be carried out at the start of the academic year. As presented in Section 6.2.2, the existing cohort did not know that a large group of Chinese students were going to join them. There were no activities organised by the school to let the two cohorts to introduce themselves. The gap was there without a way to close it.

> Obviously, we are all doing Engineering so I'm sure we all have an interest in that, and I'm sure there are common interests among the group ... it's just that we don't know ... they've got no reason to speak to each other. And I know that sounds a bit strange, but what I would do is, when they first come over, don't have the first week of lectures, have the first week sort of team building, exercises, general sort of games where everyone gets involved and then if you sort of had to ... If we had to speak to the Chinese and they had to speak to us and it happened, then we'd know a few names so when we go on for lectures and we've got assignments and things then we'd probably speak to people and say, 'Oh, how's that going?', whereas if we go into a lecture and all the Chinese sat together and the English sat together, there's never really any reason for them to speak to each other (William, British Student).

William pointed out that one of the barriers that hindered their integration was a lack of contact. Students did not know their 'common ground'. Common ground identified through individual contact could help students to overcome the language barrier in the communication. As Charlie pointed out:

> The main reason that there is no integration, I think it's because, obviously, all the Chinese people, they are in a different

> country and they are just together. I think a lot of the reason that the home students are put off is because they don't speak Englis. They speak Chinese to each other and it's like a barrier, because obviously unless we speak Chinese we can't interact, so if there was individual contact then people would find common ground and would start to talk and then it wouldn't matter if Chinese people spoke Chinese to each other because you could approach then. Now, we don't know what we have in common; we don't know what everyone is like and they don't know what we're like (Charlie, British Student).

Jacky demonstrated how the two groups could learn from each other's strengths and make up for their own deficiencies in their studies.

> I think it would be a better experience because you get over that sort of thing at the start, and then you sort of create a rapport and you would be able to tap into each other's resources, like for instance, report writing or something like that, and different things that they are good at and I'm good at. And probably it would be slightly better, because the way that the home students go towards things, it could be completely different to the way Chinese students do. So having one of each sort of, you could bounce ideas off each other and then find the ultimate way of doing it (Jacky, British Student).

Therefore, the integration in the class could enhance learning and benefit both groups. The intercultural contact could also help both groups to develop their intercultural competence.

> One of the best things about being at a university where there is a lot of international students is that you can learn about other people as well and how things like that go on. They have their

> ways of learning and we've got ours and you might come up with something better so . . . It's quite nice to actually get along with some of them and see how they do things and also try and pass on to the students on the English side (Jim, British Student).

Home students were willing to integrate with Chinese students in the multicultural learning environment. In the interviews, they asked me many questions about Chinese students, such as 'why did they choose the course', 'how were they educated in China', 'are their tuition fees a lot more than they are in China', 'is there much interaction between teachers and students in China', 'what are their future plans after graduation', 'are there a lot of jobs waiting for them in China' and many other questions that could have been answered directly by Chinese students.

As presented in Chapter 5, making friends with home students was the Articulation Programme Students' expectation while they were in China. Both groups showed the willingness to know each other, which was in contradiction with the current segregation in the class. From a customer perspective, home students argued that the school should take more responsibility in promoting the integration.

> I don't think it's their fault that they don't integrate and it's just as much our fault as theirs, if anyone was to blame. It's just the school needs to do something if they really care. I don't see why they would but, at the end of the day, everyone is paying, They've got their money; that's fine! [Laughs]. But if they'd wanted to chat, I guess the school could organise something and then that's a way of making it less daunting (Charlie, British Student).

Apart from the school, staff could also have taken some actions to integrate the students in their teaching. As Max suggested below, staff could arrange seating to change the current 'front-back' division in the class and design some games for students to introduce themselves.

> That might be a good idea, a way of maybe for the first couple of lectures that maybe some sort of seating arrangement, so you're deliberately not sitting next to someone you know, and also yes maybe some games would be a good idea where you all introduce yourself (Max, British Student).

Changing the classroom to be more interactive among students could engage more students into the discussion.

> In class, you could just get everyone talking. And like a professor, he turns the place into a forum rather than a lecture. He'll put something on the board and then get everyone talking and doing this and that. That's quite good because at the end everyone is shouting at each other because everyone has different opinions so it gets, you know ... it's like when you meet anyone for the first time, you have to get everyone moving and talking and mixing up otherwise people will just stay in their set groups (Charlie, British Student).

Staff could design more group assignments and lab work to create individual contact opportunities.

> They've asked us for help but haven't asked to join the group or anything, but, they have asked 'Oh, have you got this?' and I think we've asked them a few times and they've helped us. I think it's because there's more group assignment this year than last year(Jacky, British Student).

Students hoped to improve integration in a low-stake learning environment.

> And so big puzzles that you have to sort and problems that they

> have to solve in groups and things like that ... I mean, things like that would get people talking, and obviously it's fun, there's no grades relying on it so you're not worried in case someone doesn't pull their weight and things like that, and just things like that would be interesting and it gives you an opportunity to get to know people ... When you start to think about the grades ... Yes, you don't want anyone to drag you down (William, British Student).

The preference of '*no grades relying on it*' illustrated why the group project discussed in Section 6.2.3.4 did not work to facilitate the integration. Group work could also be designed to combine the different strengths of each group member, which could foster 'listening' in the group. Only through each member's contribution can the task be successfully accomplished.

> You need to have games at the start. Or you could do quizzes, like, where you have to get into groups with some English and some Chinese and there'll be questions that maybe sometimes on the English know and sometimes only the Chinese know. And then at least the English will listen to the answers and the Chinese will listen to the answers, so they are learning a little bit about the other cultures that way. I really do think that if you did have some games and things, a reason to talk to each other, then after that it would be so much easier because you have spoken to them before (William, British Student).

The above quotations showed vividly how active the home students could be in integrating with the Chinese students facilitated by proper instructed interventions. They welcomed the integration, but could not find a way to break the ice and talk to the Chinese. Owing to the increasing position of Chinese economy, this kind of contact would be more valued.

> There're not many people that realise ... They still think that the Western world, like, America and Europe is going to be the bigger industrial nations forever, and it's not. China probably will be in a few years. So it would be better to have more integration and to become friends with some of them so we do have contacts (William, British Student).

Students also suggested going to China to meet the Chinese students before their coming to the UK. This interaction in China will be taken in the environment where Chinese students feel comfortable. Home students could also get information about Chinese students' previous learning experience.

> So maybe something like, over the Easter holiday maybe, in the first year, the English students go over to China and maybe even sit in a few lectures over there, and then you would also get interaction with them where they are comfortable, and then when they come over here, we might possibly know them a bit better. A lot of people would be up for that, would be willing to do it, especially if they could do some classes in there as well. I think a lot of students would love that; you get to see some Chinese Culture, you get to see various places and you get to do some teaching ourselves or at least give a few lectures. And in some of the lectures, I think a lot of people would absolutely love that. I know if I was offered it, I would certainly have taken it (Max, British Student).

In this case, when Chinese students come to the UK, both of the groups will then have somebody they know. They will not be strangers.

> That would be good because you come back and you would know the person and you would keep in touch, and then when they come back then you would meet up, and I think it would be

better for them as well because then when they come over they're not strangers (Jacky, British Student).

One example given by the Chinese students might support the possible results of the above suggestion. Min Min and Ping Ping went to a workshop held in Germany, where they worked in teams with students from the UK, France and Germany. One home student in their class, Jason, went there too. After one week's study, they got to know each other. When they came back, Min Min and Ping Ping started to know some of the other home students in the class through Jason.

6.4 Conclusions

This chapter focused on the interaction between the Articulation Programme Students and the UK-based cohort, mainly home students. The findings indicated that a lack of suitable interventions at the initial stage, the competition for insufficient resources, double-language barriers and different questioning behaviour led the Chinese and UK students to self-categorize themselves into ' Us ' and ' Them '. The significant differences perceived by Chinese Articulation Programme Students and the home student cohort contributed to the generation of group identities and to visible and invisible divide in the class. The size of a sojourners' group became an influential factor in segregation in the class. Home students felt threatened by the presence of such a large cohort of Chinese students. The separation had a negative impact on peer learning.

This unexpected learning environment in the class triggered students' questioning the structure of the Articulation Programme. Studying abroad as a group, which used to be considered as a facilitator to their study in the UK before leaving China, hindered the programme students' integration with the existing cohort in the class. This chapter showed that international students travelling abroad individually were easier to integrate with home students than students travelling as a group. The Articulation Programme Students were wired into their monocultural circle and relied largely on their own group members.

Participants' outside classroom experiences showed that structured interventions, such as 'Student Community Action' activities, could enlarge students' friendship circle and facilitate their transition in the new learning environment. Culturally mixed accommodation was a controversial place for international students to make friends with home students. Simply being exposed to this kind of environment would not necessariling lead to successful intercultural communication or intergroup integration. The encouragement, empathy and friendship given by home students were important to facilitate international students to overcome their language deficiency and to participate successfully in communication. Intercultural competence became a crucial factor in the integration in a culturally mixed environment, both inside and outside the class. How to create an integrated multinational class deserves attention from all stake-holders. Running a successful articulation programme should take the experiences of all students into consideration.

Chapter 7 Discussion and Conclusions

7.1 Introduction

This chapter provides a critical discussion on the findings presented in the previous two chapters by relating them with the existing literatures. It first explores the connections of personal factors (motivations for studying abroad, attitudes towards pre-departure preparation, language competence, and autonomy) with the transition process. The functions of social factors in transition are then emphasised. It moves on to a discussion on the impact of the unique feature of the Articulation Programme, studying abroad as a group, on the students' interaction with the home students. The final part of this chapter answers the research question by providing a conclusion from the evidence collected in the study. The contribution to knowledge is specified, followed by the implications for practice and recommendations for further research.

7.2 Individual Transition Experience: Different Journeys and Different Outcomes

Evidence found in this research has supported Burnett and Gardner's (2006) argument that the existing models of international students' transition experience cannot cover the individual complexities that constitute any sojourner's path of acculturation. The participants of this research experienced different journeys during their transition from Southeast China University to

North Britain University. The outcomes of their transition experiences were different, which challenged the 'happy-ending' presumed in the existing intercultural development models. Oberg's (1960) cultural shock theory gives a final stage of complete adjustment; Lysgaard's (1955) U-shaped curve theory shows a better integration into the foreign community; Kim's (2001) stress-adaptation-growth model suggests that stress can promote transition in a positive way; and the developmental models reviewed presume that the individual sojourners will move to the stage of 'integration', 'double-swing' or 'internalisation'. Findings of this research suggest that these ideas might be too optimistic. Not all the participants moved to the stage of *integration*, *personal growth*, *double-swing*, *independence* or *internalisation* argued in these models. In contrast, some of the students achieved quite negative outcomes at the end.

The Articulation Programme Students' transition experience was an individual journey depending largely on autonomy guided by their personal agency. They responded differently to the changes in their transition from the Chinese campus to the British campus. In the process, they constructed their own third space when being confronted with a new learning environment (Feng, 2009). This third space is unique and located somewhere different for each learner (*ibid.*), and 'will make different sense at different times' (Kramsch, 1993, cited in Feng, 2009: 75). In the process of transition in the third space, the three broad response categories identified in this research represented three key types of experiences within the participants' group and were presented in terms of Direct Interaction, Indirect Interaction and Avoiding Interaction. They responded differently to the academic changes in their transition process driven by various level of autonomy. When looking at the social environment, there were some variations away from the model. One example was Xiao Ming's frustration in making friends with his British flatmates no matter how hard he had tried to interact directly with them. This demonstrated that the empathy, encouragement and support from the other interlocutor were important for international students' successful communication. Ying Ying's own closed group culture blocked her direct interaction with the home students. However, Xiao Jie who gradually avoided the interaction with the learning environment made friends on internet through team working in PC games. These variations indicate that the social environment is more complex than the academic environment and requires a further study.

The Articulation Programme Students' transition experiences were closely related to their motivations for studying abroad, attitudes towards predeparture preparation, language competence, and autonomy. These factors were reciprocally related. In general, this research supports the findings of Chirkov *et al.* (2007) that international students who are self-determined in their decision to study abroad achieve more positive outcomes in their transition abroad compared to those who are driven by non-self-determined reasons. Those who perceived studying abroad as an interesting and enjoyable journey demonstrated great autonomy in the process of transition. The participants, who agreed with their parents' opinions that studying abroad could benefit their future career, also took an active attitude towards their intercultural study. They accepted the value of studying abroad and transformed external regulation into self-regulation. This kind of internalisation was facilitated by pre-departure preparation which aimed to increase students' competence, relatedness and autonomy in their transition. Their transition process was also autonomously driven and led to positive outcomes. Therefore, the results confirm the arguments of self-determination theory (Ryan and Deci, 2000) that intrinsic motivation, as well as internalised extrinsic motivation, can result in high-quality learning and creativity. This study also matches the findings of Ryan and Connell (1989), whose research demonstrates that positive coping strategies are more likely to be adopted by these students. Strong evidence lends support to the argument of Koestner and Losier (2002) that intrinsic and identified regulation can generate positive outcomes and successful adaptation to school transitions. Therefore, the open attitude and willingness to encounter both life and learning in Britain is the main pre-requisite for overseas students' successful study abroad(Gill,2005).

Participants whose studying abroad was pushed by their decisive parents demonstrated less autonomy in their transition process. These students were not competent enough to interact with the new learning environment while studying abroad and thus unlikely to internalise their extrinsic motivation (Ryan and Deci,2002). Some of them, like Fang Fang and Xiao Jie, tried to avoid interaction completely. Their transition was accompanied by more anxiety, frustrations and even failures. The results agree with Koestner and Losier's(2002) arguments that introjections place students at risk when they are negotiating important developmental transition. Heightened psychological distress is connected to their transition(*ibid.*), as found in Fang Fang's case. In line with self-determination theory, these students, overly controlled by their parents, exhibited less initiative towards their study abroad and learned less well than those who were autonomously driven.

Evidence from this research agrees with Ryan and Deci's (2000) argument that support for the three basic psychological needs of relatedness, competence, and autonomy can enhance the internalisation of students' extrinsic motivation. Pre-departure preparation was an effective way of competence support, as well as a personal resource development for living abroad, lending power to the participants and building up their confidence and autonomy. It facilitated the participants to internalise the extrinsic motivation by improving their competence in coping with the changes in the new learning environment. Therefore, participants with intrinsic motivation or internalised extrinsic motivation showed great autonomy in their active preparation for the new learning environment. Participants with negative feelings towards studying abroad showed much less autonomy in pre-departure preparation than students who intended to stay longer in the UK. These students were more likely to accept 'positive feedback' from the previous students about the study in the UK. How to prepare these students for their study abroad needs further attention from the programme educators on both sides.

The findings of this research have supported the argument in the existing literature that pre-departure knowledge is crucial for sojourners' smooth transition abroad(Alred, 2003; Tsang, 2001; Black, 1988). The predictability of the new situation and students' anticipatory familiarity were increased by well-designed preparation activities conducted by sending and receiving universities, and this also reduced the uncertainty faced by the participants (Tsang, 2001). This, in a sense, enhanced their readiness and ability to be open and flexible in a new learning environment (Alred, 2003). Evidence shown in this research matches the findings of Zhou, Topping and Jindal-Snape (2009) which identified that pre-departure preparations can help Chinese international students' successful adaptation to the UK educational system. This study supports the findings of Gill(2005:232) that it is difficult for overseas Chinese students to cope with their challenges in the transition caused by a lack of preparation for academic culture and norms in British universities.

Bilingual education conducted at Southeast China University reflects the country's longing for *Zhuanye Waiyu Fuhexing Rencai*(talents with integrated skills in specialisation and a foreign language) to compete in the globalised world(Feng, 2005:540). It also demonstrates that English teaching in China has moved from pure linguistics to professional knowledge teaching through the media of English and Chinese. This has become a selling point for the Articulation Programmes and a way to make China's education system more competitive. As presented in Chapter 5, the practices in the programme had been conducted unevenly due to the language competence of the lecturers, attitudes towards bilingual education and the contents of the subjects. However, evidence showed that this approach was an effective way to prepare students' studying abroad. Teaching in English and Chinese had built a bridge between English terminology and Chinese concepts. Disciplinary knowledge and language skills were obtained simultaneously. This preparation helped students to overcome the initial difficulties in understanding academic language in the UK.

Early intervention aimed to prepare students academically, linguistically and psychologically for their further study in the UK, and ameliorated students' transition experience. Exposure to the authentic learning activities provided by staff from the receiving university had given students a chance to become familiar with approaches to teaching and learning and the requirements of UK education before their departure. This research argues that education transition is a mutual adaptation which is experienced by all the stakeholders in the transition process. The evidence supports Zhou and Todman's (2008) argument that international students' transition experience can be viewed as a reciprocal adaptation process between them and the staff at the host university. Meanwhile, the academic exchange between sending and receiving universities facilitated the participants' transition abroad. The exchange of information at staff level made the four years' teaching more coherent, which built an invisible bridge for Chinese students' transition.

Through cultural study before their departure, students became familiar with the signs or cues that might potentially lead to anxiety in the new environment abroad. The environment might be new, but it was no longer totally strange. This highlights the importance of preparation before departure. Sojourners are supposed to learn cultural differences in social interaction to fulfil their mission effectively abroad (Argyle, 1982: 63-69). Therefore, students coming from a globalised society are bombarded with information about different countries, especially those they intend to pursue their study in. For the Articulation Programme Students, a naivety of the host culture is unlikely to be true, as their intercultural contact starts in their study in the home country. The visiting of academic staff from the host country, language preparation with native-speakers, internet surfing and feedback from relatives or friends abroad all expose students to intercultural contact. Therefore, we cannot put them in an ethnocentric position even at the start of their transition experience. Chinese students on Articulation Programmes may experience the same difficulties that other international students face in their transitional stage. However, the cultural, linguistic and academic challenges faced by such students may have been decreased by the closing of the 'cultural gap' between their home context and the new context. Similarly, the closing of the 'language gap' and the 'academic gap' due to pre-departure preparation may also have an impact.

Different features on the new campus, classroom practices, and assessment requirements created new challenges for all students. Driven by different levels of autonomy, the participants developed different ways in interacting with the changes in the new learning environment. Three significant patterns (Direct Interaction, Indirect Interaction and Avoiding Interaction) representing the key types of experiences were identified. Among these three groups, students who interacted directly with the new learning environment had high levels of confidence in their ability to accomplish the learning abroad and produce desirable outcomes (Bandura, 1997). They demonstrated high resilience towards the highs and lows in the transition and believed that consequences were under their own personal control. Facing the distractions of easy access to the Internet and more privacy in accommodation, students in this group improved their self-management skills.

This research partly supports the argument that second language competency will influence international students' acculturation experience (Duru and Poyrazli, 2007; Lee, Koeske and Sales, 2004; Yeh and Inose, 2003; Poyrazli *et al.*, 2002; Mori, 2000). Language competence did have a connection with transition. The participants with higher language competence showed a willingness to ask for help, meet new people and participate in class discussions which, as proved by Duru and Poyrazli (2007), reduced the level of their acculturative stress. While some participants, like Xiao Yu and Xiao Yong, interacted with the new learning environment through their peers because of the lack of confidence in language. This supports MacIntyre's (1995) theory on recursive relations within anxiety, cognition, and behaviour. A lack of linguistic competence caused stress, which on the other hand affected their second language acquisition by blocking direct interaction with the learning environment. Some participants, like Fang Fang and Xiao Jie, retracted gradually when confronting language problems.

However, participants with lower language competence, but high level of autonomy, were observed to interact directly with the changes. For example, although Xiao Qiang's English was not good, he tried to communicate with staff via drawings and formulas. His deficiency in language did not hinder his direct interaction, which became a way for him to improve his language instead. The challenges stimulated him to adopt new strategies to enhance his abilities to cope with difficulties, and thus triggered his development and learning (Brooker, 2008: 7). Participants, like Xiao Feng, who spoke good English, avoided the interaction because of the lack of autonomy. When he did not find teachers at the office, he just gave up. This research argues that the language barrier is not the most significant problem for the participants, which conflicts with Mori's (2000) and Smalley's (1963) viewpoints. Instead, the sojourner's autonomy is crucial in their transition, and greatly influences their academic performance.

This research has found that social support is a facilitator for students' successful transition, which is consistent with the arguments of existing literature (Brown, 2009; Montgomery and McDowell, 2009; Duru and Poyrazli, 2007; Ye, 2006; Lee, Koeske and Sales, 2004; Yeh and Inose, 2003; Tsang, 2001; Searle and Ward, 1990; Adelman, 1988; Berry *et al.*, 1987; Bochner 1982). It assisted the participants' coping with uncertainty and enhanced their perceived mastery and control (Adelman, 1988). This was particularly important for those who were weak in English and interacted indirectly with the new environment. Compared with students who avoided the interaction completely, these students had higher connectedness and were more willing to seek help from other group members. This increased their social connections with social and academic environments and decreased their acculturative stress (Duru and Poyrazli, 2007; Lee and Robbins, 1998).

Consistent with Furnham and Bochner's (1982) international students' friendship pattern theories, a conational network was the most important social network in the participants' transition experience. The unique feature of the Articulation Programme, studying abroad as a group, bound the compatriot group together. Their conational network was largely within their own group formed in China. Therefore, it was more monocultural compared with other non-programme Chinese overseas students. This research, on one hand, found that the support by the conational group was the main effective source of support for Articulation Programme Students at the initial stage, which was consistent with the findings of Gill's (2007) and Li, Chen and Duanmu's (2010) studies. On the other hand, it identified that as time passed by, some of the participants, especially those interacting directly with the new environment built up their secondary network: bonds with host nationals, and a third network: multicultural friendship relationships. Thus, conational support became less dominant. These students obtained various network resources to deal with the difficulties in their transition. However, those who were in the Indirect Interaction group still relied largely on their compatriot group. They only had part of the resources: their Chinese classmates. To support these students, I agree with Bochner's (1982) argument that conational contacts should not be 'administratively interfered with, regulated against, obstructed, or sneered at' as they have served a very important function in international students' study transition. Those who were in the Avoiding Interaction group misused this kind of support, which verified the arguments that co-national relationships could be harmful (Ward, Bochner and Furnham, 2001), associated with more acculturative stress (Poyrazli *et al.*, 2004), and freeze international students' worldviews (Kosic *et al.*, 2004). Being indulgent and confined in this kind of monoculture limited these students' socialisation with the outside world.

The bicultural network and the multicultural circle were easily found in the Direct Interaction group. Their interactions with academic staff, working colleagues, flatmates, and other volunteers provided them with various channels to set up bonds with host nationals. Through direct interaction with the environment, participants built up various contacts with native or international contacts, such as Xiao Ming's relationship with his colleagues, Min Min's relationship with the volunteers, and Xiao Hua's relationship with his flatmates and football team players. These contacts enabled them to develop local networks, understand local cultures and acquire social skills. This facilitated their sociocultural adjustment process (Li and Gasser, 2005), helped overcome the initial challenges (Elsey, 1990; Gill, 2007) and alleviated their psychological adjustment (Kashima and Loh, 2006).

However, this research, as well as studies in the existing literature (Gu, Schweisfurth and Day, 2010; Montgomery, 2010; Middlehurst and Woodfield, 2007; Volet and Ang, 1998), has found that it is not easy for international students to make friends with host nationals. For instance, in this research, the multicultural classroom could have been an ideal place to set up these networks, but failed to be so due to the separation situation presented in Chapter 6. Internationally mixed accommodation, in Xiao Ming's case, also failed to be a place for students to get to know each other and build long-standing cross-cultural friendships, which has also been argued by the study of Bochner, Hutnik and Furnham (1985). Therefore, this research argues that simple exposure to a culturally-mixed environment cannot foster the intercultural competence and integration of international and home students. This has echoed the findings of Brown (2009), whose research does not uphold the claim of Hofstede (1991) that the presence of international visitors can foster cultural awareness in the host society.

Therefore, both sending and receiving universities should take more responsibility to help Articulation Programme Students build up bonds with members of the host and other international cultures. In this research, the receiving university set up specific arrangements to facilitate sojourners' settlement in the new environment, which have not reached their full potential. For instance, Fang Fang did not go to see the international advisors until she failed the academic year. Therefore, some 'taken-for-granted' methods may not be effective. Personalised support is therefore argued to give special help to those who are confronted with problems in transition.

The existing literature has suggested that international students under transition suffer a lot of stress from academic challenges in the host university

(Sovic, 2008; Ying, 2005). Evidence found in this research supports the argument that formative assessment can be a way to nurture students' transition by helping them cope with the challenges. The large proportion of formative assessment in the six modules(EN0213, EN0214, EN0215, EN0216, EN0217 and EN0219) transformed Yan Yan, Ling Ling and Li Li from students who did 'cram' for examinations to those who would work hard on their learning during the term, which facilitated their success in the transition. This supports Hussey and Smith's (2010) assertion that increasing proportions of formative assessment can be a guide to facilitate students' transfer from surface learning to deep learning, and is a means to monitor their transition. This is more important for students who are less autonomous in their learning especially those in the Avoiding Interaction group. More could be done to facilitate Articulation Programme Students' transition by assessment. The module of Project Design(EN0213) is an example which supports this argument.

First, the assessment task was an extension of the Course Design students had in the last semester in China. Students were looking forward to continuing this kind of tasks in the UK. Therefore, these assessment practices were bridged through which the two stages of teaching and learning were connected. Second, it was less risky compared with examinations, and had reduced students' stress. Being asked to write three reports and give one presentation together, students had more chances to accumulate the points. Third, it paid attention to the process rather than the results. During the learning process, timely feedback from the staff and peers was provided at weekly workshops, which not only benefited both teaching and learning (Biggs, 2003), but also avoided the problem caused by examinations: which were too late for early feedback (Light and Cox, 2001). Timely feedback enabled the participants to identify gaps by comparing their current performance with the assessment standards(Nicol and Macfarlane-Dick, 2006; Carless, 2003). Finally, as the only module that assessed students' attendance, it became a means to monitor the transition of the participants, especially those with low self-management skills. For instance, Fang Fang and

Xiao Jie, who had been absent from many classes, went to each of the workshops and made contributions to their group project. Considering these students' previous learning experience in China, this kind of assessment acted as a bridge for their transition abroad.

International students, especially those coming from collectivist societies, are connected closely with a concern about plagiarism in Western universities (Ryan, 2000). Chinese learners have been described as passive and rote learners, adopting surface learning styles, relying largely on mechanical memorisation without understanding and lacking creativity and original thinking (Ramburuth and McCormick, 2001). These are all considered by western scholars as low-level cognitive learning styles. As Feng (2009) has warned, these essentialist or reductionist views of culture are context dependent and cannot be generalised to all students. The nature of collectivist culture in China may have changed due to the 'One-Child Family Policy' and the independent and creative education in the last two decades. It might not be appropriate to view 'Chinese International students' as a fixed term nor to ignore the country's fast developing situation as well as the change in the sojourners' attributes before their arrival. Understanding international students' transition experience through their national cultures or cultures of learning will lead to the tendency of stereotyping individuals (Holliday, 2010; Montgomery, 2010; Feng, 2009; Tian, 2008; Gieve and Clark, 2005; Kumaravadivelu, 2003; Stephens, 1997).

Evidence in some studies (see Montgomery 2009; Peacock and Harrison, 2009) demonstrates how these stereotypes could influence students' integration in class to a certain extent. For example Montgomery's (2009) study shows that there is remaining evidence of negative stereotypes and prejudice about Chinese students, such as poor language competence and reluctance to contribute to group discussion. These opinions have prevented the formation of multicultural group work in her study. Peacock and Harrison (2009) also observed a specific issue of interaction between British students and Chinese students who were viewed to be 'the most culturally distant, to be the most likely to exhibit self-excluding behaviours, to have the poorest language skills, and to share the fewest cultural reference points' (p. 507).

Not all 'Chinese students' observed in this study shared the above features. Taking a microscope perspective on the participants' transition experience individually, I found the participants, especially those who were in Direct Interaction group, responded well to the new requirements of assessment practices in the host university. They demonstrated great ability to be independent and critical in their learning. The authentic assessment practices at both universities helped the students link the knowledge they learned in class to real life practice. Their so-called passive and cure-seeking behaviours have changed, which demonstrates that students' learning behaviours are not fixed, as described in the culture of learning. They can be changed in the same 'culture', but by different practices. It is largely up to how staff carry out their teaching and assessment practices.

7.3 Studying Abroad as a Group: Us & Them Unavoidable?

This research finds that the transition of this group of students was unavoidably affected by the unique feature of the Articulation Programme: studying abroad as a group. Their group formed earlier before coming to the UK when they were considered as a special group on the Chinese campus. As 'Students in Sino-British Class', they received a certain degree of discrimination and isolation on campus, which drove them to become a close group. When these students arrived at the English campus, they came across an existing cohort of students in class. Consistent with Social Identity Theory (Tajfel, 1981) and Self-Categorisation Theory (Turner *et al.*, 1987), this research finds that without structured intervention by the school and staff, the interaction between these two cohorts in the same class resulted in two social and psychological groups: Us & Them. Neither the sending nor the receiving universities informed their students about the possible change of classroom culture, which led to their quite negative feeling about their first meeting in the class. Being 'shocked' and 'overwhelmed' by the presence of the 'whole bunch of Chinese' sitting in the front, the existing cohort (predominantly British) felt 'vulnerable', 'irritated' and 'frustrated' in the newly merged classroom. This supports the argument of Bochner (1982) that cross-cultural contact can be either a threatening or an enhancing experience.

> It will be threatening if the other person is regarded as a deindividuated outsider intruding on a group's established territory, undermining the values and diluting the cultural identity of its member. The contact can also be enhancing, if the other person is regarded as a different but interesting individual, whose presence does not constitute a territorial infringement but instead an opportunity to learn something about the world at large (Bochner, 1982:37).

The size of a group is identified as a factor that has influenced the integration between international students and home students. In the classroom researched in this study, the group of Chinese students were numerically large, but home students were the dominant cultural group as part of the host culture in the university and country. A dominant cultural group tends to feel threatened by the presence of cultural minority groups whose size increases (Nesdale and Todd, 1998). Evidence from this study supports Peacock and Harrison's (2009) findings that where the ratio of international to home students is higher, less interaction between the groups is observed. Work groups tend to crystallise around national and language groupings.

This Chinese-dominant classroom was not in keeping with the Articulation Programme Students' expectation, and caused their feeling of being disappointed with the programme and their study abroad. These negative feelings were worsened by the competition for insufficient resources in this large and culturally dramatically changed classroom, such as seating and attention from the staff. This supports the experiment results of Sherif(1967) that the competition for insufficient resources will cause hostility between groups. Their cooperation in class, such as the assessment of the Group Project (EN0213), was conducted within their own groups. Therefore, the formation of groups not only influences the choice of friends, but also increases the solidarity and cooperativeness within each group (Sherif, 1967). Group work was mainly conducted monoculturally caused by the segregation in the class and the lack of structured intervention by staff. It failed to be an opportunity to prepare students to function in an international and inter-cultural context (De Vita, 2002; Volet and Ang, 1998; Knight and de Wit, 1995). I am reluctant to attribute the ‘monocultural’ phenomenon to ‘culture’. The Articulation Programme Students and the existing cohort chose their group members from their own group. As the group of the participants were all from China, their academic groups were indeed ‘monocultural’. However, the existing cohort, although mainly British, was more diverse in culture. They had students from other countries. Nina, a female student from Kuwait, was in a group with home students. Her group members were students who repeated the second year. These students knew each other very well and were willing to work together. Therefore, a lack of enough contact might be blamed for the ‘monocultural’ phenomenon. ‘Culture’ should not be over-emphasised in understanding the segregation in intercultural group work.

The ‘front-back’ seating became a visible geographic divide in the class. The different classroom behaviours in asking and answering questions split the two groups invisibly. The double-language barriers in the class hindered the peer learning in the class. These meaningful differences between the ingroup and the outgroup were perceived by the groups of students as the important attributes or common experience shared by their ingroup members, and contributed to the generalisation of their group identities (Schmitt, Spears and Branscombe, 2003). Once this social categorisation is done, the tendency for ingroup favouritism and outgroup derogation is evident (Hewstone, Rubin and Willis, 2002). When the group characteristics are prominent, individuals categorise themselves and others in terms of their belonging to groups and interact on intergroup behaviour rather than an interpersonal level (Byram, 2008).

Here, the findings support Gaertner and Dovidio's (1986) argument that seating is a factor in reducing group bias. Their research shows that manipulation of the seating arrangement can reduce group bias through changing group representations. Therefore, at the beginning of the academic year, staff could integrate the groups by arranging them in a mixed seating pattern. Poor group dynamics in the class can cause these students to become anxious, which leads to worry and rumination in answering questions in a second language (MacIntyre, 1995). The splitting situation was strengthened by the obstacle of communication: double-language barriers. As Byram (2008) argues, the presence of another language is one indicator of group difference, which accentuates the presence of group characteristics. The power of the number of the Chinese group in the class resulted in two main languages in the class: Chinese and English. Home students described their feeling as being intimidated by when surrounded by the Chinese language, even within their own country (the UK). For the existing cohort, not knowing the strangers' language and their perspectives caused anxiety and uncertainty (Gudykunst, 2005).

Evidence from this study suggests that international students who travel abroad individually are easier to integrate with home students than students travelling as a group. It is easier for the host nationals to accept them. This matches the findings of Zhou and Todman (2008) that students coming in a group have fewer chances to learn about a different culture and practice less in English than students coming individually. The possible reason might be that contact would appear to be best promoted in an unequal ration condition, and members of a minority group experience significantly more contact than members of equal-sized groups (Nesdale and Todd, 1998: 1210). This could partly explain the ingroup and outgroup distinction theories which are closely related to individuated-deindividuated distinction. As Bochner (1982: 35) has pointed out, 'deindividuated persons tend to be treated less favourably than individuated ones'. Hypothetically, outgroup members are more deindividuated than members of the ingroup, which leads to the further hypothesis that individuating the outgroup members could reduce discrimination against them (Bochner, 1982: 13). Decategorisation allows members of each group to perceive each other as separate individuals and thus enhance the integration.

Compared with home students, Chinese students were more disappointed with the divide in the class, especially those with high expectations to make friends with British students. For home students, they had their own life, friends, and family members in their country. Some of them borrowed loans from the government and had to do a part-time job to cover the expenses. The motivation of their taking the Engineering course was to find a job after graduation. There was no 'luxury' time for them to hang out with the Articulation Programme Students who had more spare time. Making friends with international students was not their 'centre of gravity' in their social lives and motivations (Montgomery, 2010), and was limited by their economic situation.

The separation in the class had an impact on the learning of both sides. As Chickering and Reisser (1993) argue, a student's most important teacher is often another student. However, both groups did not know how to break the ice to ask for help. Peer learning was constrained within their own groups. The isolation might affect their self-confidence, as some of them felt uneasy sitting in a class in such a manner. Both the Articulation Programme Students and the existing cohort demonstrated willingness to know each other, which was a great contradiction to the current segregation in the class. Both groups showed their understanding of the benefit of integration on their learning experience and future career. However, they were still wired into their own group. The helplessness in breaking the circle reviews a gap in the pre-departure preparation. Currently, it has involved the Chinese Articulation Programme Students and the British staff. The current situation asks educators and policy-makers to engage the existing cohort, mostly home students, in the process as well. As an influential part of the class, the preparation for this cohort's readiness in communicating with new-comers will not only have impact on the Articulation Programme students' transition experience, but also the success of the programme as a whole. Meanwhile, the increasing tuition fees paid by home students require universities to take care of their benefits as customers as well. They argued from the customers' perspectives that the school should take more responsibility in promoting the integration (see also Peacock and Harrison, 2009).

A lack of preparedness for both groups and early structured intervention, such as icebreaking activities, means the integration of the two groups in the class is hard to realise, leading to separation and bias. The status of separation and bias strengthened the distinction between in and outgroup membership. This research cannot predict that with proper preparation and structured activities, the 'Us' and 'Them' phenomenon can be avoided. This research is a preliminary study to explore the impact of a large group of Chinese students in an overseas classroom. The intention is to raise the level of attention given to the issue and invite more research studies in this area. The following solutions suggested can be viewed as initial proposals for guidance to enhance the integration in the intercultural classroom.

The first solution to enhance the integration in this multinational class is to develop a common ingroup identity by creating the 'We'. As discussed in Chapter 3, Gaertner and Dovidio's (2000) Common Ingroup Identity Model based on the idea of recategorisation of different groups into one group might be useful in diminishing the discrimination between groups. The Articulation Programme Students, and the existing cohort share a common superordinate category (Engineering students on the same campus). Gaertner and Dovidio (2000: 48) propose that increasing the salience of existing common superordinate memberships, such as a school or introducing factors like common goals, can achieve common ingroup identity. Once this kind of identity is perceived, more positive thoughts, feelings, and behaviours are believed to develop toward the former outgroup members (*ibid.*). Within this positive context, more elaborate and personalised impressions will soon develop (*ibid.*). Setting up a common ingroup identity can make both sides feel part of the community and thus enhance their commitment to the university, as suggested by the findings of Dovidio *et al.* (2001:177). They are more willing to recommend the university to others and have higher intention to complete their degree at that university (Snider and Dovidio, 1996, cited in Gaertner and Dovidio, 2000: 140). By expanding the inclusiveness of one's ingroup to include students who would otherwise be considered as outgroup members, the perceptions of the memberships can be transformed from subordinate 'Us' and 'Them' to a more inclusive superordinate 'We' (Gaertner and Dovidio, 2000; Gaertner, Dovidio and Bachman, 1996). The likelihood of positive interracial behaviours is supposed to be increased, and the intergroup attitudes (prejudice), cognition (stereotypes) and behaviour (discrimination) can be decreased (Dovidio *et al.*, 2001). In the process of transforming the perceptions of the memberships from subordinate 'Us' and 'Them' to a more inclusive superordinate 'We' (Gaertner, Dovidio and Bachman, 1996; Gaertner and Dovidio, 2000), we cannot presume that the distinction of two groups will vanish completely. 'The distinction between "us" and "them" can be blurred which results in a stage where people become partially "them", i. e. incorporate some of "their" characteristics without however losing their own ethnic identity' (Bochner, 1982: 37). Considering the fact that the Articulation Programme Students have been in a close group for two years, it is impossible for them to abandon their own group identity completely. Therefore, they could keep their identity as 'Sino-British Articulation Programme Students' while developing the Common Ingroup Identity with the existing cohort as 'Engineering students' on the same campus. During the process, personalised intergroup interactions are encouraged for them to know each other individually.

Building a low-stake learning environment can be another way to improve the communication between the two groups of students. Cross-cultural group work may be seen as sufficient to promote the integration of international students and host nationals in a multicultural class. However, this research finds that when students are assessed by group work, the desire to have a mixed-culture group is given lower priority than academic performance. Both groups had the same concerns about working with students from other groups (rather than simply being divided by nationality). Both sides worried that a lack of familiarity with each other's past performance and the language barrier could prevent effective group work and pull down their grades. Unbalanced numbers made the minority group (not Chinese in this case) feel intimidated and excluded. It was a kind of protection for them to form their own group to conduct group projects. These barriers prevented them from stepping forward to get to know the other group. Other studies (Strauss, U and Young, 2011; Peacock and Harrison, 2009; Volet and Ang, 1998) have also identified the same phenomena.

Therefore, this research argues that more effective group work conducted in low stakes assessment environments could enable students to perceive the strength of working in multicultural groups. Low stakes assessment environments created by formative assessment can exert a positive influence on students' perceptions of intercultural group work (Montgomery, 2009). This kind of structured interventions can be taken at the start of their meeting in the class. As Bochner (1982:20) has commented, 'the better we get to know other people the more do we come to regard them as we regard ourselves'. Without this, the unfamiliarity between each group will hinder the possibility of facilitating intergroup integration through academic group work. This kind of cooperation should be a series of activities to produce a cumulative effect rather than a one-off event (Sherif, 1967). This can explain why the effort some staff members devoted, such as organising football matches, produced a very weak effect.

14 out of 50 Articulation Programme Students achieved over 70% in the group project. Students' final assessment results also showed that the standard of the course had been improved owing to the Chinese students' participation. This can provide strong evidence to dismiss the concern that the presence of

international students might reduce academic standards at the host university (See Devos, 2003). My participants' positive achievement in the group project can be the evidence to remove the stereotypes that may act as barriers to the development of educationally rich and rewarding inter-cultural interactions via multicultural group work (De Vita, 2002: 159). Therefore, more effective design of group work could be conducted to enable students to perceive the strength of working in multicultural groups. This will eliminate their concerns about the complexities of working with students from different countries and improve their intercultural competence.

In the process of reducing intergroup bias, enhancing intercultural competence can be an additional facilitator. Students are likely to have intercultural experience when they meet others from different social groups with different values, beliefs and behaviours (Byram, 2008: 206). Studying in a multicultural environment could be a valuable opportunity for students to develop intercultural competence. The participants' social experience in the new learning environment shows that their attendance as a group arouses group awareness in the existing cohort as well. In the sudden culturally changed environment, their socialisation in the class whilst acting as groups provides them with a sense of security and enhances favouritism towards insider group members (Tajfel, 1981). This formation of ingroups also provides opportunities for experience of otherness, other groups' cultures including their conventions, beliefs, values and behaviours (Alred, Byram and Fleming, 2003). Therefore, the intergroup encounter experience encourages students to question the given conventions and values within their group and will lead students to become 'intercultural' (*ibid.*).

However, experience alone is not enough. As Alred, Byram and Fleming (2003: 4) have pointed out, the experience of otherness only creates a potential for questioning the taken-for-granted aspects of one's own self and environment, but being intercultural requires more than that:

> It is the capacity to reflect on the relationships among groups

> and the experience of those relationships. It is both the awareness of experiencing otherness and the ability to analyse the experience and act upon the insights into self and other which the analysis brings (Alred, Byram and Fleming, 2003:4).

Therefore, reflection, analysis and action are also necessary apart from experience. Although there is some evidence that students experienced some level of the intercultural experience, the defensive attitudes towards each other in the classroom hindered the potential integration and cultivation of the ability to reflect on the relationships among groups and the experience of those relationships. The findings of this research are in line with the study of Savicki (2008) in suggesting that adequate preparation is necessary for learners' intercultural competence.

Findings in this research demonstrate that both the Chinese students and the UK cohort expressed a high level of interest in getting to know each other. However, some knowledge and skills are necessary to function effectively in this type of multicultural class and adequate preparation is necessary for learners' intercultural competence (Savicki, 2008). As Volet and Ang (1998) have argued, successful intercultural contact can only be achieved if both parties are prepared to make it work. Currently, the pre-departure preparation in China included English language teaching with the aim to increase language competence. It also included some elements of cultural learning and an appreciation of the similarities and differences between British and Chinese culture, which focused more on static facts rather than process knowledge. Consistent and holistic training on intercultural competence has not been carried out. In addition, the home student cohort did not benefit from the preparation. Intercultural competence education should be one important part of the preparation for both parties in Articulation Programmes. Being interculturally competent can help students to break the ice, move out of their own circles and become more integrated. As Byram (2008: 69) has pointed out, acting interculturally requires members of both groups to be willing to suspend their deeper values acquired in early socialisation in order to understand and empathise with the values of others that are incompatible with one's own. Both partner universities need to provide training to enhance students' abilities to become ' aware of cultural similarities and differences ' , and able to ' act as mediator between two or more cultures, two or more sets of beliefs, values and behaviours ' (Byram, 2008 : 75).

The study supports Byram's (2008) argument that the success of interaction is dependent on both groups of interlocutors involved in intercultural communication. To provide constructive solutions for intercultural integration, we need to define ' interlocutors ' in the context of transnational articulation programmes. The situation is more complex than in cases where students travel as individuals. The parties not only include both groups of students, but the two teaching teams in sending universities and receiving universities. Many research studies argue that institutions play a critical role in fostering positive intercultural interactions amongst all students, and the responsibilities for the lack of interaction should be shared between home students and international students (Denson and Zhang, 2010; Sovic, 2009; Volet and Ang, 1998). This is correct beyond all doubt. The institution, in the form of the senior management, can set up and support agreements with overseas institutions and take steps to foster an international ethos on campus. However, most of what affects students directly happens within their programme and with their immediate peers. While students may have some concerns, it is likely that they will accept the situation as they find it, unless there is some clear and obvious way to raise issues and propose action. This is probably why the issue remains intractable and still puzzles many educators and researchers in this area. In fact, between the management level and the student group, there is an influential body which is more concrete, direct and effective—the staff teaching team. This is where development could most usefully take place.

To facilitate the intercultural integration in a transnational articulation programme, the coherence in both teaching and management is a key influential factor. A better understanding between the two teaching teams will benefit the integration amongst students. The harmonious understanding is formalised at the management level when signing up numerous memoranda and contracts to set up the transnational educational programmes. The universities could also provide more opportunities for academic exchange, design cooperative modules for both teams of staff to lecture together and conduct collaborative research projects. The two teaching teams themselves can adopt some creative solutions to facilitate the integration of their students. Before students meet in the UK, both teams can develop intercultural competence education in their courses. With more opportunities for academic exchange, academics can give seminars in both countries. They can design some modules to involve both of the groups. This can readily be facilitated by e-learning approaches. Steps could be taken to allocate each Articulation Programme Student an e-learning system account as soon as they enrol in the programme in their home country. A space could be set up on the e-learning platform for the two groups of students and staff to exchange information. Activities focussing on the common interests and concerns of engineering students across national boundaries would foster the process of changing 'Us' and 'Them' to 'We'. This could support staff and students on both sides of the articulation partnership to get to know each other. It would enable some relationships to be formed before the groups join for their final two years of study and students could start to develop their intercultural competence.

When two groups of students first meet in the class, staff at the host universities can conduct structured interventions, such as mixing seating, building in time for group discussion, and producing a low-stake assessment environment to support students to undertake group work in mixed cultures. The Schools can organise some social activities outside the classroom for their students to foster long-term friendship, which has been argued as an effective way to solidify learning about culture and to reduce anxieties (Harrison and Peacock, 2009). To enhance the intercultural integration needs more joint effort from the universities, staff, and the students to promote an ideal intercultural campus and classroom.

7.4 Transition and the Impact on the Teaching and Learning Context at Two Campuses

The transition experience of the Chinese Articulation Programme Students and the intention to facilitate this transition has an impact on both universities, making the two teaching and learning contexts more connected. As presented in Chapter 2, the Articulation Programme, as one of the formats in Chinese-Foreign Cooperation in Running Schools (CFCRS), is encouraged by the Chinese Government to introduce high quality education resources from cooperative universities abroad. Southeast China University takes this as a way to extend their international cooperation and thus improve their teaching and research. North Britain University also values the Articulation Programme Students' contribution to their revenue and the internationalisation of their university culture. Therefore, both universities start to link with each other closely. The exchange of information at a staff level makes the four years' teaching more coherent, which is a way of building an invisible bridge for Chinese students' transition. Teaching and learning has become more internationalised at both universities. In agreement with Zhou and Todman (2008), evidence from this research shows that participants' transition experience has an impact on the teaching at the host university. The presence of this large cohort of Chinese students has motivated some of the academic staff to modify their teaching to adjust to their learning, not only because of their weak points but because of their strengths as well. Both staff and students adjusted their teaching and learning strategies in the process of adaptation, which resulted in gains for both parties (*ibid.*).

The current research also adds a new dimension to Zhou and Todman's (2008) work by including the perspectives of home students and other international students to triangulate the findings. The impact on peer learning is an important finding. The adjustment carried out by British staff to support

Articulation Programme Students' transition has caused some complaints from the other students in class. The social disintegration and unfamiliarity amongst students at the initial stage hindered the peer learning. Meanwhile, studying with Chinese students enables home students to reflect on their past learning experiences and this highlights a gap among secondary school, college and university education, which could be a potential obstacle to young people studying Engineering. This verifies the argument of Lam's (2006) research in Hong Kong that sojourners' adaption process is a reciprocal adjustment between them and their local counter-parts. These findings remind us that we should never overlook the impact of sojourners on local people and local culture (Byram and Feng, 2006). The strength of the large group culture has influenced the teaching and learning practices at the UK partner university, which has meant that change also occurred in the host context. Instead of passively adapting to the learning culture in the UK, the large group of Chinese students, who have become the majority in the classroom, actively influence the teaching and learning practices in the university. Thus, international students are no longer being considered as a source of income generation and as problematic, but as 'a source of cultural capital and intentional diversity, enriching the learning experience both for home students and for one other, expanding staff horizons, building a more powerful learning community and thus deepening the HE experience as a whole' (Brown and Jones, 2007: 2). Therefore, where there are carefully planned and well-designed bridging programmes, change becomes a two-way process.

7.5 Conclusions

This study aims to explore transnational Articulation Programme Students' transition experience between the educational context in China and the UK, with the objectives to investigate the factors that have influenced students' transition and the impact of students' transition on the educational context at both universities. The main research question of this study is: How do Chinese

Articulation Programme Students experience their transitional stage from China to the UK?

This research finds that international students' transition experience is a complex journey and cannot be oversimplified by any of the existing models. Understanding their transition experience from the perspectives of national cultural theory or culture of learning theory is more likely to fall into the trap of stereotyping. Therefore, a microscopic perspective focusing on individual factors together with a contextual perspective focusing on situational factors are suggested to make a better understanding of their intercultural transition. The findings indicate that Articulation Programme Students' transition experience is an individual process, in which they construct their own third space in confronting changes in the new learning environment. The process of transition is influenced by their personal factors, such as motivations for studying abroad, attitudes towards pre-departure preparation, language competence and autonomy, as well as situational factors, such as social support and formative assessment practices. Autonomy was identified as more crucial in transition than language competence. In their different responses to the new learning environment, three broad categories that represent the key types of experience were identified: Direct Interaction, Indirect Interaction, and Avoiding Interaction. Many factors, such as 'Internet', 'Privacy' and 'Peer support', can be 'double-edged' in that they can have negative or positive impacts depending upon the student's transition response.

These students' transition experiences have great impact on the learning environment. A lack of proper interventions at the initial stage, the competition for insufficient resources, double-language barriers and the different questioning behaviour in the class lead these two groups of students to self-categorise themselves into 'Us' and 'Them'. The separation in the class has a negative impact on the peer learning in the class. Both groups demonstrate a willingness to integrate with each other. Therefore, developing a low-stake learning environment, enhancing intercultural competence and developing Common Ingroup Identity (Engineering students on campus in this case) are suggested to promote integration in class. The transition experience of the Chinese Articulation Programme Students and the intention to facilitate this transition have impact on both universities, making the two teaching and learning contexts more connected and internationalised. The exchange of information at staff level makes the four years' teaching more coherent, and is a way of building an invisible bridge for Chinese students' transition.

This study has made contributions to the existing knowledge in the following facets:

First, it focuses on the intercultural transition experience of transnational Articulation Programme Students, which is an under-studied area due to the complexity of the new phenomenon of Transnational Higher Education. The findings have implications for global cooperation as such not confined to China and the UK.

Second, it advances the understanding of international students' transition experience by extending the scope of perspectives from international students only to other stakeholders in the process, such as home students, parents, academic staff and administrative staff at both universities. The intention of including various voices in the study is to provide a comprehensive and holistic understanding of the phenomenon by triangulating the themes generated from the grounded data.

Third, this study pays attention to the process by propelling the research time range forward to the last semester in China. 15 months' fieldwork in China and the UK provides educators on both sides with an in-depth analysis of the learning experience of the Articulation Programme Students including their motivations for studying abroad and attitudes towards pre-departure preparation.

Fourth, the unique feature of the Articulation Programme, i. e. studying abroad as a group, provides a precious chance for intercultural research to explore the interaction with home students and the impact of a large cohort of Chinese students on the teaching and learning environment on the host university. The findings generated in this research contribute to the existing knowledge which focuses on the international students' transition individually.

Fifth, the diversities in the participants' transition experiences challenge the cultural stereotype posed on the homogeneous address of Chinese students abroad and lend strong support to the argument that the transition experience is not culturally determined, but depends largely on students' autonomy, guided by their personal agency. Situational factors, such as social support and formative assessment practices, can facilitate their transition, but their usefulness depends on students' autonomy and response to what is on offer.

Finally, it develops a conceptual model of intercultural transition grounded in the theories of motivation, autonomy, second language learning, intercultural competence, and social identity to provide an explanation of the process of transition. This model includes both personal and social dimensions in which the social groups operate in China and the UK. It is not just about how individuals make the transition experience, but considers the broader social context and the wider material context. This detailed explanatory model is situated in the day-to-day lived experience of students and staff, rather than relying on a small number of structural variables to explain and model the learning experience.

This research portrays a comprehensive picture of the Articulation Programme Students' experience in their transitional stage from China to the UK. The findings provided some useful suggestions for policy makers and teaching staff on how to bridge the two stages of teaching and learning effectively and how to successfully facilitate students' transition. The stakeholders in the transition experience can benefit from the findings generated from this study.

For students who are going to take Transnational Higher Education programmes, their willingness to take the action and their confidence in performing the tasks are very important. Meanwhile, the pre-departure preparation deserves great attention in order to generate familiarity with the academic culture of the partner university, build up language and intercultural competence, and also develop psychological confidence to cope with the challenges in the transition. They are suggested to make direct interaction with the new learning environment, demonstrate high autonomy, enlarge their group circle to include others, and avoid binding with their own group all the time.

For home students at the receiving university, they are suggested to understand the benefits of studying in a multinational classroom. To improve the integration in the class, they need to take initiative to talk to and work with the international students, improve their intercultural competence to become a better interlocutor for international students, and thus become a global citizen. Meanwhile, it is important for them to suspend the stereotypes depicted in the media or traditional ideology on international students and get to know these students individually.

For the two staff teams involved in the transnational cooperation, they are suggested to adjust teaching practices to facilitate students' transition. For instance, the staff at the sending universities could make full use of the academic exchange to become familiar with the teaching and learning practices at the receiving universities. They are suggested to understand students' future development at the secondary stage abroad and increase the percentage of formative assessment in teaching. The staff at the receiving universities are suggested to take more responsibility in students' pre-departure preparation. They can conduct a whole process of teaching, including assessment practices, to become more familiar with students' previous learning experience. Both teams work together to make the four years' teaching more coherent. In facilitating the integration in a multi-cultural class, staff at the host universities can carried out structured interventions, such as mixing seating, building in time for group discussion, and producing a low-stake assessment environment to support students to perform group work in mixed cultures.

For policy-makers at both universities, they are suggested to provide more opportunities for academic exchange. For instance, they could design cooperative modules for two teams of staff to lecture together. This might be more helpful for the two staff teams to become familiar with each other's teaching practices. Collaborative research projects could also be conducted to improve the quality of the cooperation. In promoting the integration in the class, both organisations are suggested to include intercultural competence education in their courses. They could also design some modules to involve both of the groups in the first year. New ways of group work could be carried out to facilitate the distance cooperation. For instance, this could include making full use of the E-learning Portal.

Three issues have been identified for future research.

How to prepare students to study abroad, especially those who are under difficult transition?

How to build a low-stake learning environment through formative assessment to enhance integration in a multicultural class?

How to create the inclusive 'We' in a class with a high ratio of international students?

Although this research has tried to discuss the above issues based on the relevant theories, it did not give systematic suggestions due to the lack of empirical evidence. Relevant studies could be done to extend this research.

Against the background that transnational cooperation in higher education is becoming increasingly common in the globalised world, this study invites the attention to focus on the intercultural transition experiences of the students with the aim to improve the teaching and learning practices in Transnational Higher Education. It demonstrates that the transition is a complex journey which can trigger development as well as demolish confidence. The consequences of the transition are various and depend on factors in personal and social dimensions. This research encourages studies examining the journeys of transition to take a microscopic perspective focusing on individual factors together with a contextual perspective focusing on situational factors to avoid the trap of stereotyping.

References

Adelman, M. B. (1988) 'Cross-cultural Adjustment: a Theoretical Perspective on Social Support', *International Journal of Intercultural Relations*, 12(3), pp. 183 - 204.

Adler, P. (1975) 'The Transitional Experience: an Alternative View of Culture Shock', *Journal of Humanistic Psychology*, 15(4), pp. 13 - 23.

Allen, H. W. and Herron, C. (2003) 'A Mixed-Methodology Investigation of the Linguistic and Affective Outcomes of Summer Study Abroad', *Foreign Language Annals*, 36(3), pp. 370 - 385.

Allport, G. W. (1954) *The Nature of Prejudice*. Massachusetts: Addison-Wesley.

Alred, G. (2003) 'Becoming a "Better Stranger": a Therapeutic Perspective on Intercultural Experience and/as Education', in Alred, G., Byram, M. and Fleming, M. (eds.) *Intercultural Experience and Education*. Clevedon: Multilingual Matters LTD, pp. 14 - 30.

Alred, G., Byram, M. and Fleming, M. (2003) 'Introduction', in Alred, G., Byram, M. and Fleming, M. (eds.) *Intercultural Experience and Education*. Clevedon: Multilingual Matters LTD, pp. 1 - 13.

Altbach, P. G. (2009) 'The Giants Awake: The Present and Future of Higher Education Systems in China and India', in *Higher Education to* 2030: *Vol. 2 Globalisation*. OECD, pp. 179 - 203.

Altbach, P. G. and Knight, J. (2007) 'The Internationalization of Higher Education: Motivations and Realities', *Journal of Studies in International Education*, 11(3 - 4), pp. 290 - 305.

Argyle, M. (1982) 'Inter-cultural communication', in Bochner, S. (ed.) *Cultures in Contact: Studies in Cross-cultural Interaction: Vol.* 1. Oxford: Pergamon Press, pp. 61 – 79.

Assessment Reform Group (2002) *Testing, Motivation and Learning.* [Online]. Available at: http://arg. educ. cam. ac. uk/TML%20BOOKLET%20complete. pdf(Accessed:23 April,2007).

Bandura, A. (1997) *Self-efficacy: The Experience of Control.* New York: W. H. Freeman and Company.

Bennell, P. and Pearce, T. (2003) 'The internationalisation of higher education: exporting education to developing and transitional economies', *International Journal of Educational Development*, 23, pp. 215 – 232.

Bennett, M. J. (1986) 'A Developmental Approach to Training for Intercultural Sensitivity', *International Journal of Intercultural Relations*, 10, pp. 179 – 196.

Berdrow, I. (2009) 'Designing effective global competence development opportunities', *International Journal of Management in Education*, 3 (3/4), pp. 335 – 345.

Berry, J. W. (1997) 'Immigration, Acculturation, and Adaptation', *Applied Psychology: an International Review*, 46(1), pp. 5 – 68.

Berry, J. W. (2006) 'Contexts of acculturation', in Sam, D. and Berry, J. (eds.) *The Cambridge Handbook of Acculturation Psychology.* New York: Cambridge University Press, pp. 27 – 42.

Berry, J. W., Kim, U., Minde, T. and Mok, D. (1987) 'Comparative Studies of Acculturative Stress', *International Migration Review*, 21 (3), pp. 491 – 511.

Berry, J. W. and Sam, D. L. (1997) 'Acculturation and Adaptation', in Berry, J. W., Segall, M. H. and Kagitcibasi, C. (eds.) *Handbook of Cross-Cultural Psychology: Vol. 3 Social Behavior and Applications.* 2nd edn. London: Allyn and Bacon, pp. 291 – 326.

Biggs, J. (2003) *Teaching for Quality Learning at University.* 2nd edn. Berkshire: Open University Press.

Billing, D. (1997) 'Induction of New Students to Higher Education', *Innovations in Education and Teaching International*, 34 (2), pp. 125 – 134.

Black, J. S. (1988) 'Work role transitions: A study of American expatriate managers in Japan', *Journal of International Business Studies*, 19, pp. 277 – 294.

Blaikie, N. (2007) *Approaches to Social Enquiry: Advancing Knowledge*. 2nd edn. Cambridge: Polity Press.

Bochner, S. (1982) 'The social psychology of cross-cultural relations', in Bochner, S. (ed.) *Cultures in Contact: Studies in Cross-cultural Interaction: Vol.* 1. Oxford: Pergamon Press, pp. 5 – 44.

Bochner, S., Hutnik, N. and Furnham, A. (1985) 'The Friendship Patterns of Overseas and Host Students in an Oxford Student Residence', *The Journal of Social Psychology*, 125 (6), pp. 689 – 694.

Brewer, J. D. (2000) *Ethnography*. Buckingham: Open University Press.

Brewer, M. B. (1996) 'When Contact is not Enough: Social Identity and Intergroup Cooperation', *International Journal of Intercultural Relations*, 20 (3/4), pp. 291 – 303.

British Council (2013) *The Shape of things to come. Research report.* [Online]. Available at http://www.britishcouncil.org/sites/britishcouncil.uk2/files/the_shape_of_things_to_come_2.pdf (Accessed: 13 January, 2014).

Brockington, J. L. and Wiedenhoeft, M. D. (2009) 'The Liberal Arts and Global Citizenship: Fostering Intercultural Engagement through Integrative Experiences and Structured Reflection', in Lewin, R. (ed.) *The Handbook of Practice and Research in Study Abroad: Higher Education and the Quest for Global Citizenship*. New York: Routledge, pp. 117 – 132.

Brooker, L. (2008) *Supporting Transitions in the Early Years*. Berkshire: Open University Press.

Brown, L. (2009) 'A Failure of Communication on the Cross-Cultural Campus', *Journal of Studies in International Education*, 13 (4), pp. 439 – 454.

Brown, L. and Holloway, I. (2007) 'The initial stage of the international sojourn: excitement or culture shock?', *British Journal of Guidance and Counselling*, 36(1), pp. 33 – 49.

Brown, S. and Jones, E. (2007) 'Introduction: Values, valuing and value in an internationalised Higher Education context', in Jones, E. and Brown, S. (eds.) *Internationalising Higher Education*. Oxon: Routledge, pp. 1 – 6.

Bryman, A. (2008) *Social Research Methods*. 3rd edn. New York: Oxford University Press.

Burnett, C. and Gardner, J. (2006) 'The One Less Travelled By ...: The Experience of Chinese Students in a UK University', in Byram, M. and Feng, A. (eds.) *Living and Studying Abroad*. Clevedon: Multilingual Matters Ltd., pp. 64 – 90.

Burr, V. (2003) *Social Constructionism*. 2nd edn. East Sussex: Routledge.

Byram, M. (1997) *Teaching and Assessing Intercultural Communicative Competence*. Clevedon: Multilingual Matters LTD.

Byram, M. (2008) *From Foreign Language Education to Education for Intercultural Citizenship: Essays and Reflections*. Clevedon: Multilingual Matters.

Byram, M. and Feng, A. (2006) 'Introduction', in Byram, M. and Feng, A. (eds.) *Living and Studying Abroad*. Clevedon: Multilingual Matters Ltd., pp. 1 – 10.

Carless, D. (2003) 'Putting the learning into assessment', *The Teacher Trainer*, 17(3), pp. 14 – 18.

Central People's Government of People's Republic of China (2010) *National Plan for Medium and Long-term Education Reform & Development* (2010 – 2020). [In Chinese]. [Online]. Available at: http://www.gov.cn/jrzg/2010-07/29/content_1667143.htm (Accessed: 2 October, 2010).

Chan, W. W. Y. (2004) 'International Cooperation in Higher Education: Theory and Practice', *Journal of Studies in International Education*, 8(1), pp. 32 – 55.

Charmaz, K. (2006) *Constructing Grounded Theory: a Practical Guide through Qualitative Analysis*. London: Sage Publications.

Charmaz, K. and Mitchell, R. G. (2001) 'Grounded Theory in Ethnography', in Atkinson, P., Coffey, A., Delamont, S., Lofland, J. and Lofland, L. (eds.) *Handbook of Ethnography*. London: Sage Publications, pp. 160 – 174.

Cheng, X. (2002) 'Chinese EFL students' cultures of learning', in Lee, C. and Littlewood, W. (eds.) *Culture, communication and language pedagogy*. Hong Kong: Hong Kong Baptist University Press, pp. 103 – 116.

Chickering, A. W., and Reisser, L. (1993) *Education and Identity*. 2nd edn. San Francisco: Jossey-Bass Publishers.

China-Eu School of Law (2010) *About CESL*. [Online]. Available at: http://www.cesl.edu.cn/eng/ecslintro.asp (Accessed: 7 August, 2010).

Chirkov, V., Vansteenkiste, M., Tao, R. and Lynch, M. (2007) 'The role of self-determined motivation and goals for study abroad in the adaptation of international students', *International Journal of Intercultural Relations*, 31, pp. 199 – 222.

Chow, G. C. (2007) *China's Economic Transformation*. 2nd edn. Oxford: Blackwell Publishing.

Coffey, A. (1999) *The ethnographic self: fieldwork and the representation of identity*. London: Sage Publications.

Conner, D. R. (1998) *Managing at the Speed of Change: How Resilient Managers Succeed and Prosper Where Others Fail*. Chichester: John Wiley and Sons.

Cook, S. W. (1985) 'Experimenting on Social Issues: the Case of School Desegregation', *American Psychologist*, 40, pp. 452 – 460.

Corbin, J. and Strauss, A. (2008) *Basics of Qualitative Research*. 3rd edn. Thousand Oaks: Sage Publications.

Cortazzi, M. and Jin, L. (1996a) 'Cultures of learning: Language classrooms in China', in Coleman, H. (ed.) *Society and the Language Classroom*. Cambridge: Cambridge University Press, pp. 169 – 206.

Cortazzi, M. and Jin, L. (1996b) 'English teaching and learning in China', *Language Teaching*, 29(2), pp. 61 – 80.

Cortazzi, M. and Jin. L. (1997) 'Communication for learning across cultures', in McNamara, D. and Harris, R. (eds.) *Overseas Students in Higher Education: Issues in Teaching and Learning*. London: Routledge, pp. 76 – 90.

Cowie, B. and Bell, B. (1999) 'A model for formative assessment', *Assessment in Education*, 6(1), pp. 101 – 116.

Creswell, J. W. (2003) *Research Design: Qualitative, Quantitative, and Mixed Methods Approaches*. 2nd edn. Thousand Oaks: Sage Publications.

Creswell, J. W. (2007) *Qualitative Inquiry & Research Design: Choosing Among Five Approaches*. 2nd edn. Thousand Oaks: Sage Publications.

Creswell, J. W. (2009) *Research Design: Qualitative, Quantitative, and Mixed Methods Approaches*. 3rd edn. Thousand Oaks: Sage Publications.

Crotty, M. (1998) *The Foundations of Social Research: Meaning and Perspective in the Research Process*. London: Sage Publications.

De Vita, G. (2002) 'Does assessed multicultural group work really pull UK students' average down?', *Assessment & Evaluation in Higher Education*, 27, pp. 153 – 161.

Deardorff, D. K. (2009) 'Preface', in Deardorff, D. K. (ed.) *The Sage Handbook of Intercultural Competence*. Thousand Oaks: Sage Publications, pp. xi – xiv.

DeBerard, M. S., Spielmans, G. I. and Julka, D. L. (2004) 'Predictors of academic achievement and retention among college freshmen: a longitudinal study', *College Student Journal*, 38(1), pp. 66 – 80.

Deci, E. L., Connell, J. P. and Ryan, R. M. (1989) 'Self-determination in a work organization', *Journal of Applied Psychology*, 74, pp. 580 – 590.

Deci, E. L., Nezlek, J. and Sheinman, L. (1981) 'Characteristics of the rewarder and intrinsic motivation of the rewardee', *Journal of Personality and Social Psychology*, 40, pp. 1 – 10.

Deci, E. L. and Ryan, R. M. (2009) 'Self-determination theory: a consideration of human motivational universals', in Corr, P. J. and Matthews, G. (eds.) *The Cambridge Handbook of Personality Psychology*. New York: Cambridge University Press, pp. 441 – 456.

Deegan, M. J. (2007) 'The Chicago School of Ethnography', in Atkinson, P., Coffey, A., Delamont, S., Lofland, J. and Lofland, L. (eds.) *Handbook of Ethnography*. London: Sage Publications, pp. 11 – 25.

Denson, N. and Zhang, S. (2010) 'The impact of student experiences with diversity on developing graduate attributes', *Studies in Higher Education*, 35(5), pp. 529 – 543.

Devos, A. (2003) 'Academic Standards, Internationalisation, and the Discursive Construction of "The International Student"', *Higher Education Research and Development*, 22(2), pp. 155 – 166.

Doherty, C. and Singh, P. (2005) 'How the West is Done: Simulating Western Pedagogy in a Curriculum for Asian International students', in Ninnes, P. and Hellstén, M. (eds.) *Internationalizing Higher Education: Critical Explorations of Pedagogy and Policy*. Hong Kong: Comparative Education Research Centre, the University of Hong Kong, pp. 53 – 74.

Dovidio, J. F., Gaertner, S. L., Niemann, Y. F. and Snider, K. (2001) 'Racial, Ethnic, and Cultural Differences in Responding to Distinctiveness and Discrimination on Campus: Stigma and Common Group Identity', *Journal of Social Issues*, 57(1), pp. 167 – 188.

Duru, E. and Poyrazli, S. (2007) 'Personality Dimensions, Psychosocial-Demographic Variables, and English Language Competency in Predicting Level of Acculturative Stress Among Turkish International students', *International Journal of Stress Management*, 14(1), pp. 99 – 110.

Elsey, R. (1990) 'Teaching and learning', in Kinnell, M. (ed.) *The Learning Experiences of Overseas Students*. Buckingham: Society for Research into Higher Education and Open University Press, pp. 46 – 62.

Elton, L. and Johnston, B. (2002) *Assessment in universities: a critical review of research*. York: Learning and Teaching Support Network Generic Centre.

Fan, C. and Mak, A. (1998) 'Measuring social self-efficacy in a culturally diverse student population', *Social Behavior and Personality*, 26, pp. 131 - 144.

Fang, W. (2012) 'The development of transnational higher education in China: a comparative study of research universities and teaching universities, *Journal of Studies in International Education*, 16 (1), pp. 5 - 23.

Feng, A. (2005) 'Bilingualism for the minor or the major? An evaluative analysis of parallel conceptions in China', *International Journal of Bilingual Education and Bilingualism*, 8 (6), pp. 529 - 551.

Feng, A. (2009) 'Becoming Interculturally Competent in a Third Space', in Feng, A., Byram, M. and Fleming, M. (eds.) *Becoming Interculturally Competent through Education and Training*. Bristol: Multilingual Matters, pp. 71 - 91.

Fernandes, J. (2006) 'Trends in International Student Mobility: a Study of the Relationship between the UK and China and the Chinese Student Experience in the UK', *Scottish Educational Review*, 38 (2), pp. 133 - 144.

Fetterman, D. M. (2010) *Ethnography: Step-by-Step*. 3rd edn. Thousand Oaks: Sage Publications.

Finlay, L. (2003) 'Thc rcflcxivc journcy: mapping multiplc routcs', in Finlay, L. and Gough, B. (eds.) *Reflexivity: a Practical Guide for Researchers in Health and Social Sciences*. Oxford: Blackwell Science Ltd, pp. 3 - 20.

Finlay, L. and Gough, B. (2003) 'Prologue', in Finlay, L. and Gough, B. (eds.) *Reflexivity: a Practical Guide for Researchers in Health and Social Sciences*. Oxford: Blackwell Science Ltd, pp. ix - xi.

Furnham, A. and Bochner, S. (1982) 'Social difficulty in a foreign culture: an empirical analysis of culture shock', in Bochner, S. (ed.) *Cultures in Contact: Studies in Cross-cultural Interaction: Vol. 1*. Oxford: Pergamon Press, pp. 161 - 198.

Gaertner, S. L. and Dovidio, J. F. (1986) 'Prejudice, discrimination, and racism: Problems, progress and promise', in Dovidio, J. F. and Gaertner, S. L. (eds.) *Prejudice, discrimination, and racism.* Orlando, FL: Academic Press, pp. 315 – 332.

Gaertner, S. L. and Dovidio, J. F. (2000) *Reducing intergroup bias: The Common Ingroup Identity Model.* Philadelphia: Psychology Press.

Gaertner, S. L. and Dovidio, J. F. (2005) 'Understanding and Addressing Contemporary Racism: From Aversive Racism to the Common Ingroup Identity Model', *Journal of Social Issues*, 61(3), pp. 615 – 639.

Gaertner, S. L., Dovidio, J. F. and Bachman, B. A. (1996) 'Revisiting the Contact Hypothesis: the Induction of a Common Ingroup Identity', *International Journal of Intercultural Review*, 20(3/4), pp. 271 – 290.

Gaertner, S. L., Dovidio, J. F., Rust, M. C., Nier, J. A. Banker, B. S., Ward, C. M., Mottola, G. R. and Houlette, M. (1999) 'Reducing Intergroup Bias: Elements of Intergroup Cooperation', *Journal of Personality and Social Psychology*, 76(3), pp. 388 – 402.

Gaertner, S. L., Mann, J. A., Dovidio, J. F., Murrell, A. J. and Pomare, M. (1990) 'How does cooperation reduce intergroup bias?', *Journal of Personality and Social Psychology*, 59, pp. 692 – 704.

Gaertner, S. L., Rust, M. C., Dovidio, J. F., Bachman, B. A. and Anastasio, P. A. (1994) 'The Contact Hypothesis: the role of a common ingroup identity on reducing intergroup bias', *Small Group Research*, 25, pp. 224 – 249.

Gieve, S. and Clark, R. (2005) '"The Chinese approach to learning": Cultural trait or situated response? The case of a self-directed learning programme', *System*, 33, pp. 261 – 276.

Gill, S. (2005) *Learning Across Cultures: An ethnographic and narrative study of postgraduate overseas Chinese students' intercultural learning, social interaction, self reflection and meaning making at a British university.* Unpublished PhD thesis. Brighton: University of Sussex.

Gill, S. (2007) 'Overseas students' intercultural adaptation as intercultural learning: a transformative framework', *Compare*, 37(2), pp. 167 – 183.

Glaser, B. G. and Strauss, A. L. (1967) *The Discovery of Grounded Theory*. New York: Aldine Publishing Company.

Goldrick-Rab, S., Carter, D. F. and Wagner, R. W. (2007) 'What Higher Education Has to Say about the Transition to College', *Teachers College Record*, 109(10), pp. 2444 – 2481.

Gough, B. (2003) 'Deconstructing reflexivity', in Finlay, L. and Gough, B. (eds.) *Reflexivity: a Practical Guide for Researchers in Health and Social Sciences*. Oxford: Blackwell Science Ltd, pp. 21 – 35.

Grolnick, W. S. and Apostoleris, N. H. (2002) 'What Makes Parents Controlling?', in Deci, E. L. and Ryan, R. M. (eds.) *Handbook of Self-determination Research*. Rochester: the University of Rochester Press, pp. 161 – 181.

Grolnick, W. S. and Ryan, R. M. (1989) 'Parent styles associated with children's self-regulation and competence in school', *Journal of Educational Psychology*, 81, pp. 143 – 154.

Gu, Q. and Maley, A. (2008) 'Changing Places: A Study of Chinese Students in the UK', *Language and Intercultural Communication*, 8 (4), pp. 224 – 245.

Gu, Q., Schweisfurth, M. and Day, C. (2010) 'Learning and growing in a "foreign" context: intercultural experiences of international students', *Compare*, 40(1), pp. 7 – 23.

Guba, E. G. and Lincoln, Y. S. (1989) *Fourth Generation Evaluation*. London: Sage, Publications.

Guba, E. G. and Lincoln, Y. S. (2008) 'Paradigmatic Controversies, Contradictions, and Emerging Confluences', in Denzin, N. K. and Lincoln, Y. S. (eds.) *The Landscape of Qualitative Research*. 3rd edn. London: Sage Publications, pp. 255 – 286.

Gudykunst, W. B. (2005) 'An Anxiety/Uncertainty Management (AUM) Theory of Effective Communication: Making the Mesh of the Net Finer', in Gudykunst, W. B. (ed.) *Theorizing about Intercultural Communication*. Thousand Oaks: Sage Publications, pp. 281 – 322.

Gullahorn, J. T. and Gullahorn, J. E. (1963) 'An extension of the U-curve hypothesis', *Journal of Social Issues*, 19(3), pp. 33 – 47.

Gürüz, K. (2008) *Higher Education and International Student Mobility in the Global Knowledge Economy*. Albany: State University of New York Press.

Guthrie, D. (2009) *China and Globalisation: The social, economic and political transformation of Chinese society*. 2nd edn. London: Routledge.

Hall, S. and Toll, S. (1999) *Raising Intercultural Awareness in preparation for periods of residence abroad: a review of current practice in UKHE*. [online]. Available at: www. lancs. ac. uk/users/interculture/docs/ria. rtf (Accessed: 2 October, 2010).

Hammersley, M. (2001) 'On "Systematic" Reviews of Research Literatures: a "narrative" response to Evans & Benefield', *British Educational Research Journal*, 27(5), pp. 543 – 554.

Hammersley, M. and Atkinson, P. (2007) *Ethnography: Principles in practice*. 3rd edn. London: Routledge.

Harrison, J. K., Chadwick, M. and Scales, M. (1996) 'The Relationship Between Cross-Cultural Adjustment and the Personality Variables of Self-Efficacy and Self-Monitoring', *International Journal of Intercultural Relations*, 20(2), pp. 167 – 188.

Harrison, N. and Peacock, N. (2010) 'Cultural distance, mindfulness and passive xenophobia: using Integrated Threat Theory to explore home higher education students' perspectives on "internationalisation at home"', *British Educational Research Journal*, 36(6), pp. 877 – 902.

Hattie, J. (1999) *Influences on student learning*. Inaugural lecture: Professor of Education, University of Auckland.

Hewstone, M., Rubin, M. and Willis, H. (2002) 'Intergroup Bias', *Annual Review of Psychology*, 53, pp. 575 – 604.

Ho, W. C. (2006) 'Popular culture in mainland Chinese education', *International Education Journal*, 7(3), pp. 348 – 363.

Hofstede, G. (1984) *Culture's Consequences: International Differences in Work-Related Values*. Abridged Edition. Newbury Park, Sage Publications.

Hofstede, G. (1991) *Cultures and Organizations: Software of the Mind*. New York: McGraw-Hill.

Hofstede, G. (2001) *Culture's Consequences: Comparing Values, Behaviors, and Organizations Across nations*. 2nd edn. Thousand Oaks: Sage Publications.

Hofstede, G. and Hofstede, G. J. (2005) *Cultures and Organizations: Software of the Mind*. 2nd edn. New York: McGraw-Hill.

Hofstede, G., Hofstede, G. J. and Minkov, M. (2010) *Cultures and Organizations: Software of the Mind*. 3rd edn. New York: McGraw-Hill.

Hogg, M. A. and Terry, D. J. (2000) 'Social Identity and Self-Categorization Processes in Organizational Contexts', *Academy of Management Review*, 25 (1), pp. 121 - 140.

Holliday, A. (1999) 'Small Cultures', *Applied Linguistics*, 20 (2), pp. 237 - 264.

Holliday, A. (2010) 'Cultural descriptions as political cultural acts: an exploration', *Language and Intercultural Communication*, 10 (3), pp. 259 - 272.

Hornsey, M. J. and Hogg, M. A. (2000) 'Subgroup Relations: A Comparison of Mutual Intergroup Differentiation and Common Ingroup Identity Models of Prejudice Reduction', *Personality and Social Psychology Bulletin*, 26 (2), pp. 242 - 256.

Hou, J., and McDowell, L. (2013) 'Learning Together? Experiences on a China-U. K. Articulation Program in Engineering', *Journal of Studies in International Education*, 18(3), pp. 223 - 240.

Hou, J., Montgomery, C. and McDowell, L. (2011) 'Transition in Chinese-British Higher Education Articulation Programmes: Closing the Gap between East and West?' In Ryan, J. (ed.) *China's higher education: Reform and internationalisation*. London: Routledge, pp. 104 - 119.

Huang, F. (2007) 'Internationalization of Higher Education in the Developing and Emerging Countries: A Focus on Transnational Higher Education in Asia', *Journal of Studies in International Education*, 11(3 - 4), pp. 421 - 432.

Hussey, T. and Smith, P. (2010) 'Transitions in higher education', *Innovations in Education and Teaching International*, 47(2), pp. 155 - 164.

Imamura, M., Zhang, Y. B. and Harwood, J. (2011) 'Japanese sojourners' attitudes toward Americans: Exploring the influences of communication accommodation, linguistic competence, and relational solidarity in intergroup contact', *Journal of Asian Pacific Communication*, 21 (1), pp. 103 - 120.

Ippolito, K. (2007) 'Promoting intercultural learning in a multicultural university: ideals and realities', *Teaching in Higher Education*, 12(5 - 6), pp. 749 - 763.

Jick, T. D. (1979) 'Mixing Qualitative and Quantitative Methods: Triangulation in Action', *Administrative Science Quarterly*, 24, pp. 602 - 611.

Jindal-Snape, D. (2010) 'Setting the Scene: Educational Transitions and Moving Stories', in Jindal-Snape, D. (ed.) *Educational Transitions: Moving Stories from Around the World*. Oxon: Routledge, pp. 1 - 8.

Jindal-Snape, D. and Miller, D. J. (2010) 'Understanding Transitions Through Self-Esteem and Resilience', in Jindal-Snape, D. (ed.) *Educational Transitions: Moving Stories from Around the World*. Oxon: Routledge, pp. 11 - 32.

Kashima, E. S. and Loh, E. (2006) 'International students' acculturation: Effects of international, conational, and local ties and need for closure', *International Journal of Intercultural Relations*, 30, pp. 471 - 485.

Ke, J. (2010) 'To Promote Healthy and Orderly Development of Chinese-foreign Transnational Education'. [In Chinese]. China Education Daily, 5th March, p. 3.

Keppel, M., Au, E., Ma, A. and Chan, C. (2006) 'Peer learning and learning-oriented assessment in technology-enhanced environments', *Assessment & Evaluation in Higher Education*, 31(4), pp. 453 - 464.

Kim, Y. Y. (2001) *Becoming Intercultural: an Integrative Theory of Communication and Cross-cultural Adaptation*. Thousand Oaks: Sage Publications.

Kim, Y. Y. (2005) 'Adapting to a New Culture: An Integrative Communication Theory', in Gudykunst W. B. (ed.) *Theorizing About Intercultural Communication*. London: Sage Publications, pp. 375 – 400.

Knight, J. and De Wit, H. (1995) 'Strategies for internationalisation of higher education: Historical and conceptual perspectives', in De Wit, H. (ed.) *Strategies for internationalisation of higher education: A comparative study of Australia, Canada, Europe and the United States of America*. Amsterdam: EAIE, pp. 5 – 32.

Knight, J., and Morshidi, S. (2011) 'The complexities and challenges of regional education hubs: focus on Malaysia', *Higher Education*, 62 (5), pp. 593 – 606.

Knight, P. (2001) *A briefing on key concepts: formative and summative, criterion & norm-referenced assessment*. York: LTSN Generic Centre ASS No. 7.

Koestner, R. and Losier, G. F. (2002) 'Distinguishing Three Ways of Being Internally Motivated: A Closer Look at Introjection, Identification, and Intrinsic Motivation', in Deci, E. L. and Ryan, R. M. (eds.) *Handbook of Self-determination Research*. Rochester: the University of Rochester Press, pp. 101 – 121.

Kosic, A., Kruglanski, A., Pierro, J. and Mannetti, L. (2004) 'The social cognition of immigrants' acculturation: Effects of the need for closure and the reference group at entry', *Journal of Personality and Social Psychology*, 86(6), pp. 796 – 813.

Kosic, A., Mannetti, L. and Sam, D. L. (2006) 'Self-monitoring: A moderating role between acculturation strategies and adaptation of immigrants', *International Journal of Intercultural Relations*, 30, pp. 141 – 157.

Kumaravadivelu, B. (2003) 'Problematizing Cultural Stereotypes in TESOL', *TESOL Quarterly*, 37(4), pp. 709 – 719.

Lam, C. M. H. (2006) 'Reciprocal Adjustment by Host and Sojourning Groups: Mainland Chinese Students in Hong Kong', in Byram, M. and Feng, A. (eds.) *Living and Studying Abroad*. Clevedon: Multilingual Matters Ltd, pp. 91 – 107.

Lazarus, R. S. and Folkman, S. (1984) *Stress, Appraisal, and Coping*. New York: Springer Publishing Company.

Leask, B. (2008) 'Internationalisation, Globalisation and Curriculum Innovation', in Hellstén, M. and Reid, A. (eds.) *Researching International Pedagogies: Sustainable Practice for Teaching and Learning in Higher Education*. Hong Kong: Springer, pp. 9 – 26.

Lee, J., Koeske, G. F. and Sales, E. (2004) 'Social support buffering of acculturative stress: a study of mental health symptoms among Korean international students', *International Journal of Intercultural Relations*, 28, pp. 399 – 414.

Lee, R. M. and Robbins, S. B. (1998) 'The Relationship between Social Connectedness and Anxiety, Self-Esteem, and Social Identity', *Journal of Counseling Psychology*, 45(3), pp. 338 – 345.

Li, A. and Gasser, M. B. (2005) 'Predicting Asian International Students' Sociocultural Adjustment: a Test of Two Mediation Models', *International Journal of Intercultural Relations*, 29, pp. 561 – 576.

Li, G., Chen, W. and Duanmu, J. (2010) 'Determinants of International Students' Academic Performance: A Comparison between Chinese and Other International Students', *Journal of Studies in International Education*, 14(4), pp. 389 – 405.

Light, G. and Cox, R. (2001) *Learning and teaching in higher education*. London: PCP Publishing.

Loke, A. J. T. Y. and Chow, F. L. W. (2007) 'Learning partnership – the experience of peer tutoring among nursing students: a qualitative study', *International Journal of Nursing Studies*, 44, pp. 237 – 244.

Longfellow, E., May, S., Burke, L. and Marks-Maran, D. (2008) '"They had a way of helping that actually helped": a case study of a peer-assisted learning scheme', *Teaching in Higher Education*, 13(1), pp. 93 – 105.

Loots, A. G. J. (2009) 'Student involvement and retention in higher education: the case for academic peer mentoring programmes for first-years', *Education As Change*, 13(1), pp. 211 – 235.

Lysgaard, S. (1955) 'Adjustment in a Foreign Society: Norwegian Fulbright Grantees Visiting the United States', *International Social Science Bulletin*, 7, pp. 45 - 51.

Mackie, D. M. and Smith, E. R. (1998) 'Intergroup Relations: Insights from a Theoretically Integrative Approach', *Psychological Review*, 105 (3), pp. 499 - 529.

Mackie, S. (2001) 'Jumping the hurdles—undergraduate student withdrawal behaviour', *Innovations in Education and Training International*, 38 (3), pp. 265 - 275.

MacIntyre, P. D. (1995) 'How does Anxiety Affect Second Language Learning? A Reply to Sparks and Ganschow', *The Modern Language Journal*, 79 (1), pp. 90 - 99.

Mak, A. S. and Tran, C. (2001) 'Big five personality and cultural relocation factors in Vietnamese Australian students' intercultural social self-efficacy', *International Journal of Intercultural Relations*, 25, pp. 181 - 201.

Marginson, S. and van der Wende, M. (2009) 'The New Global Landscape of Nations and Institutions', in *Higher Education to 2030: Vol. 2 Globalisation*. OECD, pp. 17 - 62.

Maso, I. (2003) 'Necessary subjectivity: exploiting researchers' motives, passions and prejudices in pursuit of answering "true" questions', in Finlay, L. and Gough, B. (eds.) *Reflexivity: a Practical Guide for Researchers in Health and Social Sciences*. Oxford: Blackwell Science Ltd, pp. 39 - 51.

Mayer, K. L., Amendum, S. J. and Vernon-Feagans, L. (2010) 'The Transition to Formal Schooling', in Jindal-Snape, D. (ed.) *Educational Transitions: Moving Stories from Around the World*. Oxon: Routledge, pp. 85 - 103.

McBurnie, G. and Ziguras, C. (2007) *Transnational Education: Issues and trends in offshore higher education*. Oxon: Routledge.

McBurnie, G. and Ziguras, C. (2009) 'Trends and Future Scenarios in Programme and Institution Mobility across Borders', in *Higher Education to*

2030: *Vol. 2: Globalisation*. OECD, pp. 89 – 108.

McDowell, L. (2001) *Students and innovative assessment*. The Higher Education Academy. [Online]. Available at http://www.heacademy.ac.uk/resources.asp? process = full_record§ion = generic&id = 431 (Accessed: 16 March, 2007).

McDowell, L., Sambell, K., Bazin, V., Penlington, R., Wakelin, D., Wickes, H. and Smailes, J. (2006) *Assessment for Learning: Current Practice Exemplars from the Centre for Excellence in Teaching and Learning*. Newcastle: Northumbria University.

McInnis, C., James, R. and McNaught, C. (1995) *First year on campus: diversity in the initial experiences of Australian undergraduate students*. Commissioned project for the Committee for the Advancement of university Teaching. Canberra: Australian Government Publishing Services.

Mellors-Bourne, R., Humfrey, C., Kemp, N. and Woodfield, S. (2013) *The wider benefits of UK international education*. BIS Research Paper Number 128. London: Department for Business, Innovation and Skills.

Middlehurst, R. and Woodfield, S. (2007) *Responding to the internationalisation agenda: implications for institutional strategy*. The Higher Education Academy.

MoE (Ministry of Education of the People's Republic of China) (1998) *Undergraduate Professional Directory for Higher Education Institutions*. [In Chinese]. [Online]. Available at: http://www.moe.edu.cn/edoas/website18/84/info1212562471366584.htm (Accessed: 8 August, 2010).

MoE (Ministry of Education of the People's Republic of China) (2003) *General Information on Chinese-foreign Transnational Education*. [In Chinese]. [Online]. Available at: http://www.moe.edu.cn/edoas/website18/40/info5440.htm (Accessed: 8 August, 2010).

MoE (Ministry of Education of the People's Republic of China) (2004a) *How to Develop Chinese-Foreign Cooperation in Running Schools*. [In Chinese]. [Online]. Available at: http://www.moe.edu.cn/publicfiles/business/htmlfiles/moe/moe_337/index.html (Accessed: 8 August, 2010).

MoE(Ministry of Education of the People's Republic of China) (2004b) *Implementation Measures for Regulations of the People's Republic of China on Chinese-Foreign Cooperation in Running Schools*. [In Chinese]. [Online]. Available at: http://www. moe. gov. cn/publicfiles/business/htmlfiles/moe/moe _ 861/201005/xxgk _ 88508. html (Accessed: 27 February, 2007).

MoE(Ministry of Education of the People's Republic of China) (2006) *The Views of Ministry of Education on the Current Issues in Chinese-foreign Transnational Education*. [In Chinese]. [Online]. Available at: http://www. moe. edu. cn/edoas/website18/89/info1225950226329589. htm (Accessed:8 August, 2009).

MoE (Ministry of Education of the People's Republic of China) (2007) *Ministry of Education Notice on Further Regulating the Order in Transnational Education*. [In Chinese]. [Online]. Available at http://www. moe. edu. cn/edoas/website18/55/info27355. htm (accessed: 10 August 2009).

MoE(Ministry of Education of the People's Republic of China) (2009) *Gross Enrolment Ratio at All Levels of Education*. [In Chinese]. [Online]. Available at: http://www. moe. edu. cn/edoas/website18/level3. jsp? tablename = 1261364094322579&infoid = 1261548667642896 (Accessed:5 August, 2010).

MoE(Ministry of Education of the People's Republic of China) (2010a) *List of Undergraduate Transnational Higher Education Programmes and Institutes*. [In Chinese]. [Online]. Available at: http://www. crs. jsj. edu. cn/info_by_key. php? sort = 1 (Accessed:30 July, 2010).

MoE(Ministry of Education of the People's Republic of China) (2010b) *List of Postgraduate Transnational Higher Education Programmes and Institutes*. [In Chinese]. [Online]. Available at: http://www. crs. jsj. edu. cn/info_by_key. php? sort = 2 (Accessed:30 July, 2010).

MoE(Ministry of Education of the People's Republic of China) (2013a) *Current Situation of Chinese-foreign Transnational Education since the*

Implementation of The National Medium and Long Term Program for Education Reform and Development. [In Chinese]. [Online]. Available at: http://www.moe.gov.cn/publicfiles/business/htmlfiles/moe/s7598/201309/156992.html (Accessed: 13 January, 2014).

MoE (Ministry of Education of the People's Republic of China) (2013b) *New Achievements in Higher Education Reform and Development in Western China*. [In Chinese]. [Online]. Available at: http://www.moe.gov.cn/publicfiles/business/htmlfiles/moe/s7180/201302/147776.html (Accessed: 13 January, 2014).

Montgomery, C. (2009) 'A decade of internationalisation: Has it influenced students' views of cross-cultural group work at university?', *Journal of Studies in International Education*, 13 (2), pp. 256 – 270. [Online]. Available at: http://jsi.sagepub.com/cgi/content/abstract/13/2/256 (Accessed: 1 November, 2009).

Montgomery, C. (2010) *Understanding the International Student Experience*. Hampshire: Palgrave Macmillan.

Montgomery, C. and McDowell, L. (2004) 'Social networks and learning: a study of the socio-cultural context of the international student', in Rust, C. (ed.) *Improving Student Learning: Theory, Research and Scholarship*. Oxford: Oxford Centre for Staff and Learning Development, pp. 66 – 79.

Montgomery, C. and McDowell, L. (2009) 'Social Networks and the International Student Experience: An International Community of Practice?', *Journal of Studies in International Education*, 13 (4), pp. 455 – 466.

Mori, S. (2000) 'Addressing the mental health concerns of international students', *Journal of Counseling & Development*, 78 (2), pp. 137 – 144.

Murphy-Lejeune, E. (2003) 'An Experience of Interculturality: Student Travellers Abroad', in Alred, G., Byram, M. and Fleming, M. (eds.) *Intercultural Experience and Education*. Clevedon: Multilingual Matters LTD, pp. 101 – 113.

Naidoo, V. (2009) 'Transnational Higher Education: A Stock Take of Current

Activity', *Journal of Studies in International Education*, 13 (3), pp. 310 – 330.

National Bureau of Statistics of China(2008) *China Statistical Yearbook* 2008. [Online]. Available at: http://www. stats. gov. cn/tjsj/ndsj/2008/left_. htm (Accessed:15 July 2009).

National Bureau of Statistics of China(2009) *China Statistical Yearbook* 2009. [Online]. Available at: http://www. stats. gov. cn/tjsj/ndsj/2009/ indexch. htm (Accessed:5 August,2010).

Nesdale, D. and Todd, P. (1998) 'Intergroup Ratio and the Contact Hypothesis', *Journal of Applied Social Psychology*, 28 (13), pp. 1196 – 1217.

NG, S. W. (2011) 'Can Hong Kong export its higher education services to the Asian markets?', *Educational Research for Policy and Practice*, 10 (2), pp. 115 – 131.

Nicol, D. J. and Macfarlane-Dick, D. (2006) 'Formative assessment and self-regulated learning: A model and seven principles of good feedback practice', *Studies in Higher Education*, 31(2), pp. 199 – 218.

Oberg, K. (1960) 'Cultural shock: Adjustment to new cultural environments', *Practical Anthropology*, July-August, pp. 177 – 182.

Olcott, D. J. (2008) 'Global Connections—Local Impacts: Trends and Developments for Internationalism and Cross-Border Higher Education', in Coverdale-Jones, T. and Rastall, P. (eds.) *Internationalising the University: The Chinese Context*. London: Palgrave MacMillan, pp. 72 – 84.

Oliver, P. (2003) *The Student's guide to research ethics*. Philadelphia: Open University Press.

Oxford, E. (2008) 'Foreign Exchange', *Times Higher Education*, 7 February. [Online]. Available at: http://www. timeshighereducation. co. uk/story. asp? sectioncode = 26&storycode = 400478&c = 2 (Accessed: 15 August, 2009).

Parkinson, M. (2009) 'The effect of peer assisted learning support(PALS) on performance in mathematics and chemistry', *Innovations in Education and*

Teaching International,46(4),pp. 381 - 392.

Peacock, N. and Harrison, N. (2009) '"It So Much Easier to Go With What's Easy": "Mindfulness" and the Discourse Between Home and International Students in the United Kingdom', *Journal of Studies in International Education*, 13(4), pp. 487 - 508.

Pettigrew, T. F. (1998) 'Intergroup Contact Theory', *Annual Review of Psychology*, 49, pp. 65 - 85.

Pettigrew, T. F. and Tropp, L. R. (2000) 'Does intergroup contact reduce prejudice? Recent metaanalytic findings', in Oskamp, S. (ed.) *Reducing prejudice and discrimination*. Hillsdale, NJ: Erlbaum, pp. 93 - 114.

Pickard, A. J. (2007) *Research methods in information*. London: Facet Publishing.

Poyrazli, S., Arbona, C., Nora, A., McPherson, R. and Pisecco, S. (2002) 'Relation between Assertiveness, Academic Self-Efficacy, and Psychosocial Adjustment among International Graduate students', *Journal of College Student Development*, 43(5), pp. 632 - 642.

Poyrazli, S., Kavanaugh, P. R., Baker, A., and Al-Timimi, N. (2004) 'Social Support and Demographic Correlates of Acculturative Stress in International students', *Journal of College Counseling*, 7, pp. 73 - 82.

Poyrazli, S., Thukral, R. K. and Duru, E. (2010) 'International Students' Race-ethnicity, Personality and Acculturative Stress', *Journal of Psychology and Counseling*, 2(8), pp. 25 - 32.

Quality Assurance Agency for Higher Education (2006) *UK Higher Education in China: An overview of the quality assurance arrangements*. Mansfield: The Quality Assurance Agency for Higher Education. [Online]. Available at: http://www. qaa. ac. uk/reviews/international/china06/overview. pdf (Accessed: 1 March, 2009).

Quintrell, N. and Westwood, M. (1994) 'The influence of a peer-pairing program on international students' first year experience and use of student services', *Higher Education Research and Development*, 13 (1), pp. 49 - 57.

Ramburuth, P. and McCormick, J. (2001) 'Learning diversity in higher education: A comparative study of Asian international and Australian students', *Higher Education*, 42, pp. 333 – 350.

Ramsay, S., Jones, E. and Barker, M. (2007) 'Relationship between adjustment and support types: Young and mature-aged local and international first year university students', *Higher Education*, 54, pp. 247 – 265.

Robson, C. (2002) *Real World Research: A Resource of Social Scientists and Practitioner-Researchers*. 2nd edn. London: Blackwell Publishing.

Rotter, J. B. (1954) *Social learning and clinical psychology*. Englewood Cliffs: Prentice-Hall.

Rotter, J. B. (1966) 'Generalized Expectancies for internal vs. external control of reinforcement', *Psychological Monographs*, 80, pp. 1 – 28.

Rotter, J. B. (1990) 'Internal Versus External Control of Reinforcement: A Case History of a Variable', *American Psychologist*, 45(4), pp. 489 – 493.

Ryan, J. (2000) *A Guide to Teaching International Students*. Oxford: The Oxford Centre for Staff and Learning Development.

Ryan, J. (2005) 'The student experience: challenges and rewards', in Carroll, J. and Ryan, J. (eds.) *Teaching International Students: Improving Learning for All*. Oxon: Routledge, pp. 147 151.

Ryan, R. M. and Connell, J. P. (1989) 'Perceived locus of causality and internalization: Examining reasons for acting in two domains', *Journal of Personality and Social Psychology*, 57, pp. 749 – 761.

Ryan, R. M. and Deci, E. L. (2000) 'Intrinsic and Extrinsic Motivations: Classic Definitions and New Directions', *Contemporary Educational Psychology*, 25, pp. 54 – 67.

Ryan, R. M. and Deci, E. L. (2002) 'Overview of Self-Determination Theory: An Organismic Dialectical Perspective', in Deci, E. L. and Ryan, R. M. (eds.) *Handbook of Self-determination Research*. Rochester: the University of Rochester Press, pp. 3 – 33.

Sakurai, T., McCall-Wolf, F. and Kashima, E. S. (2010) 'Building intercultural links: the impact of a multicultural intervention programme on social ties of international students in Australia', *International Journal of Intercultural Relations*, 34, pp. 176 – 185.

Sale, J. E. M., Lohfeld, L. H. and Brazil, K. (2002) 'Revising the Quantitative-Qualitative Debate: Implications for Mixed-Methods Research', *Quality & Quantity*, 36, pp. 43 – 53.

Savicki, V. (2008) *Developing intercultural competence and transformation: Theory, research, and application in international education*. Sterling: Stylus.

Schmitt, M. T., Spears, R. and Branscombe, N. R. (2003) 'Constructing a minority group identity out of shared rejection: the case of international students', *European Journal of Social Psychology*, 33, pp. 1 – 12.

Scott, J. C. (1990) *A Matter of Record: Documentary Sources in Social Research*. Cambridge: Polity.

Searle, W. and Ward, C. (1990) 'The Prediction of Psychological and Sociocultural Adjustment during Cross-Cultural Transitions', *International Journal of Intercultural Relations*, 14, pp. 449 – 464.

Sheridan, V. (2011) 'A holistic approach to international students, institutional habitus and academic literacies in an Irish third level institution', *Higher Education*, 62, pp. 129 – 140.

Sherif, M. (1967) *Group Conflict and Co-operation: their Social Psychology*. London: Routledge & Kegan Paul Ltd.

Singh, M. (2005) 'Enabling Transnational Learning Communities: Policies, Pedagogies and Politics of Educational Power', in Ninnes, P. and Hellstén, M. (eds.) *Internationalizing Higher Education: Critical Explorations of Pedagogy and Policy*. Hong Kong: Comparative Education Research Centre, the University of Hong Kong, pp. 9 – 36.

Skelly, J. M. (2009) 'Forstering Engagement: The Role of International Education in the Development of Global Civil Society', in Lewin, R. (ed.) *The Handbook of Practice and Research in Study Abroad: Higher Education and the Quest for Global Citizenship*. New York: Routledge, pp. 21 – 32.

Skinner, E. and Edge, K. (2002) 'Self-Determination, Coping, and

Development', in Deci, E. L. and Ryan, R. M. (eds.) *Handbook of Self-determination Research*. Rochester: the University of Rochester Press, pp. 297 - 337.

Smalley, W. A. (1963) 'Culture shock, language shock, and the shock of self-discovery', *Practical Anthropology*, 10, pp. 49 - 56.

Smart, D., Volet, S. and Ang, G. (2000) *Fostering social cohesion in universities: Bridging the cultural divide*. Canberra: Australian Education International.

Sovic, S. (2008) 'Coping with stress: the perspective of international students', *Art, Design & Communication in Higher Education*, 6 (3), pp. 145 - 158.

Sovic, S. (2009) 'Hi-bye friends and the herd instinct: international and home students in the creative arts', *Higher Education*, 58, pp. 747 - 761.

Spring, J. (2009) *Globalization of Education: An Introduction*. New York: Routledge.

State Council of the People's Republic of China (2003) *Regulations of the People's Republic of China on Chinese-Foreign Cooperation in Running Schools*. [Online]. Available at: http://news.xinhuanet.com/edu/2003-09/02/content_1057903.htm (Accessed: 12 August, 2009).

Stephens, K. (1997) 'Cultural Stereotyping and Intercultural Communication: Working with Students from the People's Republic of China in the UK', *Language and Education*, 11 (2), pp. 113 - 124.

Stiglitz, J. E. (2006) 'China and the global economy: Challenges, opportunities, responsibilities', in Ho, L. S. and Ash, R. (eds.) *China, Hong Kong and the World Economy: Studies on globalisation*. Hampshire: Palgrave Macmillan, pp. 17 - 31.

Strauss, A. and Corbin, J. (1998) *Basics of Qualitative Research: techniques and procedures for developing grounded theory*. London: Sage Publications.

Strauss, P., U, A. and Young, S. (2011) '"I know the type of people I work well with": student anxiety in multicultural group projects', *Studies in Higher Education*, 36 (7), pp. 815 - 829.

Summers, M. and Volet, S. (2008) 'Students' attitudes towards culturally mixed groups on international campuses: impact of participation in diverse and non-diverse groups', *Studies in Higher Education*, 33(4), pp. 357 – 370.

Tajfel, H. (1981) *Human Groups & Social Categories: Studies in Social Psychology*. Cambridge: Cambridge University Press.

Tashakkori, A. and Teddlie, C. (1998) *Mixed methodology: Combining qualitative and quantitative approaches*. Thousand Oaks, Sage Publications.

TKI (Te Kete Ipurangi) (2007) *Assessment: Formative and Summative*. [Online]. Available at: http://www.govwentworth.k12.nh.us/ASSESSMENT.ppt 268, 15, The Garden Analogy (Accessed: 13 March, 2007).

Tian, M. (2008) "*The Chinese learner*" *or* "*learners from China*"?: *A multiple case study of Chinese masters' students in the University of Bath*. Unpublished PhD thesis. Bath: University of Bath.

Timmermans, S. and Tavory, I. (2007). 'Advancing Ethnographic Research through Grounded Theory Practice', in Bryant, A. and Charmaz, K. (eds.) *The SAGE Handbook of Grounded Theory*. London: Sage Publications, pp. 1 – 28.

Trotter, E. (2006) 'Student perceptions of continuous summative assessment', *Assessment & Evaluation in Higher Education*, 31 (5), pp. 505 – 521. [Online]. Available at: http://www.taylorandfrancis.metapress.com/index/G5155358R60Q4T66.pdf (Accessed: 7 May, 2007).

Tsang, E. W. K. (2001) 'Adjustment of mainland Chinese academics and students to Singapore', *International Journal of Intercultural Relations*, 25, pp. 347 – 372.

Tsang, E. Y. (2013) 'The quest for higher education by the Chinese middle class: retrenching social mobility?', *Higher Education*, 66 (6), pp. 653 – 668.

Turner, J. C., Hogg, M. A., Oakes, P. J., Reicher, S. D. and Wetherell, M. (1987) *Rediscovering the Social Group: a Self-Categorization Theory*. Oxford: Basil Blackwell Inc.

Turner, Y. (2006) 'Chinese Students in a UK Business School: Hearing the Student Voice in Reflective Teaching and Learning Practice', *Higher Education Quarterly*, 60(1), pp. 27 – 51.

UKCISA (UK Council for International Student Affairs) (2013) *International student statistics: UK higher education.* [Online]. Available at: http://www.ukcisa.org.uk/content/2196/International-students-in-UK-HE International-(non-UK)-students-in-UK-HE-in-2011-12 (Accessed: 9 January, 2014).

University of Manchester (2014) *Policy on Transnational Education.* [Online]. Available at http://www.tlso.manchester.ac.uk/map/collaborationsandpartnerships/policyontransnationaleducation/ (Accessed: 21 January, 2014).

Vincent-Lancrin, S. (2009) 'Cross-border Higher Education: Trends and Perspectives', in *Higher Education to* 2030: *Vol.* 2: *Globalisation*. Paris: OECD Publishing, pp. 63 – 88.

Volet, S. E. and Ang, G. (1998) 'Culturally Mixed Groups on International Campuses: an Opportunity for Inter-cultural Learning', *Higher Education Research & Development*, 17(1), pp. 5 – 23.

Walsh, E. (2010) 'A model of research group microclimate: environmental and cultural factors affecting the experiences of overseas research students in the UK', *Studies in Higher Education*, 35(5), pp. 545 – 560.

Wang, J. (2009) 'A Study of Resiliency Characteristics in the Adjustment of International Graduate Students at American Universities', *Journal of Studies in International Education*, 13(1), pp. 22 – 45.

Wang, T. (2008) 'Intercultural Dialogue and Understanding: Implications for Teachers', in Dunn, L. and Wallace, M. (eds.) *Teaching in Transnational Higher Education: Enhancing Learning for Offshore International Students.* London: Routledge, pp. 57 – 66.

Ward, C., Bochner, S. and Furnham, A. (2001) *The Psychology of Culture Shock.* 2nd edn. New York: Routledge.

Ward, C. and Kennedy, A. (1992) 'Locus of Control, Mood Disturbance, and Social Difficulty during Cross-Cultural Transitions', *International Journal of Intercultural Relations*, 16, pp. 175 – 194.

Ward, C. and Kennedy, A. (1993) 'Where's the "Culture" in Cross-Cultural Transition?: Comparative Studies of Sojourner Adjustment', *Journal of Cross-Cultural Psychology*, 24(2), pp. 221 – 249.

Ward, C. and Kennedy, A. (1994) 'Acculturation Strategies, Psychological Adjustment, and Sociocultural Competence during Cross-Cultural Transitions', *International Journal of Intercultural Relations*, 18 (3), pp. 329 – 343.

Ward, C., Leong, C. and Low, M. (2004) 'Personality and Sojourner Adjustment: An Exploration of the Big Five and the Cultural Fit Proposition', *Journal of Cross-Cultural Psychology*, 35(2), pp. 137 – 151.

Ward, C., Okura, Y., Kennedy, A. and Kojima, T. (1998) 'The U-curve on Trial: a Longitudinal Study of Psychological and Sociocultural Adjustment during Cross-cultural Transition', *International Journal of Intercultural Relations*, 22(3), pp. 277 – 291.

Welch, A. (2009) 'Mammon, Markets, and Managerialism—Asia-Pacific Perspectives on Contemporary Education Reforms', in Cowen, R. and Kazamias, A. M. (eds.) *International Handbook of Comparative Education*. Netherlands: Springer, pp. 587 – 600.

Wende, M. C. Van der (2003) 'Globalisation and Access to Higher Education', *Journal of Studies in International Education*, 7 (2), pp. 193 – 206.

Wilkins, S., and Huisman, J. (2012) 'The international branch campus as transnational strategy in higher education', *Higher Education*, 64 (5), pp. 627 – 645.

Willis, M (2006) 'Why Do Chinese Universities Seek Foreign University Partners: An Investigation of the Motivating Factors Behind a Significant Area of Alliance Activity', *Journal of Marketing for Higher Education*, 16 (1), pp. 115 – 141.

Wolcott, H. F. (2008) *Ethnography: a way of seeing*. 2nd edn. Plymouth: AltaMira Press.

World Bank(2009) 'Gross Domestic Product 2008, PPP', *World Development Indicators Database*. [Online]. Available at: http://siteresources.worldbank.org/DATASTATISTICS/Resources/GDP_PPP.pdf (Accessed: 30 October, 2009).

WTO(World Trade Organization) (1995) *General Agreement on Trade in Services*. [Online]. Available at: http://www.wto.org/english/docs_e/legal_e/26-gats.pdf (Accessed: 2 July, 2010).

WTO(World Trade Organization) (2006) *The General Agreement on Trade in Services: An Introduction*. [Online]. Available at: http://www.wto.org/english/tratop_e/serv_e/serv_e.htm (Accessed: 2 July, 2010).

Ye, J. (2006) 'An examination of acculturative stress, interpersonal social support, use of ethnic social groups among Chinese international students', *Howard Journal of Communication*, 17(1), pp. 1 – 20.

Yeh, C. J. and Inose, M. (2003) 'International students' reported English fluency, social support satisfaction, and social connectedness as predictors of acculturative stress', *Counselling Psychology Quarterly*, 16 (1), pp. 15 – 28.

Yin, R. K. (2003) *Case Study Research*. 3rd edn. London: Sage Publications.

Ying, Y. W. (2005) 'Variation in acculturative stressors over time: A study of Taiwanese students in the United States', *International Journal of Intercultural Relations*, 29, pp. 59 – 71.

Yorke, M. and Longden, B. (2007) *The first year experience in higher education in the UK*. Heslington, UK: The Higher Education Academy.

Yoshikawa, M. J. (1987) 'The Double-Swing Model of Intercultural Communication between the East and the West', in Kincaid, L. (ed.) *Communication Theory: Eastern and Western Perspectives*. San Diego: Academic Press, Inc., pp. 319 – 330.

Yoshikawa, M. J. (1988) 'Cross-Cultural Adaptation and Perceptual Development', in Kim, Y. Y. and Gudykunst, W. B. (eds.) *Cross-Cultural Adaptation: Current Approaches*. Beverly Hills, California: Sage Publications, pp. 140 – 148.

Zhou, J. (2006) *Higher Education in China*. Singapore: Thomson Learning.

Zhou, Y. and Todman, J. (2008) 'Chinese Postgraduate Students in the UK: A Two-Way Reciprocal Adaptation', *Journal of International and Intercultural Communication*, 1(3), pp. 221-243.

Zhou, Y., Topping, K. and Jindal-Snape, D. (2009) *Cultural and educational adaptation of Chinese students in the UK: Theory, process and implications*. Saarbrücken: VDM Verlag Dr. Müller Aktiengesellschaft & Co. KG.

Ziguras, C. (2003) 'The Impact of the GATS on Transnational Tertiary Education: Comparing Experiences of New Zealand, Australia, Singapore and Malaysia', *The Australian Educational Researcher*, 30 (3), pp. 89-109.

后　记

从2007年到2012年，历时五年完成的博士论文将要出版，心绪竟难以平静。毕业后一直不想去碰它，不仅是因为之前倾注了太多的心血，还有论文背后的人和事。落笔时，我已三十六周岁，女儿刚刚满月。接下来的日子忙于回国找工作、面试、上课、发论文、评职称、申报课题。静下来的时候，已离毕业三年有余。感觉英国离我已经很远，只有在某条静谧的街道或是Costa咖啡厅里才会偶尔闪现一两个镜头。

这次修改时重新拿来阅读，方觉幼稚。第一次开展历时质性研究，所有的一切都是新鲜的，没有经验，只有激情和大胆尝试。其实这项研究开始于我在英国读硕士时的一门课，课程要求撰写一篇研究预案。留学前在高校做过两年合作办学项目助理，当时合作办学正是兴盛时期，各个高校都在申报，只是不知道如何做好国内国外的教学衔接工作。我写了份研究预案，并发给英国一些高校申请读博。一天，在网上看到优质教学中心（CETL）招收博士并提供全额奖学金的消息，便投了份简历，提交了研究预案，后来进入了复试。答辩时，三位教授问我为什么要来读博，我说我想成为Dr. Hou，想解决研究预案里提出的问题，找到答案。

2007年10月1日，我开始了在CETL读博的日子。CETL全称Centre for Excellence in Teaching and Learning，我把它翻译为“优质教学促进中心”。本世纪初，英国高等教育拨款委员会在全国筹建了74家CETL，以促进教学方式及测评方式的研究和改革。这家研究中心与全校多个学院的老师合作，在课程中推行关注学习过程的发展性评价体系（Assessment for Learning）。在这里，我和来自澳洲的Kerry和德国的Nicola作为为数不多的老外，与Liz，Catherine，Angelina，Gillian，

Ruth，Martha，Mat，Linda，Mel，Kay 等英国学者一起学习、研究、工作了五年，亲身经历并感受到评价体系改革对改进教学效果的无限魔力和魅力，也促使我回国任教后立志建立这样一个研究中心以推进教学改革的进行。

那五年我得到太多人的帮助，先是导师 Liz 帮我付了国际学生和英国学生学费之间的差价，这样我和英国学生拿到的生活费就一样多了，她认为这样才公平。之后 Jennifer、Gerry、James 和 Jane 帮我联系了国内的合作高校，回国搜集数据时更是得到了国内学生和老师的极大帮助。John、Erik 和 Kerry 在硕士和读博期间为我提供了授课的机会，Sarah、Gillian、Shuting、Rose 和 Xiaoqing 在我论文答辩期间给予我无私的帮助。怀孕时泰国同学 Rung 每天帮我背书包，餐厅的阿姨每次都给我的盘子里多打一勺，因为我 eat for two，连学校的保安锁门时都会去研究室看看那个中国来的 Jessie 走了没有。这次重新修改论文，每一字每一句都会让我的思绪碰到以前，让我想起过往的点点滴滴。以为英国已经离我很远了，谁知想起来还是那么亲切，触手可及。谨以此书感谢故事里的每个人，有名的，无名的，都在我的记忆里不曾远去。

同时感谢我的家人，耐心等待我按照自己的节奏完成了论文撰写，依着我的性子从纽卡迁到多伦多再到北京，又举家南迁至长沙。支撑每一次变迁的是他们对我无尽的爱。感谢我的母校国防科学技术大学，四年的学习生活给了我扎实的专业基础、强烈的求知欲望、豁达的人生态度和坚毅的奋斗精神，感谢各位领导及同事对我回国工作后的倾力帮助。特别感谢中国社会科学出版社的编辑刘艳，是她的鼓励和支持让我在不惑之年的繁忙时刻顺利出版了这本专著。本书出版受到国家社科基金项目（15BSH032）、湖南省社科基金项目（12YBA031）和国防科技大学本科教育教学研究重点课题（U2015105）资助，在此一并感谢。

侯俊霞

2015 年 11 月 17 日于长沙